F I L M

SIMON AND SCHUSTER · NEW YORK

69/70

AN ANTHOLOGY BY THE

NATIONAL SOCIETY

OF FILM CRITICS

edited by

JOSEPH MORGENSTERN

and

STEFAN KANFER

PUBLISHED BY SIMON AND SCHUSTER
ROCKEFELLER CENTER, 630 FIFTH AVENUE
NEW YORK, NEW YORK 10020

FIRST PRINTING

SBN 671-20607-9 CLOTH
SBN 671-20608-7 PAPER
LIBRARY OF CONGRESS CATALOG CARD NUMBER: 68-19946
DESIGNED BY CARL WEISS
MANUFACTURED IN THE UNITED STATES OF AMERICA

The reviews and articles in this book originally appeared, for the most part, in the publications for which the contributors regularly write. Thanks are hereby given by the contributors as follows:

Hollis Alpert, reviews of *Bob & Carol & Ted & Alice, Stolen Kisses, The Loves of Isadora, I Am Curious* (*Yellow*), and the article "Fellini at Work," reprinted by permission of *Saturday Review*, copyright © 1968, 1969 by Saturday Review, Inc.

Harold Clurman, review of *Salesman*, reprinted by permission of *The Nation*, copyright © 1969 by The Nation, Inc.

Penelope Gilliatt, reviews of *Easy Rider, The Red and the White, The Wild Bunch, Putney Swope, The Loves of Isadora* and *I Am Curious* (*Yellow*), reprinted by permission of *The New Yorker*, copyright © 1969 by The New Yorker Magazine, Inc.

Philip T. Hartung, review of *Midnight Cowboy*, reprinted by permission of *Commonweal*, copyright © 1969 by Commonweal Publishing Co., Inc.

Robert Hatch, reviews of *Alice's Restaurant, Goodbye, Columbus, The Red and the White* and *Che!*, reprinted by permission of *The Nation*, copyright © 1969 by The Nation, Inc.

Pauline Kael, reviews of *Z, Bob & Carol & Ted & Alice, If . . . , Paint Your Wagon, In the Year of the Pig* and *Goodbye, Mr. Chips*, reprinted by

CONTENTS

III. Auteurisms

IV. On Locations

V. Documentarians

VI. Performers and Performances

FOREWORD

At the back of the New Yorker theater, a revival house in Manhattan, the management keeps a ledger book and a pencil on a string with which customers can ask for movies they'd like to see. One recent request was for "*Strange Love,* with Eldridge Cleaver and Little Shirley Temple." It never hurts to ask. Critics do so constantly, even though they devote much of their length and breath to movies already made. All the praisings, misgivings, doubtings, carpings and denouncings in this, our third anthology in as many years, also contain implicit requests for movies we'd like to see. And who knows what wish fulfillments the future may bring? Next year *Strange Love.*

JOSEPH MORGENSTERN, *Chairman*
National Society of Film Critics

THE AWARDS

THE NATIONAL SOCIETY OF FILM CRITICS, in its fourth annual awards, voted Z as the best picture of 1969. The Society named François Truffaut as the best director of the year for *Stolen Kisses,* while Vanessa Redgrave, who stars in *The Loves of Isadora,* was honored for her performance. Miss Redgrave won the best actress award. The award for the best actor went to Jon Voight in recognition of his performance in *Midnight Cowboy.*

Other awards voted by the Society named Jack Nicholson as the best supporting actor for his performance in *Easy Rider,* and Sian Phillips as the best supporting actress for her role in *Goodbye, Mr. Chips.*

The best cinematographer award was given to Lucien Ballard, who was responsible for the photography in *The Wild Bunch.*

Paul Mazursky and Larry Tucker received the best script of the year citation from the Society for *Bob & Carol & Ted & Alice.*

Two special awards were given: to Ivan Passer for a first film of great originality—*Intimate Lighting,* and to Dennis Hopper for his achievements in *Easy Rider* as director, co-writer and co-star.

Participants in the voting included Hollis Alpert of *The Saturday Review;* Harold Clurman of *The Nation;* Brad Darrach of *Movie;* Penelope Gilliatt and Pauline Kael of *The New Yorker;* Stefan Kanfer of *Time;* Stanley Kauffmann of the *New Republic;* Robert Kotlowitz of *Harper's;* Joseph Morgenstern of *Newsweek;* Andrew Sarris of *The Village Voice;* Richard Schickel of *Life;* Arthur Schlesinger, Jr., of *Vogue;* and John Simon of *The New Leader.*

VOTING FOR 1969 AWARDS—THE NATIONAL SOCIETY OF FILM CRITICS

Each critic was asked to vote for three candidates in each category. The first choice was worth three points, the second two, the third one, and a simple plurality established the winner.

BEST PICTURE

HOLLIS ALPERT: *Stolen Kisses; Z; Bob & Carol & Ted & Alice*

HAROLD CLURMAN: *Z; Adalen '31; Medium Cool*

BRAD DARRACH: *Adalen '31; Intimate Lighting; The Damned*

PENELOPE GILLIATT: *Z; Alice's Restaurant; La Femme Infidèle*

PAULINE KAEL: *Z; Bob & Carol & Ted & Alice* (no 3rd choice)

STEFAN KANFER: *Stolen Kisses; Z; La Femme Infidèle*

STANLEY KAUFFMANN: *The Red and the White; Simon of the Desert; The Wild Bunch*

ROBERT KOTLOWITZ: *La Femme Infidèle; Bob & Carol & Ted & Alice; Z*

JOSEPH MORGENSTERN: *Z; La Femme Infidèle* (no 3rd choice)

ANDREW SARRIS: *La Femme Infidèle; Stolen Kisses; Pierrot Le Fou*

RICHARD SCHICKEL: *Stolen Kisses; The Red and the White; Bob & Carol & Ted & Alice*

ARTHUR SCHLESINGER: *Z; If; Bob & Carol & Ted & Alice*

JOHN SIMON: *They Shoot Horses, Don't They?; Adalen '31; Z*

BEST DIRECTOR

HOLLIS ALPERT: Federico Fellini (*Spirits of the Dead*); François Truffaut (*Stolen Kisses*); Costa-Gavras (Z)

HAROLD CLURMAN: Costa-Gavras (Z); Bo Widerberg (*Adalen '31*); Claude Chabrol (*La Femme Infidèle*)

BRAD DARRACH: Bo Widerberg (*Adalen '31*); Ivan Passer (*Intimate Lighting*); Luchino Visconti (*The Damned*)

PENELOPE GILLIATT: Miklós Jancsó (*The Red and the White*; *The Roundup*); François Truffaut (*Stolen Kisses*); Ivan Passer (*Intimate Lighting*)

PAULINE KAEL: Sam Peckinpah (*The Wild Bunch*) (no 2nd and 3rd choices)

STEFAN KANFER: François Truffaut (*Stolen Kisses*); Miklós Jancsó (*The Red and the White*); Sam Peckinpah (*The Wild Bunch*)

STANLEY KAUFFMANN: Miklós Jancsó (*The Red and the White*); Luis Buñuel (*Simon of the Desert*); Sam Peckinpah (*The Wild Bunch*)

ROBERT KOTLOWITZ: Claude Chabrol (*La Femme Infidèle*); Costa-Gavras (Z); Luchino Visconti (*The Damned*)

JOSEPH MORGENSTERN: Costa-Gavras (Z); Claude Chabrol (*La Femme Infidèle*); François Truffaut (*Stolen Kisses*)

ANDREW SARRIS: Claude Chabrol (*La Femme Infidèle*); François Truffaut (*Stolen Kisses*); Luis Buñuel (*Simon of the Desert*)

RICHARD SCHICKEL: Sam Peckinpah (*The Wild Bunch*); François Truffaut (*Stolen Kisses*); Miklós Jancsó (*The Red and the White*)

ARTHUR SCHLESINGER: Federico Fellini (*Spirits of the Dead*); Costa-Gavras (Z); Lindsay Anderson (*If*)

JOHN SIMON: Ivan Passer (*Intimate Lighting*); Bo Widerberg (*Adalen '31*); Sidney Pollack (*They Shoot Horses, Don't They?*)

BEST ACTOR

HOLLIS ALPERT: Robert Redford (*Butch Cassidy and the Sundance Kid*); Peter O'Toole (*Goodbye,*

Mr. Chips); Dustin Hoffman (*Midnight Cowboy*)

HAROLD CLURMAN: Jon Voight (*Midnight Cowboy*); Helmut Berger (*The Damned*); Michel Bouquet (*La Femme Infidèle*)

BRAD DARRACH: Helmut Berger (*The Damned*); Nicol Williamson (*Laughter in the Dark*); Michel Bouquet (*La Femme Infidèle*)

PENELOPE GILLIATT: Nicol Williamson (*Hamlet; Laughter in the Dark*); Robert Ryan (*The Wild Bunch*); Elliott Gould (*Bob & Carol & Ted & Alice*)

PAULINE KAEL: Peter O'Toole (*Goodbye, Mr. Chips*); Jon Voight (*Midnight Cowboy*); Michel Bouquet (*La Femme Infidèle*)

STEFAN KANFER: Nicol Williamson (*Laughter in the Dark*); Peter O'Toole (*Goodbye, Mr. Chips*); Elliott Gould (*Bob & Carol & Ted & Alice*)

STANLEY KAUFFMANN: Richard Burton (*Staircase*); Peter O'Toole (*Goodbye, Mr. Chips*); Jon Voight (*Midnight Cowboy*)

ROBERT KOTLOWITZ: Jon Voight (*Midnight Cowboy*); Michel Bouquet (*La Femme Infidèle*); Wendell Burton (*The Sterile Cuckoo*)

JOSEPH MORGENSTERN: Peter O'Toole (*Goodbye, Mr. Chips*); Jon Voight (*Midnight Cowboy*); Michel Bouquet (*La Femme Infidèle*)

ANDREW SARRIS: Jon Voight (*Midnight Cowboy*); Robert Redford (*Butch Cassidy and the Sundance Kid*); Henry Fonda (*Once upon a Time in the West*)

RICHARD SCHICKEL: Robert Redford (*Downhill Racer*); John Wayne (*True Grit*); Peter O'Toole (*Goodbye, Mr. Chips*)

ARTHUR SCHLESINGER: Dustin Hoffman (*Midnight Cowboy*); Jon Voight (*Midnight Cowboy*); Robert Redford (*Downhill Racer* and *Butch Cassidy and the Sundance Kid*)

JOHN SIMON: Michel Bouquet (*La Femme Infidèle*); Jon Voight (*Midnight Cowboy*); Peter O'Toole (*Goodbye, Mr. Chips*)

BEST ACTRESS

HOLLIS ALPERT: Maggie Smith (*The Prime of Miss Jean Brodie*); Natalie Wood (*Bob & Carol & Ted & Alice*); Ingrid Thulin (*The Damned*)

HAROLD CLURMAN: Vanessa Redgrave (*The Loves of Isadora*); Jane Fonda (*They Shoot Horses, Don't They?*); Geraldine Page (*Trilogy*)

BRAD DARRACH: Dyan Cannon (*Bob & Carol & Ted & Alice*); Vanessa Redgrave (*The Loves of Isadora*); Barbra Streisand (*Hello, Dolly!*)

PENELOPE GILLIATT: Jane Fonda (*They Shoot Horses, Don't They?*); Vanessa Redgrave (*The Loves of Isadora*); Barbra Streisand (*Hello, Dolly!*)

PAULINE KAEL: Barbra Streisand (*Hello, Dolly!*); Jane Fonda (*They Shoot Horses, Don't They?*); Vanessa Redgrave (*The Loves of Isadora*)

STEFAN KANFER: Vanessa Redgrave (*The Loves of Isadora*); Jane Fonda (*They Shoot Horses, Don't They?*) (no 3rd choice)

STANLEY KAUFFMANN: Vanessa Redgrave (*The Loves of Isadora*); Maggie Smith (*The Prime of Miss Jean Brodie*); Claire Bloom (*Three into Two Won't Go*)

ROBERT KOTLOWITZ: Ingrid Thulin (*The Damned*); Liza Minnelli (*The Sterile Cuckoo*) (no 3rd choice)

JOSEPH MORGENSTERN: Vanessa Redgrave (*The Loves of Isadora*); Liza Minnelli (*The Sterile Cuckoo*); Jane Fonda (*They Shoot Horses, Don't They?*)

ANDREW SARRIS: Jane Fonda (*They Shoot Horses, Don't They?*); Pat Quinn (*Alice's Restaurant*); Dyan Cannon (*Bob & Carol & Ted & Alice*)

RICHARD SCHICKEL: Vanessa Redgrave (*The Loves of Isadora*) (no 2nd and 3rd choices)

ARTHUR SCHLESINGER: Vanessa Redgrave (*The Loves of Isadora*); Verna Bloom (*Medium Cool*); Ingrid Thulin (*The Damned*)

JOHN SIMON: Verna Bloom (*Medium Cool*); Jane Fonda (*They Shoot Horses, Don't They?*); Vanessa Redgrave (*The Loves of Isadora*)

BEST SUPPORTING ACTOR

Majority vote—1st ballot

HOLLIS ALPERT: Gig Young (*They Shoot Horses, Don't They?*)
HAROLD CLURMAN: Jack Nicholson (*Easy Rider*)
BRAD DARRACH: Jack Nicholson (*Easy Rider*)
PENELOPE GILLIATT: Jack Nicholson (*Easy Rider*)
PAULINE KAEL: Brian Keith (*Gaily, Gaily*)
STEFAN KANFER: Jack Nicholson (*Easy Rider*)
STANLEY KAUFFMANN: Jack Nicholson (*Easy Rider*)
ROBERT KOTLOWITZ: Jack Nicholson (*Easy Rider*)
JOSEPH MORGENSTERN: Elliott Gould (*Bob & Carol & Ted & Alice*)
ANDREW SARRIS: Jack Nicholson (*Easy Rider*)
RICHARD SCHICKEL: Gig Young (*They Shoot Horses, Don't They?*)
ARTHUR SCHLESINGER: Harold Blankenship (*Medium Cool*)
JOHN SIMON: Jack Nicholson (*Easy Rider*)

BEST SUPPORTING ACTRESS

HOLLIS ALPERT: Sian Phillips (*Goodbye, Mr. Chips*); Delphine Seyrig (*Stolen Kisses*); Celia Johnson (*The Prime of Miss Jean Brodie*)

HAROLD CLURMAN: Verna Bloom (*Medium Cool*); Celia Johnson (*The Prime of Miss Jean Brodie*); Delphine Seyrig (*Stolen Kisses*)

BRAD DARRACH: Dyan Cannon (*Bob & Carol & Ted & Alice*); Verna Bloom (*Medium Cool*); Sally Kirkland (*Coming Apart*)

PENELOPE GILLIATT: Sian Phillips (*Goodbye, Mr. Chips*); Celia Johnson (*The Prime of Miss Jean Brodie*); Maggie Smith (*Oh! What a Lovely War*)

PAULINE KAEL: Sian Phillips (*Goodbye, Mr. Chips*); Celia Johnson (*The Prime of Miss Jean Brodie*) (no 3rd choice)

STEFAN KANFER: Verna Bloom (*Medium Cool*); Sian Phillips (*Goodbye, Mr. Chips*); Bonnie Bedelia (*They Shoot Horses, Don't They?*)

STANLEY KAUFFMANN: Celia Johnson (*The Prime of Miss Jean Brodie*); Mona Washbourne (*The Bed Sitting Room*); Catherine Burns (*Last Summer*)

ROBERT KOTLOWITZ: Delphine Seyrig (*Stolen Kisses*); Dyan Cannon (*Bob & Carol & Ted & Alice*); Pat Quinn (*Alice's Restaurant*)

JOSEPH MORGENSTERN: Dyan Cannon (*Bob & Carol & Ted & Alice*); Delphine Seyrig (*Stolen Kisses*); Sian Phillips (*Goodbye, Mr. Chips*)

ANDREW SARRIS: Delphine Seyrig (*Stolen Kisses*); Bonnie Bedelia (*They Shoot Horses, Don't They?*); Rita Moreno (*Marlowe*)

RICHARD SCHICKEL: Dyan Cannon (*Bob & Carol & Ted & Alice*); Delphine Seyrig (*Stolen Kisses*); Verna Bloom (*Medium Cool*)

ARTHUR SCHLESINGER: Verna Bloom (*Medium Cool*); Pat Quinn (*Alice's Restaurant*); Maggie Smith (*Oh! What a Lovely War*)

JOHN SIMON: Susannah York (*They Shoot Horses, Don't They?*); Celia Johnson (*The Prime of Miss Jean Brodie*); Dyan Cannon (*Bob & Carol & Ted & Alice*)

BEST SCREENPLAY

HOLLIS ALPERT: Paul Mazursky and Larry Tucker (*Bob & Carol & Ted & Alice*); Waldo Salt (*Midnight Cowboy*); Jorge Semprun and Costa-Gavras (Z)

HAROLD CLURMAN: Jorge Semprun and Costa-Gavras (Z); Lindsay Anderson (*If*); Waldo Salt (*Midnight Cowboy*)

BRAD DARRACH: Luchino Visconti, Nicola Badalucca and Enrico Medioli (*The Damned*); Susumi Hani (*Nanami*); Paul Mazursky and Larry Tucker (*Bob & Carol & Ted & Alice*)

PENELOPE GILLIATT: Jorge Semprun and Costa-Gavras (Z); Paul Mazursky and Larry Tucker (*Bob & Carol & Ted & Alice*); Joan Littlewood and Charles Carlton (*Oh! What a Lovely War*)

PAULINE KAEL: Paul Mazursky and Larry Tucker (*Bob & Carol & Ted & Alice*); Alvin Sargent *The Sterile Cuckoo*) (no 3rd choice)

STEFAN KANFER: Jorge Semprun and Costa-Gavras (Z); Miklós Jancsó, Gergij Mdvani and Gyula Hernădi (*The Red and the White*)

STANLEY KAUFFMANN: Miklós Jancsó, Gergij Mdvani and Gyula Hernădi (*The Red and the White*); Luis Buñuel (*Simon of the Desert*); Sam Peckinpah and Walon Green (*The Wild Bunch*)

ROBERT KOTLOWITZ: Alvin Sargent (*The Sterile Cuckoo*); Jorge Semprun and Costa-Gavras (*Z*); Paul Mazursky and Larry Tucker (*Bob & Carol & Ted & Alice*)

JOSEPH MORGENSTERN: Paul Mazursky and Larry Tucker (*Bob & Carol & Ted & Alice*); Jorge Semprun and Costa-Gavras (*Z*); Alvin Sargent (*The Sterile Cuckoo*)

ANDREW SARRIS: Paul Mazursky and Larry Tucker (*Bob & Carol & Ted & Alice*); Claude Chabrol (*La Femme Infidèle*); Ivan Passer, Vaclav Sasek and Jaroslav Papousek (*Intimate Lighting*)

RICHARD SCHICKEL: Paul Mazursky and Larry Tucker (*Bob & Carol & Ted & Alice*) (no 2nd and 3rd choices)

ARTHUR SCHLESINGER: Paul Mazursky and Larry Tucker (*Bob & Carol & Ted & Alice*); David Sherwin (*If*); Jorge Semprun and Costa-Gavras (*Z*)

JOHN SIMON: Jorge Semprun and Costa-Gavras (*Z*); Ivan Passer, Vaclav Sasek and Jaroslav Papousek (*Intimate Lighting*); James Salter (*Downhill Racer*)

BEST CINEMATOGRAPHY

HOLLIS ALPERT: Haskell Wexler (*Medium Cool*); Conrad Hall (*Butch Cassidy and the Sundance Kid*); Jean Rabier (*La Femme Infidèle*)

HOWARD CLURMAN: Lucien Ballard (*The Wild Bunch*); Jorgen Persson (*Adalen '31*); Miroslav Ondriček (*If*)

BRAD DARRACH: Jorgen Persson (*Adalen '31*); Milton Moses Ginsberg (*Coming Apart*); Susumi Hani and Yuji Okumara (*Nanami*)

PENELOPE GILLIATT:	Miroslav Ondriček (*If*); Lucien Ballard (*The Wild Bunch*); Raoul Coutard (*Pierrot Le Fou*)
PAULINE KAEL:	Lucien Ballard (*The Wild Bunch*); Haskell Wexler (*Medium Cool*); Raoul Coutard (*Pierrot Le Fou*)
STEFAN KANFER:	Haskell Wexler (*Medium Cool*); Conrad Hall (*Tell Them Willie Boy Is Here*); Lucien Ballard (*The Wild Bunch*)
STANLEY KAUFFMANN:	(Abstained)
ROBERT KOTLOWITZ:	Miroslav Ondriček (*If*); (no 2nd and 3rd choices)
JOSEPH MORGENSTERN:	Lucien Ballard (*The Wild Bunch*); Tamás Somló (*The Red and the White*); Raoul Coutard (Z)
ANDREW SARRIS:	Raoul Coutard (*Pierrot Le Fou*); Laszlo Kovacs (*Easy Rider*); Lucien Ballard (*The Wild Bunch*)
RICHARD SCHICKEL:	Lucien Ballard (*The Wild Bunch*); Miroslav Ondriček (*If*); Tamás Somló (*The Red and the White*)
ARTHUR SCHLESINGER:	Raoul Coutard (Z); Miroslav Ondriček (*If*); Brian Brobyn (*Downhill Racer*)
JOHN SIMON:	David Watkin (*The Bed Sitting Room*); Tonino delli Colli (*Once Upon a Time in the West*); Tamás Somló (*The Red and the White*)

Voting Tabulation (1st choice = 3 points, 2nd choice = 2 points, 3rd choice = 1 point)

BEST PICTURE

21 POINTS	Z
11 POINTS	*Stolen Kisses*
10 POINTS	*La Femme Infidèle*

BEST DIRECTOR

12 POINTS	François Truffaut (*Stolen Kisses*)
11 POINTS	Costa-Gavras (Z)

9 POINTS — Claude Chabrol (*La Femme Infidèle*)
9 POINTS — Miklós Jancsó (*The Red and the White* and *Roundup*)

BEST ACTOR

18 POINTS — Jon Voight (*Midnight Cowboy*)
14 POINTS — Peter O'Toole (*Goodbye, Mr. Chips*)
9 POINTS — Michel Bouquet (*La Femme Infidèle*)
9 POINTS — Robert Redford (*Downhill Racer* and *Butch Cassidy and the Sundance Kid*)

BEST ACTRESS

24 POINTS — Vanessa Redgrave (*The Loves of Isadora*)
16 POINTS — Jane Fonda (*They Shoot Horses, Don't They?*)
5 POINTS — Verna Bloom (*Medium Cool*)
5 POINTS — Maggie Smith (*The Prime of Miss Jean Brodie*)
5 POINTS — Ingrid Thulin (*The Damned*)

BEST SUPPORTING ACTOR

Majority vote—1st ballot

Jack Nicholson (*Easy Rider*)

BEST SUPPORTING ACTRESS

13 POINTS — Sian Phillips (*Goodbye, Mr. Chips*)
12 POINTS — Verna Bloom (*Medium Cool*)
12 POINTS — Dyan Cannon (*Bob & Carol & Ted & Alice*)
12 POINTS — Celia Johnson (*The Prime of Miss Jean Brodie*)
12 POINTS — Delphine Seyrig (*Stolen Kisses*)

BEST SCREENPLAY

22 POINTS — Paul Mazursky and Larry Tucker (*Bob & Carol & Ted & Alice*)
18 POINTS — Jorge Semprun and Costa-Gavras (*Z*)
6 POINTS — Alvin Sargent (*The Sterile Cuckoo*)

BEST CINEMATOGRAPHY

16 POINTS	Lucien Ballard (*The Wild Bunch*)
11 POINTS	Miroslav Ondriček (*If*)
8 POINTS	Haskell Wexler (*Medium Cool*)

SPECIAL AWARDS TO IVAN PASSER AND DENNIS HOPPER

by majority vote

I:

PICK OF THE LITTER

Every age need not be a renaissance; it is only necessary for our own to be one. To that end, critics and audiences create their own masterpieces and their own masters. As counter response, other critics affect to find nothing but litter in the province of Art. Film, no less than painting or publishing, suffered just such extreme oscillations in the Sixties. Extravagant claims were made for some very minor creators; other gifted film makers found themselves derided for falling short of aims they never attempted.

1969 was a year of some wretched, boring work including *Hail Hero*, which dishonestly capitalized on the headlines from Vietnam. And *The Lost Man*, which decided that the Irish rebellion and the black revolution were one. And *Teorema*, which fused homosexuality, Christianity and infelicity. It would have been facile to use these failures as indicators of the year's bleak harvest. Yet there were at least eight films which aroused enough praise and/or controversy to defend the year, and, just possibly, the decade. We are not, as yet, living in a renaissance. But, as this handful of arguments and analyses demonstrates, neither is it obligatory to dwell in the dark.

—S.K.

Z

EXILES

Pauline Kael

Z is almost intolerably exciting—a political thriller that builds up so much tension that you'll probably feel all knotted up by the time it's over. The young director Costa-Gavras, using everything he knows to drive home his points as effectively as possible, has made something very unusual in European films—a political film with a purpose and, at the same time, a thoroughly commercial film. Z is undoubtedly intended as a political act, but it never loses emotional contact with the audience. It derives not from the traditions of the French film but from American gangster movies and prison pictures and "anti-Fascist" melodramas of the forties (*Cornered, Crossfire, Brute Force, All the King's Men, Edge of Darkness, The Cross of Lorraine,* et al.), and, like those pictures, it has a basically simple point of view. America stopped making this kind of melodrama (melodrama was always the chief vehicle for political thought in our films) during the McCarthy era, so Costa-Gavras has the advantage of bringing back a popular kind of movie and of bringing it back in modern movie style. Z has been photographed by Raoul Coutard, Godard's cameraman, in Eastmancolor used in a very strong, almost robust way, and although the photography is perhaps a little too self-consciously dynamic and, at times, not as hard-focused as it might be, the searching, active style doesn't allow you to get away. Remember when the movie ads used to say, "It will knock you out of your seat"? Well, Z damn near does.

There hasn't been an exciting anti-Fascist suspense film around for a long time, and the subject of Z is so good that the audience is not likely to resent the use of melodramatic excitement the way it would now if the film were anti-Communist, like those Hollywood films of the early fifties in which our boy Gregory Peck was ferreting out Communist rats. Z is based on the novel by the Greek exile Vassili Vassilikos about the assassination of Gregorios Lambrakis, in Salonika, in May, 1963. Lambrakis, it may be recalled, was a professor of medicine at the University of Athens who was also a legislator and a spokesman for peace. He was struck down by a delivery truck as he left a peace meeting—a murder planned to look like an accident. The investigation of his death uncovered such a scandalous network of corruption and illegality in the police and in the government that the leader of the opposition party, George Papandreou, became Premier. But in April, 1967, the military coup d'état overturned the legal government. Z reenacts the murder and the investigation in an attempt to demonstrate how the mechanics of Fascist corruption may be hidden under the mask of law and order; it is a brief on the illegality of the present Greek government.

Jorge Semprun, the Spanish writer, who worked on the screenplay and wrote the dialogue, has said, "Let's not try to reassure ourselves: this type of thing doesn't only happen elsewhere, it happens everywhere." Maybe, but not necessarily in the same way, though some Americans are sure to take the conspiracy in Z as applying to our political assassinations, too. This movie has enough layers of reference without anyone's trying to fit the American political assassinations into it; our freaky loners, on the loose in a large, heterogeneous country, are part of a less tightly structured, more volatile situation. It's ironic that what apparently did happen in the Lambrakis affair should resemble the conspiracy fantasies of Mark Lane and other Americans about the death of President Kennedy. And to see how the network of crime and politics works to conceal the assassination in Z is aesthetically satisfying. One can easily recognize the psychological attraction, for both left and right, of spinning conspiratorial systems that make things grand and orderly. (Z opens with a witty treatment of right-wing paranoia.)

Z could not, of course, be made in Salonika; it was shot in Algeria, in French, as a French-Algerian co-production. The director,

Costa-Gavras, is a Greek exile. (He was a leading ballet dancer in Greece before going to France, where he studied filmmaking and made his first picture, *The Sleeping Car Murder.*) The score, by Mikis Theodorakis, who is now under house arrest in Greece (where his music is banned), is said to have been smuggled out. Yves Montand, who is the Lambrakis figure here, was recently seen as the Spanish hero of *La Guerre Est Finie,* which Semprun, an exile from Spain, also wrote, and other actors from the Spanish setting turn up here, too. The Algerian locations, being the sites of actual tortures and demonstrations, add their own resonances; the hospital where injured men may be mistreated instead of treated plays its former role. The atmosphere is thus full of echoes, and the movie—consciously, I think—reactivates them. The subject touches off our recollections of Greece, of Algeria, of Spain, which combine to make us feel, "Yes—this is the way it happens," and to evoke images of and fears about all rightist terrorism.

On the one hand, there are the weak and corrupt and degenerate, the bullies and criminals—in a word, the Fascists. On the other, there are the gentle, intelligent, honorable pacifists—in a word, humanitarians. But Costa-Gavras gets by with most of this, because, despite our knowledge that he's leaning on us, he has cast the actors so astutely and kept them so busy that they miraculously escape being stereotypes. Some of them—particularly those who play the right-wing leaders, such as Pierre Dux in the role of a general—manage to suggest more than one notorious political figure. The cast of famous names and faces from the confused, combined past of many other movies forms a familiar, living background. I'm not sure exactly how Costa-Gavras has accomplished it, but in this movie—in contrast to so many other movies—the fact that we vaguely know these people works to his advantage, and enables him to tell the story very swiftly. It does not surprise us that François Périer, as the public prosecutor, is weak; that Renato Salvatori enjoys hitting people; that the magnificent Irene Papas is a suffering widow; that Charles Denner is half-Jewish; that Jean-Louis Trintignant is civilized and intelligent; and so on. All their earlier make-believe characters have merged in our memories; by now, when we see these actors they seem like people we actually used to know. I have sometimes found myself nodding at someone on the street before I realized that that was no old friend, it was

David Susskind. There is the same sort of acquaintance with these actors, whom we have come to take for granted, and the ambience of known people seems to authenticate the case.

Not all the elements are convincing. The staging of the crowd at the peace rally and of the police lines surrounding it doesn't feel right; it's confusing that the leader who dies appears to be beaten less than a man who survives; the motives of one of the assassins, who turns himself in, are obscure. Marcel Bozzufi, the actor playing this assassin, gives the most flamboyant performance in the film; it's enjoyable, because the movie needs to be lifted out of its documentary style from time to time, yet you are as much aware of Bozzufi's performance—even though it's a good one—as you were in *Open City* when the Gestapo chief came on faggy. There are scenes, such as Georges Geret acting a shade too comic with an ice pack, and Magali Noel being excessively vicious as his vicious sister, that are too much in the standard Jules Dassin–Edward Dmytryk tradition. And, as in the Hollywood forties, the martyred man is such a perfect nondenominational Good Man—like Victor in *Casablanca*—that one never really understands his politics or why the police and the military want to get rid of him. This is an ironic element in the book, where a possible explanation is offered—that the Fascists were afraid not of the left but of liberals, like this man, who were beginning to cooperate with the Communists. In the movie, though, we get the impression that this pure peacenik-liberal and his friends *are* the left and that they are mistaken for Communists (who probably don't exist at all) by the paranoid right.

But the pace, the staccato editing, the strong sense of forward movement in the storytelling, and that old but almost unfailingly effective melodramatic technique of using loud music to build up the suspense for the violent sequences put so much pressure on you that these details don't detract much. There is a serious flaw at the end, however, where the wrap-up comes too fast. All the way through, Z stays so close to the action that it doesn't explain the larger context, and by the end we have been battered so much that we want to understand more, so that we won't have been riding this roller coaster just for the thrills. The explanations of what happened to whom and how this incident precipitated the change in government, and then the reversals of fortune after the military coup, go by at dizzying speed, and this is a psychological miscalculation. We have an almost physical need for synthesis from a movie as powerful as this. We want to know who was protected by the new rightist regime and who was sacrificed; we want to see the larger political meaning of the events. We don't want just to use the film masochistically, to feed our worst fears or to congratulate ourselves for being emotionally exhausted.

In a thriller, the director's job is to hold you in his grip and keep squeezing you to react the way he wants you to, and Costa-Gavras does his job efficiently—in fact, sensationally. Is it valid, morally, to turn actual political drama—in this case, political tragedy—into political melodrama, like Z? I honestly don't know. The techniques of melodrama are not those of art, but if we accept them when they're used on trivial, fabricated stories (robberies, spy rings, etc.) merely to excite us, how can we reject them when the filmmakers attempt to use them to expose social evils and to dramatize political issues? Yet there is an aesthetic discrepancy when the methods are not worthy of the subject; when coercive, manipulative methods are used on serious subjects, we feel a discomfort that we don't feel when the subjects are trivial. It's one of the deep contradictions in movies that in what should be a great popular, democratic art form ideas of any kind seem to reach the mass audience only by squeezing it. I anticipate that some people may ask, "What's the problem? The movie is telling the truth." And others may say, "Whether it's accurate or not, it's convincing, and that's all a critic need fret about." Neither of these arguments clears away my basic uneasiness about the use of loaded melodramatic techniques, particularly now, when they can be so effectively blended with new semidocumentary methods to produce the illusion of current history caught by the camera. Given the genre, however, the men who made this film have been intelligent and restrained. I don't think Costa-Gavras ever uses violence except to make you hate violence, and such humanitarianism in filmmaking is becoming rare.

Melodrama works so well on the screen, and when it works against the present Greek military government it's hard to think ill of it. People will say of the moviemakers not that they're "laying it on" but that they're "laying it on the line." The truth is, they're doing both. Z is a hell of an exciting movie, and it carries you along, though when it's over and you've caught your breath you know perfectly well that its techniques of excitation could as easily be used by a smart Fascist filmmaker, if there were one (fortunately, there isn't), against the left or the center.

THE THRILLER AS POLITICS

ARTHUR SCHLESINGER, JR.

In May 1963 Gregorios Lambrakis, a progressive leader in the Greek parliament, was killed as he left a peace meeting in Salonika. The police pronounced his death a motor accident. But the autopsy cast doubt on this theory; and an examining magistrate, defying official pressure to close the case, conducted a long and patient investigation. The trail finally led to a secret right-wing organization and from there to officials of the police and the army.

The trial in 1966 stirred nationalist emotions. The murderers got off with light sentences and the officials behind the crime were acquitted, though forced into retirement. Six months later the colonels set up their dictatorship in Athens and rehabilitated the instigators of the murder. Vassili Vassilikos, a young Greek writer in exile, soon wrote a novel about the Lambrakis affair called Z (from *Zet*: "He lives"), and Constantin Costa-Gavras, a French director of Greek origin, has now made it into this exceptionally strong and arresting film.

Let me say at once that the film is not cast as a political polemic. Its form is that of a detective story: a murder, a mystery, doubts, frustrations, breakthroughs, solutions. People who have never heard of Lambrakis, or for that matter of Greece, will find this the most absorbing suspense thriller of the year. But, because of the passionate artistry which emerges when intensity of conviction is joined to intensity of control, Z transcends the thriller form and becomes the most memorable political film of the decade, rivaled only by Resnais's *La Guerre est finie* in 1966.

The power of the film comes in great part from its humanism. Both Costa-Gavras' direction and the dialogue of Jorge Semprun, himself a refugee from the Spanish dictatorship, move beyond melodrama to the complexities of social relationships. The political types are marvelously delineated. One has so often seen the deputy and his supporters, decent men in a brutal world, at liberal Democratic caucuses and ADA meetings. Even the right-wing terrorists are perceived with a measure of sympathy. Most are ignorant, distraught people responding, as they think, to high motives of religion and patriotism. Violence suffuses the picture, but for once it is an organic part of the drama.

All this is reinforced by great technical proficiency—the swift, insistent pacing of the narration, the lucid beauty of the photography (by Raoul Coutard, who has served Godard and Truffaut so well in the past), the conviction of the acting. Yves Montand, with that seamed, haunted face, is fine and sensitive as the deputy, knowing the risks involved but doing what he had to do. Jean-Louis Trintignant, sardonic and dispassionate as the magistrate, Irene Papas, magnificent in grief as the deputy's wife, and the supporting cast are all superb.

In a way Z is a sequel to the Resnais film. It has the same author in Semprun and the same hero in Montand. Where the earlier picture showed the exhaustion of the impulse of communist conspiracy, Z shows the capacity of decent democrats to fight back in the open so long as speech, the press, and the courts remain free. The only way the Greek Right could dispose of the Lambrakis murder was to establish the dictatorship of Papadopoulos. Z might well have been called *La Guerre n'est pas finie.*

EASY RIDER

ON THE ROAD

JOSEPH MORGENSTERN

Time and again I wanted to reach out and shake Peter Fonda and Dennis Hopper, the two motorcyclist heroes of *Easy Rider*, until they stopped their damned-fool pompous poeticizing on the subject of doing your own thing and being your own man. I dislike Fonda as an actor; he lacks humor, affects insufferable sensitivity and always seems to be fulfilling a solemn mission instead of playing a part. I didn't believe in these Honda hobos as intuitive balladeers of the interstate highways, and I had no intention of accepting them as protagonists in a modern myth about the destruction of innocence. To my astonishment, then, the movie reached out and profoundly shook me.

Easy Rider is a silly movie in many ways, a vulnerable, romantic ballad that goes soft in the head whenever it tries to turn its characters into Christ figures or celebrates the pastoral purity of a life beyond exurbia. Fonda and Hopper, riding together on a cross-country search for personal freedom, defer reverentially to a rancher for being able to "do your own thing in your own time," though for all they know the old coot beats his Mexican wife and lives off soil bank subsidies. At a hippie commune in the mountains, Fonda surveys an engaging troop of city kids trying to sow seeds in unplowed soil, then announces solemnly: "They're going to make it." Who does he think he is, Luther Burbank?

Fonda neither approves nor disapproves of what he finds along the way. He judgeth not. He is like Christ in his tenderness, like a test pilot in his coolness, riding along and not judging, getting busted for no good reason and not judging, picking up a whore and not judging (and not doing much of anything else with her, either, overt sexuality having been suppressed in our heroes by all the pot they puff, or possibly by kidney trouble resulting from engine vibrations).

If Fonda plays a sententious squirt with ample sententiousness, Hopper plays a vague, desperate vagrant with considerable charm. The results might have been happier if Hopper, who directed the film, had also awarded himself the larger lead role. There's an authentic emptiness about both of them, a genuine displaced persona, until you begin to dig what the movie is really into, man, what kind of beautiful vibrations it's actually trying to give off, until you realize that it's not supposed to be emptiness at all, man, but like, well, you know, it's supposed to be like *eloquence*, man.

Yet the amazing, confusing thing about *Easy Rider* is that it really is eloquent in almost every passage that isn't marked Hush —Eloquence at Work. It's an important movie that's sure to involve a large audience in its story of two foolish, decent hippies set upon by indecent squares. Produced by Fonda, released through Columbia Pictures and written by Fonda, Hopper and Terry Southern, *Easy Rider* is a linear descendant of the cheap, violent and topical melodramas that Fonda did for American-International Pictures: *The Wild Angels* (also motorcycles) and *The Trip* (LSD). *Easy Rider* has the immediacy of these earlier movies, but it uses violence sparingly, to devastating effect. And it develops its single, strong idea through flashes of brilliant writing and performance that more than make up for the foolishness, and through dazzling photography (by Lazslo Kovacs) that reminds us of how ravishingly beautiful parts of the nation remain.

Easy Rider is not consistently well made, but it's purposefully made, and the purpose pays off. The photography dotes on the grandeur of Western roads, but it also notes the corruptive presence of poverty, factories, tin-roofed shacks and abandoned automobiles that serve as mute witnesses, omnipresent extras. A good movie is a time-and-motion study, and Hopper, in this auspicious directorial debut, takes plenty of time to study parades, graffiti, textures of walls, fields of flowers and, in one 360-degree shot reminiscent of the great Mozart scene in Jean-Luc Godard's *Weekend*, the faces of hippies at a planting prayer. When the material is rich, as it is in a jail sequence and a sinister roadside café scene that both bear the stamp of Terry Southern's writing, Hopper's direction takes all the time needed to set it in motion and sustain it there. And Jack Nicholson gives a fine, crucial performance as George Hanson, a sly, sad, funny lush of a lawyer who says: "You know, this used to be a hell of a good country. I don't know what happened."

In the final analysis it doesn't much matter if Fonda, Hopper or Southern were confused about the details of their heroes' confusion. What matters is the end result, and that is memorable. *Easy Rider* is not, as it first seems, a misguided myth about innocence. It is stronger than that. Neither of these two riders with names from American mythology—Wyatt and Billy—is conspicuously innocent. They've gotten the money for their odyssey by pushing dope. Their machines help pollute the fragile land with fumes and noise, though you might not know it from a succession of lyrical transitional passages in which the only thing that pours out of their exhaust stacks is folk music. They look strange and doubtless smell stranger. But they are trying to go straight, to become relatively harmless people. And their supposedly straight compatriots—we, the other people, the great washed masses—cannot abide their troubling presence. That is the true subject matter of *Easy Rider:* the wanton destruction of harmlessness. It is a movie myth, to be sure, but its essential truth is brought home by what we ourselves know of our trigger-happy, hate-ridden nation in which increasing numbers of morons bear increasing numbers of arms.

INTO THE EYE OF THE STORM

Penelope Gilliatt

Easy Rider is the real thing. Ninety-four minutes of the reason so many Americans trust film fiction more than wrapped-up actuality reports. Ninety-four minutes of the connective tissue binding Americans to a continent that, to go by those actuality reports, they would be entitled to loathe. Ninety-four minutes of what it is like to swing, to watch, to be fond, to hold opinions, and to get killed in America at this moment. The film was produced by Peter Fonda, directed by Dennis Hopper, and written by both of them, together with Terry Southern. It is beautifully simple. It goes almost like the country's traditional frontier myth, but run backward. Two young men—Peter Fonda as Wyatt and Dennis Hopper as Billy—set off from the West Coast on motorbikes and ride in the direction that is now the harder one. They are traveling not away from sophistication but into it, and the lonely part is the easy part. They begin on the far side of the Mexican border. By smuggling dope across the frontier and selling it to a gum-chewing young capitalist disguised as a fellow hippie, they make enough money to live life their own way. The soft, hot wind of the continent blows on their faces as they ride east. Wyatt's long hair flows back from the flat planes of his cheeks. The handlebars of his bike are as high as his eyebrows while he leans back in the saddle, a patch of the Stars and Stripes on his jacket and another on his fuel tank. Billy, riding a cycle laden like a pack mule, lopes along beside him. His long hair is like the ears of a water spaniel, and he has an interesting nervous laugh when he gets high on pot every night. Motels turn them away, but it is easy enough to camp out. They are making for Mardi Gras in New Orleans. They are in no hurry. Some instinct, perhaps, warns them not to get there too fast—something telling them, against the precepts of this nation of goals, that the point will be contained in the getting there and that arrival may be a death. Day after day, they ride through the bright Western sunlight and into the dusk. They pass slowly through the brown beauty of the West, past wedge-shaped mountains raised like black axes in the desert. They stop for a meal with a quiet rancher who halted here long ago in his tracks westward and doesn't now know what the initials L.A. stand for, although he probably once understood them. "When I was a young man, I was headed for California," he says, "but you know how it is. . . ." He is the man of lost objectives, the American idea of failure in a nutshell, but he may really have done well, implies this ballad in praise of ease. The two young heroes can't altogether imitate him. They threw away their watches at the start of the journey in symbolic scorn for the organized, but they can't come to rest. The uncovered size of America draws them on, and they have to keep going. They pick up a hitchhiker in some dusk, and a taillight suddenly glows red as one of them makes the slow, swerving start with him aboard. The passenger, a stammering, benign man with a print scarf around his forehead who says it's hard to say where he's from because it's a very long word, leads them to a commune of hippies living in a barn and scratching a fine life out of land in drought. The two riders are offered a meal with them, conducted and filmed with ceremony. The camera goes through a three-hundred-and-sixty-degree shot that starts on one man's face, passes slowly around a ring of the hippies—a full circle of those long falls of hair and big, rested mouths, seen over a sound track of offscreen chat and clucking hens—and comes back to the first man as he says a Digger's thanksgiving. A mime troupe comes into the hippies' barn, and there is a switch of mood like the shift into the players' scene in *Hamlet*. One of the film's wonderful small moments of acting comes when Billy gets nervy and Wyatt makes a small pacifying gesture with his hand. "We're eating their food," he says. They go swimming in a scene of pure play. "This could be the right place," says the hitchhiker, but Wyatt can't accept it. "I'm hip about time," he says, "but I just got to go." Quietly acted, the character powerfully expresses the sense of a strong man who has an instinct to keep on the move but also a nagging prescience that he is going to crash.

Cut to another America. Wyatt and Billy join a drum-majorette parade in a small town, Wyatt cheerfully paddling his bike with his feet among the crowd of plump girls with pear-shaped thighs. For its own reasons, the town throws the hippies into jail—"for parading without a permit, man," as far as Billy can make it out. Their companion in the night cells is a boozing wit of a Southern lawyer, marvelously played by Jack Nicholson. Already fine, the film takes on the weight of the first-rate as soon as he appears. The character is called George Hanson. Son of a rich man, defender of civil-liberties cases, he is gifted with surreal comic visions and with the peculiar radical sagacity that can sometimes appear in the black-sheep members of highborn classes. He breezily talks his way out of the clink, still half sloshed, patronizing the cops with panache, and stumbles into the sun in his white suit with the historic dash of fallen gentlemen. He is like one of the wise fools of Russian literature. He knows from the very start what his new hippie friends are in for in the South, and he must also know that his own pleasure in the present is no protection against the future revenges of his class.

This man, the droll sophisticate of the film, is also its classic buffoon. He is the natural victim of the bigots he was born among, a boozing dandy from the square world whom the hippies instantly know for a brother. So now he rides with them, wearing a football helmet for a skid lid, and chatting slumberously about a whorehouse in New Orleans. Sometimes he peers at the road over spectacles pushed to the end of his nose, as if the whole journey were some interesting new find in Sanskrit, and sometimes he inspires flights of quiet farce when the three of them coast along on their bikes in the positions of figure skaters. He has a sort of genius for pleasure. At good moments—raising a bottle of Scotch to his mouth in the middle of an idea, for instance—he will suddenly flap one arm against his side like a cockerel's wing. By the campfire one night, he relinquishes Scotch to try his first joint. It takes him into a brilliant daydream that a race of visiting Venusians are among us—a species with no caste sense and no monetary system, "now mating with people in all walks of life, in an advisory capacity," he explains seraphically.

They ride past waving horsemen, and billboards for Coca-Cola, and cafés selling homemade pie. The film's affection for America even rubs off onto their first sights of sedate, making-it civilization. Then there is a scene in a Southern café, and the ballad takes the turn it was bound for. Incited by who knows what—by long hair, by aliens in their midst, by the sight of ease's style—the drawlers in the café talk loudly of Yankee queers, and the trio walk out. Danger stinks in the air. That night, the Jack Nicholson character gets pounded to death in his sleep and the two others have their blooding by the South. They mourn him without mention, eating a meal with their faces shaved for the first time since the start of the ride while a Kyrie Eleison pop song plays on the sound track. In their own mood of memorial, they go on to the brothel he talked about. Nothing quite works, even though it is Mardi Gras. Wyatt doesn't want his girl. Billy's hooker, sitting becalmed in black lace stockings with a pie slice of bare leg showing at the top, looks spectacularly enervating. The brothel décor itself, a ropy mixture of the religious and the erotic, is the baroque manner at its dregs, and the acid trip that the four take is a bad one, full of hints of extinction, and gaudy about them. The film's own attitude toward death is one of repose. It is an equivalent of its attitude toward the journey: The point is the journeying. Wyatt sees a lettered sign saying, "Death only closes a man's reputation and determines it as good or bad." After this, the film has an eyeblink shot of something on fire beside a road. When the two are back on their bikes, the rednecks of the land do their worst, and the shot turns out to be as prophetic as it looked.

Easy Rider is constructed like a ballad with a recurring fourth line. Between the verses describing the heroes' hardening encounters with America, there are repeated campfire scenes and mute cycle-riding sequences overlaid with pop music. Millions of words have been written explaining every element in such films' substance —hippies, idle violence, American restlessness; the reviving thing about this picture is that it doesn't explain, it embodies. The cant of cool is here made eloquent. The long ride and its laconic happiness tell the tale of a very American style of behavior, sped by the sense of a huge continent to cover, and wide open to worry. "This used to be a hell of a good country. I can't understand what's going on in it," says the character played by Jack Nicholson, in two sentences that hold the whole idea of the picture. It is a bright movie that sets out on such a simple thought and that recognizes such a blood brother to the hippies in a stray from middle-aged, drinking, formally educated America. George Hanson actually possesses more of the hippie perception of trouble than Billy does. Billy vaguely thinks that things are as they are because "everybody's got chicken." "Oh, they're not scared of you," says Hanson. "They're scared of what you represent to them. Freedom. . . . But don't ever tell anybody they ain't free, 'cause they're gonna get real busy killin' and maimin' to prove they're free." Wyatt, who thinks more than Billy does—one of the interesting marks of the film is that the three main performances seem to come out of three different imaginative worlds, separated so distinctly that it is as if the styles of the roles themselves were sealed apart by pot—sees things unrolling on a course that hits the nerve of America. As Wyatt and Hanson pursue it, their trek east is a myth truer to the country's extant frontier-pushing impulse than the plot of any Western. With the new sort of roamer's infallible ear, the two men not only know exactly when life is prospering but also when something is about to go badly wrong. "We blew it," Wyatt says, ahead of trouble. *Easy Rider* speaks tersely and aptly for this American age that is both the best of times and the worst of times. Because the picture is also very alert, humorous, beautiful, and modestly put, it seems to leave the balance tipped a little toward the best.

SPACE ODYSSEY 1969

STEFAN KANFER

> *When you read about Mark Twain's Mississippi raftsmen and pilots, or Bret Harte's Western gold miners, they seem more remote than the cannibals of the Stone Age. The reason is simply that they are free human beings.*
>
> —GEORGE ORWELL

The two men straddle motorcycles instead of horses, and they smoke marijuana instead of tobacco. But the central characters in *Easy Rider* are as remote as the freedom they are seeking. Wyatt (Peter Fonda) is a vague, unshaven pothead who likes to refer to himself as "Captain America." His manic sidekick Billy (Dennis Hopper) has a droopy Stephen Crane mustache and shiny eyes fixed on some wild interior vision. Flush from the profits of dope selling, the cyclists symbolically cast off their wristwatches and head for that persistent American symbol of adventure, The Road.

In the course of this alternately acute and naive odyssey, Wyatt and Billy carom from ranch to hippie commune to jail to the New Orleans Mardi Gras. En route, they pick up a Civil Liberties lawyer named George Hanson. As it emerges in the film, the lawyer's part is only a mug shot of a wry, wistful boozer. But in his first major role, Jack Nicholson proves that he knows far more about acting than either of his co-stars. His elegies for a vanished life are melancholy without being pathetic; his marijuana-flavored description of a UFO takeover of the U.S. is a perfect comedy within a flawed tragedy.

With the single exception of Nicholson, *Easy Rider*'s authentic force resides not in its professional but its amateur performances. Filming throughout the Southwest, first-time Director Hopper let the townspeople "rap" as they pleased, then caught them on camera. The result is a harrowing gallery of American primitives, from mindless high-school girls to the redneck truck drivers who case the cyclists' long hair and ad-lib: "Looks like refugees from some gorilla love-in . . . We ought to mate 'em up with . . . black wenches. That's as low as you can git."

Ironically, the film has less to say when the stars step forward. Their visit with the hippies is sticky and overlong; only the owner of a motorcycle or a gasoline company could remain entranced by the endless sequences of Wyatt and Billy throttling down endless roads. Moreover, the riders often lack perspective on themselves. Their "search for America" is rather like eyes looking for a face; they are part of what they seek.

Still, these are minor lapses in a major movie. In terms of contemporary mores and methods, *Easy Rider* has told its story from the far side of the generation gap. For once the aura of evil that clings to drug-and-motorcycle movies is gone. Like other films directed to—and by—youth, *Easy Rider* could have settled for catcalls and rebellion. Instead the film has refurbished the classic romantic gospel of the outcast wanderer. Walt Whitman might not have recognized the bikes—but he would have understood the message.

Jack Valenti, president of the Motion Picture Association of America and author of the movies' new rating system, may be astonished to learn that he is the father of *Easy Rider* (rated R). In a speech before the M.P.A.A. in 1967, Valenti said he was weary, weary, weary of the excesses in drug and motorcycle films. He wished for theaters full of Doctor Dolittles. Waiting in the wings, the next speaker made a perverse resolution: to make a good movie about drugs and motorcycles.

Like most of Peter Fonda's fantasies, it should have faded with the morning. For Fonda is a loser by every Hollywood definition. He is not only known as Henry's son but as Jane's brother. At 20, he was admittedly "paranoic"; at 24, he escaped the Army when his draft board found him too unstable for military service. His vanilla screen-acting style was best expressed in such films as *Tammy and the Doctor*. Offscreen, Fonda began a new vocation—as an alcoholic who ended at least one motorcycle ride in a Hollywood hospital. When he was discharged, he gave up vodka and took up marijuana. "That changed my whole mind," recalls Fonda. "My conscience began to show. I was no longer competitive. I grew my hair and sometimes a beard." Getting busted for possessing pot simply confirmed his new convictions. "I began to get less offers from Hollywood. I developed the reputation of being a difficult person."

If Fonda was difficult, his close friend and fellow Easy Rider was impossible. A compatriot of James Dean, Director Dennis Hopper has become the caricature of the surly, inarticulate "man, like I mean" Method actor. He had once announced to Fonda that "the first movie I make will have to win at Cannes." But his appearances in films belied the boast. The mad stare, the simian stance could have been reproduced, everyone thought, by a dozen actors. Everyone but Peter Fonda. He persuaded Terry Southern (*Dr. Strangelove*) to collaborate on the *Easy Rider* script, and talked American International Pictures, creators of the beach and motorcycle placebos, into producing a film starring nobodies and directed by a weirdo. When A.I.P. refused to put up enough money to launch the project, Fonda made the ultimate rich boy's sacrifice: He took a loan on his trust fund.

Ranging around the Southwest, Director Hopper abruptly changed into a budget-watching craftsman. He avoided expensive featherbedding by hiring personnel outside the regular Hollywood trade unions, and used friends who worked for scale. He surrounded them with ordinary passersby whose faces no Central Casting agent could reproduce.

When he told the high school girls "I want one of you to ask us if you can go for a ride on our bikes," the girls were way ahead of him. "Don't tell us any more," said one. "We know how to flirt." The drugstore loafers needed no instructions in hostility. "Are you a Commie? You on welfare? You got V.D.? Or hepatitis?" The questions followed the movie makers as they filmed onlookers from Arizona to Baton Rouge. On film, they retain the sting of spontaneity and conviction. The only query that could have hurt—Can you make a movie?—was never asked.

There was, however, a kind of answer. *Dr. Dolittle,* starring Rex Harrison and 1,000 animals, has gone on to become one of the screen's biggest losers. There is no guarantee that the Fonda-Hopper movie, starring no one of consequence, will be any more profitable. But this spring, at the Cannes Film Festival, first prize for a new director went to Dennis Hopper for his work on *Easy Rider*. If such a rakehell film can get international approbation, there are only two courses open to the Motion Picture Association: prohibition of drug-and-motorcycle movies—or of speeches by Jack Valenti.

A LYRIC, TRAGIC SONG OF THE ROAD

RICHARD SCHICKEL

Easy Rider is, in the smallest, sociological sense, a historic movie. In it, motorcycles are for the first time on screen converted from a malignant to a benign symbol, and the kids who ride them are seen not as vandals or threats to the Establishment but as innocent individualists in desperate unavailing flight from The System.

Sheer romanticism? Of course. But then the endless cycle of cycle-gang pictures to which we have been subjected in recent years is also an exaggeration, a commercialized compound of the worst figments of our most dismal imaginings about what's going on across the generation gap. At the very least, *Easy Rider* is a useful corrective. At its inconsistent best, it is an attempt to restate, in vivid, contemporary terms, certain ageless American proccupations.

In form, it is a loose, lovely-to-look-at, often laughing, often lyric epic about two young men (Peter Fonda and Dennis Hopper, who respectively produced and directed the film and collaborated with Terry Southern on the screenplay) who somehow believe the American road is still free, open and fit for decent adventurings. They—and we—should know right at the beginning that they are probably doomed to discover otherwise. Without quite knowing it, they are seeking a pure and purifying experience—a refreshed intimacy with their senses as well as the land and its people. But the means by which they finance their trip (the proceeds of cocaine smuggling) and their goal (New Orleans at Mardi Gras) are, in that order, impure and trivial.

Still, at first it seems the road retains its legendary qualities as a place that promises escape, a way of changing one's luck. These promises are, of course, important to all of us—always have been—and as they proceed eastward (an interesting reversal of our traditional westering impulse), our hopes about the quality of the experience we are sharing with them rise. They investigate two aspects of the simple life—stopping briefly at a family ranch and for a longer time at a hippie commune where idealism and impracticality coexist in nicely loony fashion. Sitting around the campfire with the shaggy type who is their guide to the commune, Fonda inquires whether he has ever wanted to assume another identity. Well, maybe Porky Pig, comes the reply.

It's funny in context, anyhow, and an indication that the film is not going to ride easy on youth's present sure sense of superiority to the adult, middle-class culture. Its makers are more sympathetic to the kids than to their parents, but the deck is not entirely stacked. Later on, in a small town jail, they encounter an alcoholic civil liberties lawyer (wonderfully played by Jack Nicholson). He springs them and they attempt to spring him from his bag (largely parental) by taking him along to New Orleans. Among their first suggestions is a liberating joint or two of pot. But, in the movie's best scene, they discover that, free as they are, they can't match the half-mad visionary intensity their straight friend achieves grooving on the mystery of UFOs. The joke is on their attitudes and expectations—and on us. For the implication is that the paranoid style increasingly evident in middle-class life may be a form of mind-bending at least as funny—and ultimately scary—as the drug scene.

Indeed, it is that paranoia—based on a fear of freedom—that ultimately turns this movie into tragedy. Even drugs cannot turn Mardi Gras into the liberating carnival of the spirit and the senses they hoped it would be. It is too uptight. And the road to it, and away from it, does lead through modern America. Inevitably, they must collide with the casual, unthinking brutality of a nation that talks much of freedom but will not tolerate radical expressions of it and will, on occasion, mindlessly kill dreams it does not understand and approve.

Easy Rider often fails to develop fully and exploit its best dramatic and comic potentials. It often lacks the technical skill to realize all its ambitions. Most damaging of all, perhaps, is its failure to let us really know its principals. Fonda comes on as an inarticulate novice saint, while Hopper gives off a vague air of anarchical menace, but neither really lets us inside his skin. They are too much in love with the idea of themselves as victims to show us the defects and imbalances that led them off on their quest—and to the sad waste of its ending. But despite all this, and a rather self-congratulatory air that hangs over this determinedly independent production, the film has a marvelous quality of being alive to its own possibilities and to the possibilities, good and bad, of the land it moves across.

BOB & CAROL & TED & ALICE

A CRITICAL SITUATION

Hollis Alpert

When I saw *Bob & Carol & Ted & Alice* at a sneak preview held in a theater, some 2,500 people laughed their heads off. Curious as to what made the film so successful, I went to see it again at a screening held for critics in Columbia Pictures' New York projection room. It still provoked laughter, but hardly the uproarious kind, and the experience was different, not only in degree but in kind. For one thing, next to me sat a critic with a little penlight who, from time to time, would jot down a line of dialogue on a note pad. Very distracting, both for him and for me.

Later, the film was selected to open the New York Film Festival. Again, the large audience had a happy time. There was not only laughter, but cheering and prolonged applause at the end. Columbia obviously had itself not only an audience hit, but a critical success. Or had it? For out came *The New York Times* the next day with a violent attack on the film, and also on the festival for exhibiting it.

Now, *B & C & T & A* is hardly a cause to get overly excited about, but it does seem to me that it is the victim of some unfair treatment. The *Times,* even though it well knew the film was not due for its general release for some weeks, ran an even more scathing review of the picture in its Sunday edition, and its reviewer referred to it nastily again in a review of *another* picture. That makes no fewer than three bad reviews, well in advance, from *The New York*

Times. *Time* magazine also took up its cudgel against the picture. It called its attitude toward sex "sniggering" and its ending "a cop-out," even though the *Times* had already employed the same terms.

It's hardly the critic's duty to defend a film company's right to make an extra buck, but it does seem to me that there is little point to film reviewing unless the readership is fully and fairly informed about the kind of experience it is likely to get if it invests its money in movie tickets. And I can affirm that, unless seen in an audience atmosphere, this film's values do not emerge fully. As it happens, under those conditions, *B & C & T & A* plays beautifully. It is what might be called a contemporary comedy of sexual manners; it is bright, original, funny, and, in its way, tender as it shows two youngish married couples attempting to stay abreast of what they assume to be changing sexual mores.

California, as we have been made aware by enterprising journalists for *Playboy* and *The New York Times Magazine*, among other swinging publications, has been taking the lead in such group activities as "touch therapy," and it is to a "sensitivity institute," much like Esalen, that Bob and Carol (who are played with rare zest by Robert Culp and Natalie Wood) go for fuller understanding of themselves and their marriage. They come out beatifically, almost mystically convinced that they are now more "honest" toward each other and "sensitive" toward others than they were before, and naturally they attempt to convince their best friends, another married couple called Ted and Alice (wonderfully played by newercomers Elliott Gould and Dyan Cannon) of the benefits of their new outlook.

Out of these beginnings grows the hilarity. To be sure, it is in the tradition of typical sex farce when Bob, determined to be honest, confesses an infidelity to Carol, and she reacts in terms of her new sensitivity schooling. She is so happy about her liberation from old-hat morality that *she* hurries to engage in an affair, less for enjoyment than for the chance to let her husband in on the happy secret. But it is all in how it is done. The fresh touch and the cutting edge are provided by Larry Tucker and Paul Mazursky, the latter on his first outing as a director. They have taken the relatively affluent Southern California urban middle class and gently satirized its sun-loving, fun-loving, youth-loving attributes.

After a typical dinner party, for example, the two friendly

couples engage in a bit of bravado pot-puffing. When the two husbands gravely discuss the ins and outs of marital infidelity, they do it in a corner of the swimming pool, while the kids splash happily all about them. Best of all is the scene between Ted and Alice in the privacy of their bedroom, as they face the classic marital dilemma of whether they are in the mood for lovemaking. What makes it comedy far superior to the witless general run is the tolerant understanding of the authors and their obvious affection for the characters.

And it is because of this tolerance and affection that the final scenes, dealing as they do with an abortive experiment at mate-swapping, neither offend nor "cop out," as some critics have claimed. In terms of today's relaxed standards, the film easily could have gotten away with an orgy at the end, thus satisfying those voyeurs who pay $25 for a front-row seat at *Oh! Calcutta!* But the film is quite clearly and plainly dealing with four American middle-class humans, California variety, none of whom are quite ready for such ventures in human "touch sensitivity." Tucker and Mazursky allowed B & C & T & A to keep their dignity, while they deepened their understanding of human relationships. This was not only a tasteful, but a nice and acceptable thing to do. Of course they could have been a little more daring—daring is the easiest and cheapest thing to come by these days. They could have been a little less slick, too, but Hollywood craftsmen, whether used by Mazursky or Nichols or Frankenheimer, find it difficult to be anything but slick. Allowing for a desultory moment or two, Tucker and Mazursky have made the year's best comedy, one that at last may even signify Hollywood's coming of age. This is adult fun, neither cheap, nor sly, *nor* sniggering.

WAITING FOR ORGY

PAULINE KAEL

Bob & Carol & Ted & Alice has been widely attacked in advance: It opened the New York Film Festival, and the *Times* has had at it three times already, calling it a "sniggery" movie, and the news magazines have been jumping on it, too. *Time* was outraged that it was chosen to open "a presumably serious film festival." If one laughs at it, as I did (and I didn't snigger), one may suspect either (a) that even as good an American commercial comedy as this is *too* American and *too* commercial for the kind of fusty film-festival thinking that splits movies into art versus entertainment or (b) that there is something about the film that bugs people. It's both, I think.

When I see those ads with the quote, "You'll have to see this picture twice," I know it's the kind of picture I don't want to see once. It's practically a penance to sit through some of these movies, and a new Pasolini or a "late" Bresson lasts one a long time. The movie press has not suddenly become avant-garde; it's just embracing the European cultural values it feels safe with. European films have not struck out in any major new directions this year; they've been rather dull—which can hardly be said of American movies at this time. When one considers some of what has been urged on us as "art" this last year—all those films that *look* like art (*Teorema*) —it's clear that a commercial comedy doesn't fit into this framework of austere mortification of the audience. If you ever wanted to go see *Bob & Carol & Ted & Alice* again, it would be because it was funny, not because you didn't get it the first time. It's true it's not a work of depth that would yield up more with subsequent viewings, but it's almost schizophrenic for the movie critics to attack a movie for having just those entertaining qualities that drew them to movies in the first place. It's so damned easy to be cultured.

Bob & Carol & Ted & Alice is a slick, whorey movie, and the liveliest American comedy so far this year. It's unabashedly commercial, and in some ways it's the kind of commercial picture that succeeds with audiences by going just a little farther than they expect, but titillation is no longer easy, and this particular kind of titillation is so unconcealed that maybe it has earned the right to be called honestly comic. There is nothing hidden in this movie—the acrid commercial flavor is right there, out front. Because it's funny, and because it's marital-situation comedy and it's set in the middle-class southern California of so much tawdry Americana, it's easy to say this is Doris Day–land, and those bothered by the acridity may use that as a way of putting the film down. Superficially, the picture looks like a Day, and the people live in the same style (they did in *The Graduate* also), but this movie is made up of what was left out of the optimistic Doris Day comedies. (What a perfect name. *Sui generis.*) This is the far side of middle-class marriage, after Doris Day fades out. The period is late 1969, when the concept of legal marriage is being undermined and the members of the middle class who are trying to be swingers are nervous—culturally uneasy about clinging to something square, and personally tantalized by thoughts of the sex possibilities they're missing. The movie works its way through cuteness and "sophistication" and out the other end of nowhere. It's tawdry, all right, but the tawdriness is *used*. This is the kind of movie in which a modern husband who has just had an affair comes home unexpectedly to find another man in bed with his wife and decides that the sensible new behavior is to have a friendly drink. This solution is hardly satisfactory; the tension is unresolved. The scene is badly played, but still it nags at one: Is there a better solution?

A sophisticated popular comedy isn't Hollywood's stock-in-trade anymore; the times are too volatile. This picture is a bit more unusual than it may seem, and it raises some of the problems that may plague actors in the next few years. Paul Mazursky and Larry Tucker, who wrote *Bob & Carol & Ted & Alice*, also wrote last year's *I Love You, Alice B. Toklas!*, which had some very funny dialogue but was directed (by Hy Averback) in a loose scat style that didn't give the movie much distinction. Mazursky has directed this time, and the material takes on a far more self-aware aspect. The occasional attempts at visual effects (such as a sex fantasy on a plane) are disastrously shoddy, but Mazursky, directing his first picture, has done something very ingenious. He has developed a style from satiric improvisational revue theater—he and Tucker were part of the Second City troupe—and from TV situation comedy, and, with skill and wit, has made this mixture work.

During the past three or four years, many directors have tried to put revue humor on film, and, except for some of the early comedy sequences in *The Graduate*, it has failed, painfully—as in *Luv*, *The Tiger Makes Out*, the Eleanor Bron-William Daniels bits of *Two for the Road*, parts of *Bedazzled*, the Elaine May role in *Enter Laughing*, *The President's Analyst*, and so on. Revue theater is a form of actors' theater; even when the material isn't worked up by the actors—even when it is written by a Murray Schisgal (or, in England, transformed into more serious drama by Harold Pinter) —the meaning comes from the rhythm of clichés, defenses, and little verbal aggressions, and this depends on the pulse and the intuition of the performers. It would be as difficult to write out as dance notation. Typically, as in the Nichols-and-May routines, the satire is thin and the thinness is the essence of the joke. We laugh at the tiny, almost imperceptible hostilities that suddenly explode, because we recognize that we're tied up in knots about small issues more than about big ones, and that we don't lose our pretensions even when (or especially when) we are concerned about the big ones.

This style developed here (and in England) in the fifties, when college actors went on working together in cabarets, continuing and developing sophomoric humor. That word isn't used pejoratively; I *like* sophomoric college-revue humor, and one has only to contrast its topicality and freshness with the Joe Miller Jokebook world to understand why it swept the country. In revue, the very latest in interpersonal relations—the newest clichés and courtship rites and seduction techniques—could be polished to the point of satire almost overnight. The Lenny Bruces and Mort Sahls and the standup comics might satirize the political *them*, but cabaret, with its interacting couples, satirized *us*. We laugh at being nailed by these actors who are cartoons of us, all too easy to understand, and though there's a comic discomfort in listening to what our personal and social rituals might sound like if they were overheard, it's a comfortable form of theater—the disheveled American's form of light domestic comedy.

But it didn't work in the movies. A skit builds by the smallest of inflections, and each inflection becomes important because we construct the whole ambience from the performers—mainly from their voices. And that's what, in the past, killed this kind of acting on the screen: The performers did too much with voices and pauses, and when the director interrupted them with camera shifts and cuts, the performers lost their own rhythm and rapport. In relation to how it was being used, their acting was overdeveloped in a specialized way, and the result was, oddly, that they seemed ugly and rather grotesque and terribly stagy. And the milieu always felt wrong, because we didn't need it; instead of getting our bearings from the performers we looked at the sets and lost our bearings. This is still a problem in *Bob & Carol & Ted & Alice*—the houses the couples live in get in the way of our accepting the situations—but some of the other problems have been solved.

Mazursky has designed most of the picture in a series of sequences focusing on the actors, letting the rhythm of their interplay develop, and he has taken the series of revue sketches on the subject of modern marital stress and built them into a movie by using the format of situation comedy, with its recurrent synthetic crises. What is so surprising—and yet it should have been obvious—is that he has found useful dramatic elements in situation comedy. It's pleasant to stick to the same people throughout a movie, instead of wandering around and having the continuity broken into all the time, and it's relaxing to be in a form with controlled expectations, where there's no threat of violence, or even of direct assault on our emotions. This TV format is probably the best and most straightforward way to make revue material work on film, and it gives Mazursky a few small miracles (largely from Elliott Gould and Dyan Cannon), but, as a result of the long scenes, there's almost no way to conceal the failures.

Revue theater has attracted actors of a different kind from ordinary theater; frequently they are actor-writer-directors, literary satirists as well as satirical actors, and since their acting is so close to directing, they frequently become directors or comedians, but few of them have really become big *actors*. The kind of acting they've learned to do—which is both more demanding and, in some areas, less demanding than conventional acting—is *different*, and a basic trouble with *Bob & Carol & Ted & Alice* is that Natalie Wood can't do it. The design of the film is for two contrasting marriages—one a "good" marriage (Robert Culp, as a documentary filmmaker, and Natalie Wood), the other a mismatch (Elliott Gould, as a lawyer, and Dyan Cannon), yet a mismatch so recognizably common (she's bored and he's bewildered) that it's almost the typical perfect match. But there's no possibility of our believing in the good marriage. Natalie Wood doesn't seem to have any substance as a human being, so there's nothing at stake, as there would be with a fuller-dimensioned woman in the role. Her resources as an actress are skinny; she has nothing to draw upon but that same desperate anxiety and forced smile and agitation she's always drawn upon.

The whole area of screen acting is probably going to be a big can of worms in the next few years. We are already looking for closer identity between actor and role in many movies; we have become too acute about nuances (partly because of revue) to accept the iron-butterfly kind of star acting anymore. We never had the slightest illusion we were seeing Doris Day and Brian Keith as they were off-screen, and that hardly concerned us. In the kind of acting now being required, it *does* concern us, partly because of nudity and sex scenes, the influence of non-actors in *cinéma-vérité* roles, and the effect of TV news and talk shows, but mainly because of a new interest in less structured and less stereotyped approaches to character than in past movies. I think it's almost impossible to watch *Bob & Carol & Ted & Alice* without wondering how much the actors are playing themselves. Natalie Wood is still doing what she was doing as a child—still telegraphing us that she's being cute and funny—and she's wrong. When she tries hard, she just becomes an agitated iron butterfly. An actress's armor becomes embarrassing when character armor is the subject of the movie—and it's the subject of this movie, as it has always been the basic subject of revue.

With this material—concerning how much people are hiding from themselves—we begin to ask questions about the actors, to wonder whether they are what they appear to be. The performances that work best force us to a speculative invasion of the privacy of the actors; what would have once seemed gossip is now central not only to the performance but to the conception itself. With the camera coming in closer and closer, the inescapable question is: Can you act it if you're *not* it? Playing the bitch who sets the mechanism of "Let's have an orgy" in motion, Dyan Cannon—who looks a bit like Lauren Bacall and a bit like Jeanne Moreau, but the wrong bits—is most effective (really brilliant), I think, just because you don't like her, and I don't mean simply the character she plays; we react to her in the way untutored people used to react to actors, identifying them with their roles. We don't think she's just playing a bitch. And, on the same basis, we *like* Gould—not just because of his performance but because of an assumption, which is probably false, but which this kind of acting imposes, that he is what he's playing. Culp, who has the most difficult role, is solidly competent, and yet he fails somewhat, because he is too much the conventional actor *type*—Robert Cummings crossed with Timothy Leary.

But there is something else in this movie that bothers people. I don't think it's because it's *conventional* that they're somewhat unnerved by it; it's because, though it *looks* conventional, it *isn't*, and it doesn't quite give them what they want. The press loved Woody Allen's *Take the Money and Run*—a limply good-natured little nothing of a comedy, soft as sneakers. And it would probably feel more comfortable with this if it were soft or if it *were* "sniggery"; then it could be put down more easily as just another commercial picture. Maybe, like Dyan Cannon in the movie, the press and the audience want an orgy—and think it's a cop-out when they don't get one. An orgy would be the simplest thing in the movie world to give us right now, but it wouldn't be consistent with the idea of this movie, which, as in revue, is the comedy of recognizing that we (those on the screen and we in the audience) are not earthshakers or sexual new frontiersmen. This light domestic comedy no longer takes domesticity for granted, but after the characters begin to experiment sexually, they return for cover. Near the end, when the two couples go into one bedroom together, it's obvious that the movie could take a different turn—that if they went into two bedrooms instead of one, the cross-coupling would probably occur without any difficulty. But that would only *postpone* the return, or the movie would descend into romp and farce. The return makes perfect sense: They realize that they are about to go farther than they can handle, and they retreat to save something they still care about. Though the ending might have been better served by wit than by a "thoughtful" neo-Fellini walk, the point is clear. They need some home base and the safety of the old bourgeois traps. Forced to choose between decaying Doris Dayland and Warhol Nowheresville, they go back to what is for them, if not the good life, at least the not-bad life.

Many people in the audience have probably done just what the people in the movie do (either before or after a little wife-swapping and a small orgy or two). Why, then, do they resent it in the film? I'll make the guess that the situations are so comically close to the people in the audience that they may reject the characters for doing what they themselves have done, because that retreat cuts them off from what they want to believe in. At the beginning, the film has some satirical passages on Esalen "encounter" techniques (satire that backfired because Natalie Wood looks as if the treatment might help her), and people around me became rather hostile—not just the young, who might be expected to, because the touching is very important to them (it's a form of "truth," of approaching without being afraid, of making nonaggressive, nonhostile, "human" contact), but older people, too, because they, too, are looking for healers. The atmosphere around me was as if the Church were being satirized before an audience of early Christians. In commercial terms, the opening, with its easy targets, may be a miscalculation, and it's loosely ambivalent—as if Mazursky and Tucker were unsure and were trying to play it safe. The audience reaction to the opening may be a clue to the later discomfort: People may be so desperate to be other than what they are that they resent a movie for dealing with bourgeois values even in disruption. They may consider these characters (so like themselves) not worthy even of comic attention. And they may resent still more the suggestion that an orgy *won't* expand their consciousness, and that they might risk losing something if they try everything. They don't believe they've *got anything*. The audience is still waiting for Godot, which in this context is salvation by orgy.

INNOCENCE UPDATED

Arthur Schlesinger, Jr.

Bob & Carol & Ted & Alice can be described to readers of John Updike as *Couples* West. Let us place particular emphasis on the "West." Where Updike invested his study of promiscuity in Ipswich with appropriate New England dourness, this witty new film—written by Paul Mazursky and Larry Tucker—could only have been set in California, that citadel of Now, that home of hedonism and discontent, that terrifying premonition of all our futures.

The film's couples are in their early thirties—too old to have grown up on marijuana but too young to retire to the golf course. One funny scene shows them getting stoned, but in moments of crisis they shout for Scotch. They see themselves as swingers, though, and exist in a world of beads, turtlenecks, ruffled shirts, Nehru jackets, and dark glasses.

Carol and Bob go to a group-dynamics institute in the California hills. Purged and regenerated, they decide on a policy of total truth. Soon they involve their somewhat skeptical friends in a course of sexual experimentation. The four grope ludicrously in the pursuit of happiness until they prepare for a quadrilateral orgy in a Las Vegas hotel. Alas, they find to their shame they can't go through with it. Monogamy triumphs after all.

No doubt the young will regard the ending, in one of the film's favorite words, as a cop-out. But actually the film is not Now at all. It is an old-fashioned romantic comedy disguised as a blue picture. Twenty years ago, Jack Carson and Ronald Reagan would have starred, and everything would have been at a lower pitch. Here as elsewhere we escalate: Fornication replaces kissing, bare bosoms replace cleavage, pot replaces liquor, words like "orgasm," "impotent," "intercourse," "crap" adorn the dialogue. But the essential innocence remains.

For the rest, the satire is expert—sharply written, well and drily observed, and generally very funny. Paul Mazursky's direction is somewhat influenced, I would judge, by the Cassavetes of *Faces*. The close-ups are tight and constant; and the dialogue is filled with interruption, irrelevance, repetition, and people talking over each other. The acting could not have been better: Natalie Wood crying "beautiful" at each new expression of modern candor; Dyan Cannon giggling through a scene with a deadpan psychiatrist; Robert Culp pursuing the free life with earnest intensity; Elliott Gould struggling out from under his stoned friends as they clutch each other on the couch.

WHAT THE WORLD DOESN'T NEED NOW

JOHN SIMON

Bob & Carol & Ted & Alice (hereinafter called *BCTA*, though *&&&*, or even $$$, might be more appropriate) cops out not just at the end but right off the bat, making it a new and more contemptible genre: a cop-in.

BCTA begins, to the sounds of the Hallelujah Chorus, with a young married couple, Bob and Carol, arriving in their fancy sports car at something called The Institute, which is meant to represent Esalen. The Institute nestles in the mountains, and the first sign of it is three typical Hollywood starlets kneeling stark naked on the edge of a plateau and ostensibly sunbathing, but actually setting the tone for the film. They are much too good to be true, and their attitude, preposterous for tanning, suggests some esoteric Indian love ritual. We see other folk in various stages of jolly undress, including a grizzled patriarch in a wooden tub reading the *New York Review of Books*—after the sexual, the intellectual cachet. Or, conversely, the joke may be on those who read that magazine. A laugh for everyone, egghead or boob.

After various shots of bucolic-erotic serendipity, we see Bob and Carol in a group-therapy session. Now group therapy, more than any activity I can think of, brings out ambiguous feelings in the observer. Are these people in search of such things as "a better orgasm," as one weird-looking redhead puts it, to be taken with compassion or derision? A crying girl's false eyelashes begin to come off—is that pathos or travesty? A man introduces himself as "the group leader," and quickly corrects himself, "Well, group leader is too strong a word." Later on, he is weeping along with, and lying virtually on top of, Bob and Carol in one of their semi-private moments—is he to be viewed as a humane therapist or a ridiculous quack? The scene ends with a human pyramid piled up in a corner, everyone clinging to one another for dear life—is this meant to be touching, inspiring, or imbecile?

You have now guessed what the tone of *BCTA* will be throughout: perfectly uncommitted exploitation of socio-sexual phenomena, sometimes slanting toward the funny, sometimes toward the nasty, but even the slanting always undercut by its polar opposite. You can thus take the film any way you please—as a daring comedy essentially affirming the sexual revolution, or as a daring comedy essentially satirizing the sexual revolution—and, in either case, feel smugly up-to-date laughing at its pusillanimous japes.

So in the next scene we see our documentary film-maker, Bob, and his Carol dining in a restaurant with their friends: Ted, a young lawyer, and Alice, his wife. How anyone making documentary films can be as rich as Bob is shown to be, or how anyone successfully practicing law can be as generally cloddish as Ted, remains, like so many other questions, blithely unanswered.

Bob and Carol are dressed in dude hippie gear, Ted and Alice in classic Los Angeles expensive. Without going into the whole ludicrous scene, let us examine only a fragment of it. Bob demands to know what Ted thinks of his long hair. For a while Ted insists that it looks just fine. Bob taunts him on until Ted hesitantly concedes: "I feel it's a little long." "That's *beau*tiful!" Bob bursts out rapturously and goads on: "You think I'm a middle-aged man trying to look young?" At last Ted erupts, "O.K., I think your hair looks ridiculous!" Whereupon both Bob and Carol warble "Oh, that's *beau*tiful!" and similar expressions of ecstasy. In fact, the word "beautiful" and the ejaculations "I love you!" and "I'm so moved!" recur as refrains throughout the film, always with the same sleazy ambivalence. As an expression of legitimate feelings this is, of course, inadequate; as satire, it is too glib and easy.

What is happening? Is Bob applying Institute techniques to get Ted to express genuine emotions, and thus performing a fine therapeutic task? Then why all those jargon-ridden, ridiculous exclamations? Or are we to understand that he is dangerously meddling with Ted and Alice's peaceably conventional values, and provoking trouble both in their marriage and between the two friendly couples? In that case, why are Ted and Alice portrayed as thick squares simply begging to be kicked? In fact, all four of these creatures are made out to be comic zombies of one sort or another; no one is sympathized with and everyone is made ridiculous—sometimes with clever, accurate ridicule, more often with stale comedy turns.

Which leads me to the kind of movie this really is. Larry Tucker, producer and co-author, and Paul Mazurski, co-author and director, are graduates of The Second City cabaret. *BCTA* is really a set of cabaret skits cavalierly pasted together and sometimes inconsistent (Ted and Alice, for example, have one child, yet Ted twice refers to their "kids"). But what prevails consistently is an atmosphere of antipathy toward all four characters, not to mention the minor figures who put in unappetizing marginal appearances.

Now in the cabaret sketch everyone can be absurd or repellent, because what matters is not the people but the joke. We are not in the company of the characters long enough to have to take any of them seriously, except as exemplifying some contemporary lunacy; the important element is the conspiratorial bond between sketch-writer and audience, a chain whose links are laughs. In a full-length work, however, we must sympathize with somebody. Even in such out-and-out satire as *Candide* or *Gulliver's Travels* there is always someone for whom we can feel. In *BCTA* there are only oafs—both before and behind the camera.

Comic bit follows on comic bit. Bob commits adultery and his wife is so enlightened about it that it rather upsets him. Carol proceeds to share the wonderful, moving secret of Bob's peccadillo with Alice and Ted, which upsets the hell out of them. Next, Carol commits her little adultery, and Bob is first furious (double-standard joke), then all too sophisticatedly understanding (single-standard joke). Next, the repressed and henpecked Ted finally commits his little adultery.

Then comes Alice's scene with her psychiatrist, played by a real-life psychoanalyst. This is a funny scene but, again, a dishonest one, getting laughs from a disregard of even minimal verisimilitude (the analyst has never heard of words like "weewee" or "teetee"), from inconsistency of character (the prissy, puritanical Alice runs around in the nude in front of her young son), and from the usual ambivalent presentation (the analyst, though apparently sound and efficient, is extraordinarily unprepossessing and indulges in some peculiar, unprofessional lipsmacking).

For the grand finale, the two couples go off to Vegas for a holiday, and as they are having drinks in one of their two adjoining hotel suites, Alice—yes, Alice!—proposes a bit of wife-swapping. At first there is some embarrassment, but Alice is forthwith declared a "*beau*tiful woman" who sees "where it's at"; it is reiterated on all sides that it would be "purely, purely physical," and that "first we'll have an orgy and then we'll go see Tony Bennett."

Whereupon, instead of each rearranged couple retiring to a separate bedroom, all four orgiasts pile into the same bed—and have no fear, good people, none of the stars exposes an unseemly bit of flesh to the camera (a smidgin of Natalie Wood's arse no longer raises intimations of an "X" rating). Briefly they play footsie under the blanket, and then rue or common sense or the eye on the box office sets in, and they hastily get dressed again. They are off to hear Tony Bennett (a socially condoned obscenity). In the elevator, they still look gloomy and repentant, but as the soundtrack intones a grand cop-out song about "What the World Needs Now Is Love, Sweet Love," they begin to cheer up.

Now for the super-cop-out. They step onto the plaza in front of the hotel and here, as the ghastly song continues, they become part of one of those Fellinian closing parades (bad enough in Fellini): All kinds of people, young and old, fat and thin, hirsute and glabrous, black, yellow and white, whirl about exchanging loving looks and coming into fraternal bodily contact with one another. The whole world is united in a dance of love and brotherhood, and even the dishonest pretenses to social comment are swept away on tides of simon-pure saccharine. O *tempora!* O *mores!* O Tucker! O Mazurski!

ALICE'S RESTAURANT

Robert Hatch

For me, the central figure in *Alice's Restaurant* is not Arlo Guthrie, who plays the lead, but James Broderick, who plays Alice's husband. By and large, Guthrie is acting himself; Broderick is acting an aspect of a good many of us.

He is a man no longer quite young who finds that in this era youth has a corner on life. Like so many today—I doubt that there is a historical parallel for the impulse—he wants to be part of that scene. The reasons are obvious: The adult world has rarely offered so few satisfactions, rarely presented miseries so intractable; the efficacy of intelligent choice seems, at least for the time being, to be gone. At the same time, youth has developed a style that is often witty and that seems to offer compassion and fulfillment. It is also terribly vulnerable, since it believes in taking chances and lacks the history on which to base the odds. That's where people like Broderick's Ray Brock see their opportunity: They will contribute the wisdom of experience to the commune.

As a rule, it doesn't work out—not from failure of sympathy or because of flagging energies but because the generations run on different time tracks. The peculiar quality of the young today—those, that is, who make up what might be called the movement—is that they are willing to travel light and uncommitted. Relationships have depth, but not much length, and when the vibrations falter, there is always another scene down the road (these young, incredibly, seem never to run out of travel money). But once you have passed 30, you can no longer afford that kind of freedom. Eventually, something has to work out, because you have no time to be repeatedly starting from scratch. Ray Brock, for example, wants his marriage with Alice (Pat Quinn, very beautiful and with emotions of mercury) to work; I think the boys and girls around him see that as quaint. And at the end of the film, he is talking about land in Vermont, where they can all settle down, raise their crops and grow in love for one another. The kids have perhaps never heard of Brook Farm; in any case, theirs is a kaleidoscope utopia. They understand love, but cohesion escapes them. That is the tragedy of Ray Brock.

The picture that Arthur Penn has directed, using Arlo Guthrie's autobiographical song—"The Alice's Restaurant Massacree"—as a spine, is a triumph of unstressed understanding told in a style of relaxed professionalism (the camera work is technically superb, but does not take on that commercial gloss that was so assertive in, for example, *Pretty Poison*, made on location in the same Berkshire neighborhood). It looks like a psychedelic carnival, but it works deep into the assumptions of the time. Alice and Ray have bought a deconsecrated church in Stockbridge (the restaurant, downtown, is presumably set up to pay for the venture) and run open house and haven for vagrant hippies. The gypsies flock in. The place is, in their language, beautiful; the Brocks are good people—they offer understanding and peace.

Comes the great bust, when Arlo and a friend are arrested for littering by Stockbridge Police Chief William Obanhein (played by himself in a tone of baffled outrage tempered by curiosity), followed by Arlo's Whitehall Street army physical (he doesn't get past the "shrink"—or, more accurately, he does get past the "shrink"), the death of Woody Guthrie in Bellevue, the death also of a young addict whose return to the drug produces from Brock a shocking outburst of rage induced by disappointment. It begins the breakup of the colony.

That script is hardly a plot; indeed plot is not the preoccupation of *Alice's Restaurant*. It is concerned with a panorama of relationships that are more juxtaposed than integrated; with what people expect of one another, what they are willing to give, what they will not accept, under what circumstances they recognize responsibility and when they get in their cars and travel. Those, it might be said, are the ingredients of all plots, but here no "line" emerges because the parts are too discrete. Instead, the film offers a mosaic of great sensitivity and acumen. Aside from the entertainment joys of the picture—the wild humor, the music, the young, engaging and often very handsome cast—*Alice's Restaurant* provides a primer on youth surviving the decade of Vietnam. It should be noted, however, that Arlo Guthrie has more talent and a better mind than the general average of his generation. He can better afford, perhaps, to run free.

ARLO'S OFF-THE-RECORD MOVIE

RICHARD SCHICKEL

Its coming has been proclaimed so often that one hesitates to announce again the arrival of the New American Movie. But as far as I'm concerned, *Alice's Restaurant* clinches the matter, proving that *Faces* and *Easy Rider, Putney Swope* and *Medium Cool* are neither accidents nor a coincidence, that filmmakers from inside and outside the industrial system have succeeded in carving out a place to stand and make their own movies. It is a place where, seemingly, they have the best of two worlds, melding the individuality of the undergrounder with the possibility of getting rational financing, decent promotion, general release from the powers that be.

Alice's Restaurant is directed by Arthur Penn, whose work ranges in quality from *Bonnie and Clyde* to *Mickey One,* but whose devotion to doing things his own way has constantly remained admirable. In this case he has, in effect, illustrated and extended Arlo Guthrie's hit song, turning it into a spiritual autobiography detailing his search for a satisfying identity and a community to which he can give allegiance. It is scarcely an original idea for a work of art, but, like the original ballad, it has a charming simplicity.

Moreover, the project is just right for Penn. As *Bonnie and Clyde* proved, he has a genuine and sensitive feel for folk balladry, for the American landscape and for the smallness and loneliness people like Arlo (who plays himself) must sometimes feel when they measure themselves against its vastness. More important, in this film Penn deliberately avoids any suggestion of over-slick professionalism. His actors, many of whom are amateurs, have clearly been encouraged to avoid naturalism, to give the distinct impression of "acting out," in an almost childish way, a story that has a very loose, unfinished quality about it.

Much of what they do is marvelous to behold, particularly in the portion that is directly derived from Guthrie's original song, which, as you know, is all about the time Guthrie and a friend got busted for illegal garbage disposal. And the Stockbridge, Mass. cops took advantage of the situation to deploy hilariously the technology of modern criminal investigation that they never get a chance to use in the course of their normally sleepy rounds. This, of course, gives Arlo the criminal record that allows him to escape the draft and provides the film's second high point—his preinduction physical, where he and the U. S. Army meet in mutual (and magnificent) befuddlement.

I also like the honesty with which Arlo's benefactors, Ray and Alice Brock, are portrayed. As they run their restaurant and the deconsecrated church that becomes a refuge for troubled, dropout kids, they are shown to be good but definitely not saintly people. They are full of human error, prey to sexual and other temptations, in need of their kids (for complex reasons) as much as the kids are in need of them.

Still, one wishes the film had a slightly firmer spine. It contains too many dead spots, too many moments when everyone (Penn included) seems to be waiting around hoping something groovy will happen instead of shaping his material so that it will happen—and really mean something. For example, a potentially interesting subplot involving a youth trying—and failing—to kick junk never really engages one's sympathy as it should. Conversely, Arlo's encounters with his incurably ill father often seem awkward, too-easy plays for that sympathy. Some motorcycle races seem dragged in merely to give Penn's camera something easily cinematic to shoot. And there are moments when the film's generally pleasing simplicity of outlook crosses a shadow line and the picture becomes merely simplistic.

Nevertheless, it is important not to go to the New American Movie expecting to see the Old American Movie. What is happening is something like what happens in a piece of jazz music. The plot functions rather like the melody in jazz—as a place to take off from and a place, eventually, to come home to. It is less important than the improvisatory flights it suggests and encourages.

What stays in mind at the end of something like *Alice's Restaurant* is pretty much what stays in mind at the end of a memorable set by talented jazzmen—not their lapses but the wonderful heights they momentarily scale, seemingly by accident, as individuals engaged in a mutually supportive effort at art. And one likes these movies because of their peculiarly American sense of fun and freedom (and the blues), the sense they impart of not being an end in themselves but parts of an endless process. Of becoming. And of transcending.

MIDNIGHT COWBOY

IMPROBABLE LOVE STORY

STEFAN KANFER

They gather with the twilight in every city, swaggering under awnings and before the fluorescent lights of cafeteria windows. They like to bill themselves as "studs," but they are guys who swing from both sides of the bed. Around them swirls another kind of urban flotsam: maimed, embittered victims without a prayer of sexual gratification or a hope of companionship. From these unpromising fragments, James Leo Herlihy wrote a lyric blues ballad disguised as a novel. The film adaptation of *Midnight Cowboy* may grant that ballad too much orchestration, but it preserves its essential compassion and humor.

Joe Buck (Jon Voight) is a strutting phallus, good, he admits, for nothin' but lovin'. His muscles are like his mind, heavy and ornamental. His eyes are like attic windows, blank and blue, opening onto a pile of dusty junk. The son and grandson of prostitutes, Joe flees the loveless desolation of his Texas home and heads for Manhattan. There, in his cowboy paraphernalia, he is as out of place as a stallion in a parking lot. The demon lover swaggers before a mirror; a clown peers back.

After a series of sexual skirmishes, Joe finds himself smack in the middle of the country he left: despair. As he wanders, he comes upon Ratso Rizzo (Dustin Hoffman). A septic, crippled thief, Rizzo lives, like his nicknamesake, in the upper reaches of a condemned building, waiting for the wrecking ball. In a sense it has already arrived. Though he nourishes fantasies of a future in Miami,

Ratso is too frail to last the winter. With a final galvanic reach for life, he extends a greasy hand—and Joe Buck takes it.

Nothing overt ever transpires between them; every conversation is an exchange of slurs. They become inseparable chiefly because they share a common loss: both could sue life for alienation of affections. Joe Buck is alternately a male hustler and a gigolo; if he knows a lot about sex, he is, like Ratso, ignorant of sympathy. Neither realizes that the only place he has ever found it is in his companion. Yet by the time the two head for Florida, they have become aspects of the same person. As the thief coughs his way to death aboard a bus, the cowboy is literally beside himself with grief.

A simple tale of simple souls demands a simple style. Accordingly, Herlihy's prose was like a pane of glass, with the described objects clearly in view. Director John Schlesinger sometimes seems less interested in Buck and Rizzo than in himself, covering his film with a haze of stylistic ties and baroque decorations. Buck's involuntary memory provides him with a series of erotic flashbacks; the film illustrates them with the primitivity of a comic book. Joe's heterosexual encounters are treated with suppressed smirks. During one love session he bounces up and down on a TV remote control, so that Schlesinger can represent his athletics with quick TV clicks of Al Jolson in blackface, a bishop preaching and a Stegosaurus lunging through a forest.

Still, no amount of obfuscation can obscure the film's vaulting performances. Ratso is so unkempt that he can be smelled, so unredeemed that he can be lamented. From his debut as the open-faced Benjamin Braddock in *The Graduate,* Hoffman has progressed by stepping backward—to a supporting part. It is an act of rare skill and rarer generosity. No matter how well Ratso is performed, *Midnight Cowboy* is, after all, the tale of Joe Buck. It is a mark of Voight's intelligence that he works against his role's melodramatic tendencies and toward a central human truth. In the process, he and Hoffman bring to life one of the least likely and most melancholy love stories in the history of the American film.

Richard Schickel

Hurrying through 42nd Street or one of its equivalents—which exist in every sizable American city—we have all, at one time or another, brushed against Joe Buck, the *Midnight Cowboy*, or Ratso Rizzo, his friend. And if we have been so careless as to meet his importunate gaze, at once sly and bold, we have wondered about him—where he came from, how he lives and even, cruelly, why he lives. If we are honest we must admit that we see the Joes and Ratsos in less than human terms, as members of some alien subspecies, unknown and unknowable to us.

It is the great virtue of Director John Schlesinger's film that he insists upon the humanity of Joe and Ratso; it is its great defect that he never really proves it. What he does prove is that there is a direct relationship between their queer, sad, violent habitat and our own. Grabbing us by the arm, he forces us to slow down and look—really look—at the neon wilderness through which his cowboy rides. The grindhouse movies, all-night pizza parlors and shooting galleries are, he insists, the places where our commonly held visions of glamor, escape, heroism are reduced to parodistic least common denominators. Here we can clearly see the lunatic nature of the dreams we all share, the price of living too deeply in the media-manufactured fantasies.

In the midst of all this gaudiness we can make out something of Joe and Ratso, and we perceive that they are not exactly strangers. Joe is an up-to-date version of the eternal rube. His steed may now be a Greyhound bus, his cowboy clothes and manners may reflect not experience (despite a Texas upbringing) but the influence of popular culture, his hope of a high-priced career as a stud for hire to an eastern womankind he believes desperately in need of his talents may be comical; yet he remains heir to the long line of country cousins who have bought the Brooklyn Bridge from Ratso's forefathers. And Ratso, with his wheedling voice, his scuttling quickness, his muddled cynicism, is the city's timeless spokesman.

We are to understand that these archetypes have been flawed by their times, rendered more vulnerable than their precursors. Like the tawdry environment they inhabit, they are the products of ceaselessly, carelessly exploitative society. Controlled and consoled by the viciously moronic ideas it has implanted in them, they are on a lifelong bad trip and unable to end it.

It is a bit much. There is no end of easy targets in modern America, and Schlesinger is neither so clever nor so daring as he thinks he is in banging away at them. Still, he has this social background firmly in focus here, however we value his effort. What's disastrously wrong with the film is its foreground fuzziness. Jon Voight is admirably at ease in the title role, and Dustin Hoffman works conscientiously and well at playing Ratso. He is apparently determined to remain what he naturally is, a great character actor, instead of becoming just another movie star. But Schlesinger never fully defines their characters as individuals. To be sure, each has been given an explanatory wretched childhood, and each has a private affliction to explain further why he dropped out—Joe's a sexual trauma and Ratso's a game leg. But these are not quite enough to engage us sympathetically.

They have to be seen as literally lovable, and so, in the penniless adversity that they share, a beautiful masculine relationship begins to take shape. Slowly, too slowly, we are asked to observe that their dumbness may be a form of exemplary innocence, their inability to cope with reality a form of purity, the unacknowledged love that grows between them a kind of salvation, a sweet triumph over a mad, decadent world.

It doesn't work. One could accept mutually exploitative, explicitly stated faggery. One could imagine these men, trained the hard way in human misuse, using each other ill in their agony. To what, though, can we attribute the pretty impulse that overtakes them, converting them from a pair of dreary louts (whom we have been encouraged, much of the time, to laugh at) into tender comrades? How are we to accept the delicate suggestion that if we will only look closely at the top of the dungheap which we have been so relentlessly exploring we will find a dear, romantic pansy flowering there?

Only as a fake, I fear. Or as the act of desperate moviemakers copping a plea. It is not, in any case, the moments of hard truth that are difficult to take in this film. It is the sweet nothings it whispers in our ear that finally repel us.

RAPE UPON RAPE

JOHN SIMON

Midnight Cowboy seems to be this summer's *The Graduate*; the kids who loved Dustin Hoffman sweet and clean are just as happy to love him dirty and sweet. John Schlesinger's film is better than *The Graduate*, but it, too, suffers from an ultimate cleverness and sentimentality that fall well short of art. Very much as in Schlesinger's *Darling*, we get all the trappings and trimmings of brutal honesty; there is no evident attempt at prettification—there may even be a slight tendency to revel in the squalid—and still, still one does not quite believe what one is seeing.

Everything is calculated for maximum concision, pointedness and poignancy—everything is so blasted efficient. But art, real art, isn't like that at all. It is full of asperities, rugosities, the inexplicable. It does not get where it wants to go in the manner of a genteel equestrian cantering on a dappled gelding, but as a sleepwalker or high-wire artist making it by a combination of desperate skill and some strange, incalculable providence. *Midnight Cowboy* is just a little too knowing, pert and pat.

If, like me, you have not read the James Leo Herlihy novel on which the film is based, you may want a short synopsis. Joe Buck, a dumb but lovable and handsome Texas youth, victim of a lonely childhood, leaves his job as a small-town dishwasher, buys himself a fancy cowboy outfit, and takes a bus to fabulous New York, full of rich, frustrated women willing to pay generously for the services of a fine Texas stud.

In New York, Joe's meager savings are soon spirited away by con men and women of all sorts, including "Ratso" Rizzo, a tough little Bronx gutter rat who, pretending to set up Joe with a superpimp, sends him to a crazed religious fanatic. Egged on by absurdities spouted at him by the media, Joe is sucked ever deeper into failure—now with pathetic homosexual customers rather than women. On the verge of starvation, he reencounters Ratso, whom he threatens to beat up but goodheartedly spares. Ratso, hobbling on his deformed foot and pitiable for all his shrewdness and bluster, invites Joe to his lair in a condemned building, where the two set up a comic-pathetic housekeeping. The city rat teaches the country mouse the art of hustling and making out.

After a series of misadventures, Joe at last seems to be on to some young women (their youth is improbable, but let that pass) willing to subsidize the prowess of this Texas longhorn. But Ratso has been plagued by not only his foot but a sinister cough as well; precisely now (another bit of stretched probability) the illness comes to a terrifying head. Ratso refuses to see a doctor. All he wants is to get to his dreamed-of panacea and Eldorado: Florida.

To make this possible, Joe beats up and robs a pitiful aging homosexual who asked him up to his hotel room (where, significantly, no sexual acts were performed!) and gets on a Florida-bound bus with his fever-racked friend. There is hopeful talk now of giving up hustling and getting jobs, but as the bus nears Miami, Joe, *Erlkönig*-like, is propping up a dead Ratso.

There are in this film more dishonesties than one can easily point to. As Joe rides the bus to New York, for example, images from his childhood and young manhood come rapidly dancing by. We decipher something about a boy entrusted to a well-meaning but neglectful slut of a grandmother; and, later, about a loved and loving girlfriend who becomes the victim of a gang rape, goes mad and insanely denounces Joe, whom the gang forced to watch the vicious act. Already we are confused: How exactly do these two widely divergent unhappy experiences contribute to pointing Joe toward a career in hustling? It seems to me that a little psychologizing is a dangerous thing; we need either a good deal more of it, or none at all.

Worse yet is the glib exploitation of America the all-purpose bogey as the cause of Joe's downfall: the mass media with their mendacious siren songs; the suspiciousness and lovelessness rampant in the land; the cruel socio-economic gap between haves and have-nots; the maniacal, dehumanizing pursuit of money and success; etc., etc. But aside from the fact that these are commonplaces and remain so in the film, no matter how gussied up with superficial cleverness, there is no clear demonstration of how the society affects Joe Buck, of how his individual guilt is begotten by the community.

If, indeed, there is any guilt at all. Rather, Joe is shown as the victim of the most prodigious streak of bad luck since Pauline of the Episodic Perils, and the whole film has the quality of *Candide* rewritten in collaboration by the authors of the Grand Guignol and the Bibliothèque Rose. Everything misfires for our cowboy: People won't talk to him; or if they talk, it is only to ridicule him; and if they don't ridicule, it is only to bilk him.

He, on his part, is rather spectacularly stupid, and there is some doubt in my mind about how he could have conceived the idea of going to New York to hustle. His jinx inhabits the very objects he touches: The last cup of coffee he can afford has to be ruined by half the catsup bottle accidentally spilling into it, as well as over his pants. And if he succeeds at last in getting picked up by a homosexual, it has to be a student who proves penniless. I would have thought that even the dumbest hustler required payment in advance.

All through the ugliness, Joe manages to remain wondrously innocent. He never seems to get involved in active or passive pederasty—the closest he ever gets to it is submitting to fellatio from that pathetic student in a 42nd Street movie theater. During that act, we see Joe's pained face, and hope that he is saving his soul by thinking beautiful thoughts. One wonders why such an angelic and heterosexual fellow, upon the collapse of his pocketbook and dreams of easy living, does not opt for some kind of homely but honest labor. The "midnight cowboy" we see on the stage in Mart Crowley's *The Boys in the Band* is every bit as good-natured, stupid and blond as Joe, but neither so pure nor so heroic—and, therefore, believable.

Ratso is a much more convincing character, and though his heart, too, is basically as pure as filtered canal water, at least he chisels and swipes things, bickers and curses. But once we put Ratso and Joe together, doubts arise again. Are we to believe in the tender Platonic love of a male whore and his pimp under the cover of brawling and banter? Well, we used to be asked to believe in the female whore with the heart of gold and untapped reserve of love. Did we believe it then? Sometimes, as in the case of Cabiria, who was a kind of halfwit—and not even she would have shared a beautiful experience with her procurer.

Still, it may be unduly captious to reject out of hand the thesis of the film, that such a relationship can and does spring up. The question is how well is it demonstrated, how searchingly and persuasively is it explored? Reasonably well, considering how much of the footage is devoted to other, often only marginally relevant matter. Yet that "considering" is in itself a damaging concession. Thus there is a crazy drug-pop-psychedelic orgy sequence—enlisting the services of some of the gang from Warhol's films and some from the musical *Hair*—that is as slick as it is tangential.

Some of the other atmospheric material is good, however, and almost all of the Joe-Ratso interplay (parts of it, apparently, based on improvisations) is delightful and affecting. This is due in large measure to extremely winning performances by Jon Voight and Dustin Hoffman, the former accomplishing the difficult task of reconciling militant stupidity with charm, the latter able to turn scrounging into a gallant, Robin-Hoodish activity. There may be something a mite schematic about the way acerbic humor and mock rancor are summoned up as screens for the touching devotion between two men, but this device, as sentimental in fact as it is virile in intention, is a hallowed mainstay of American filmmaking and, before that, American fiction.

What is more disturbing about the film is its contrived, manipulative technique, adroit though it may be much of the time. I get the feeling that it is made up entirely of little skits, anecdotes, and blackout sketches, complete with final sight gag or punch line, laid end to end. I am not referring to the fragments of the past that pop up in flash frames or sharply abbreviated sequences, sometimes in deliberately scrambled order. Except for the fact that they make Joe's past unduly arcane, I don't object to them. What does bother me, though, is the patness and didacticism of episode after episode in the present.

Take a typical incident: Joe, new to New York, is walking down Fifth Avenue; suddenly, there is a man sprawled across the sidewalk. Joe is shocked and about to come to his assistance. But the mass of passersby just walk around the man (dead? in a coma?) as if he were merely a minor nuisance, say, a largish puddle. Astounded, Joe does as the New Yorkers do. At this point we notice a plaque on the building in back of the fallen man: Tiffany & Co.

It is this rubbing in that I find mildly but distinctly offensive. In the final scene, when Ratso dies on the bus just as it is about to reach Miami, his death causes a flurry of indignation among the passengers. But that is not enough: The next shot must have an ancient and repellent female rabidly coating her mouth with lipstick, in preparation for living it up at the Fontainebleau.

Women, by the way, get much the worse deal in this film which, while ostensibly holding up heterosexual values amid the homosexuality, actually exudes a homosexual sensibility, thus increasing its dishonesty. Revealing, in this respect, is the choice of actress for the young woman who gives Joe his first break, the one relatively sympathetic feminine part: Brenda Vaccaro. With the exception of Sandy Dennis, there is no more irritatingly unfeminine actress around these days than Miss Vaccaro, a cube-shaped creature who comes across as a diky kewpie-doll.

Nevertheless, the film has solid virtues as well. Much of it is very neatly directed; most of it is well acted—except for Miss Vaccaro, Viva and her fellow creeps, and a rather miscast Ruth White as Joe's sexy granny. Adam Holender has kept his color photography nicely within the bounds of the required seediness. The editing is crisp. Landscapes and cityscapes convey spacious or cramped loneliness, clean or dirty clutter. And over all of it, the irrepressible performances of Voight and Hoffman dispense their special grace.

Philip T. Hartung

Anyone feeling strong would do well to see *Midnight Cowboy*. He'll come out feeling stronger and wiser and perhaps a little less smug. He'll also see an extraordinary movie that holds one's attention throughout—in spite of its grim story and grimy view of New York as it follows Joe Buck, the title character, from his small hometown in Texas through his experiences in the big city where this hustler hopes to make a fortune off of rich, sex-starved women. No cowboy is Joe, but we do see one shot of him as a little kid on a rocking horse, and during most of the film this well-built young man wears a snazzy cowboy outfit including boots and a leather jacket with fringes. Joe is probably the most naive leading character to turn up since Booth Tarkington gave us Willie Baxter in *Seventeen*. Willie at least came from a normal Midwest family. What Joe came from, except for that Texas town and a grandmother (expertly played by Ruth White) who loved him but was too busy with other pursuits, I am not too sure. Since I didn't read James Leo Herlihy's novel from which Waldo Salt wrote his good screenplay, I found director John Schlesinger's quick-cut flashbacks a little too flashy and quick to fill in the details of Joe's past. Schlesinger used a similar technique in his *Darling* and *Petulia*, but in *Midnight Cowboy*, he seems to take it for granted that we are familiar with the original novel. I'd like to know a little more about the background that produced this tall, muscular fellow who thinks he's God's gift to women and is deadly serious about his mission in life as a hustler and stud.

Perhaps Joe is to be more pitied than scorned; but in any case he has to be laughed at in some of his misadventures. His first New York venture after strutting up Park Avenue in his absurd costume is with a tough dame who takes him up to her penthouse apartment and practically devours him before he discovers she hasn't a cent; she takes 20 bucks from *him*. Realizing that hustling is no bed of roses, he decides to try the homosexual trade on 42nd Street; but after a session with a college boy in a theater balcony, he finds himself no richer.

When he first meets Ratso Rizzo, a sweaty, unattractive Italian thief and pimp from the Bronx, Joe is taken in again, but later instead of giving lame Ratso the beating he deserves, Joe moves in with him in his dirty flat in a condemned tenement building. Perhaps these two fellows deserve each other. Joe's fortunes improve little, even under Ratso's management. The two bicker continuously and begin really to care for each other. What develops is a strong friendship that is never an overt homosexuality but a special kind of love, each with genuine concern for the other.

John Schlesinger, who with Jerome Hellman gave *Midnight Cowboy* its good production, is first-rate in his direction of the actors in these two lead roles. Newcomer Jon Voight is just right as the handsome, not-too-bright Joe Buck, the misguided lad who has no idea what life is really about. Also right in the far more difficult role of Ratso is Dustin Hoffman who is able to convey just by looking at Voight that he knows how dumb his friend is. Ratso is a product of the big city's lower depths, and while his background is probably Catholic, that religion seems to have made little impression on him. Hoffman looks as if he never bathed throughout the entire film as he coughs and sweats and suffers—and dreams of one day going to Florida, where everything is going to be all right. Joe goes out to make some money to get them both to the land of Ratso's dreams. Joe doesn't even understand the violence he uses in getting the necessary cash.

While one doesn't admire Joe or Ratso, one understands them and appreciates the compassion Schlesinger is able to convey for the two young men through their fine performances. One must also admire this good English director's feel for the locales of his story. One doesn't point with pride at the America he shows. One even cringes at the film's satirical thrusts, but this is how it is in the land of midnight cowboys.

AN ENGLISHMAN DISCOVERS AMERICA

ARTHUR SCHLESINGER, JR.

Midnight Cowboy is John (no relative) Schlesinger's first film shot in America. One feels in it the exhilaration of an imaginative director suddenly plunged into a new world of exotic sights and sounds. The concept of the American bus trip, for example, gives the film its frame. In a bravura beginning, the bus carries the cowboy from Texas to New York. The mood is lyrical though enigmatic, charged with glowing impressions of the past and hopes for the future. At the end another bus carries the cowboy and his dying New York friend from the shadows of Manhattan to the sunlight of Miami. The mood is somber but now lucid; the time of the illusion has gone.

Waldo Salt's screenplay, drawn from the novel by James Leo Herlihy, is an inquiry into the fantasy life among the lonely crowd. Joe Buck is a dishwasher in a Texas hash house who dreams of dressing up as a cowboy, going to New York and living off rich women. Ratso is another illusionist, a hustler stumbling along the streets of the big city. They meet, fight, then drift together. Both, it becomes apparent, are traumatized men, Joe Buck by youthful sexual experience, Ratso by the memory of his father. Eventually, as their own (non-queer) relationship grows, reality abolishes their world of dreams.

Midnight Cowboy has the advantage of two entirely remarkable performances by Jon Voight as Joe Buck and Dustin Hoffman as Ratso. Voight, with slow, courteous speech and a self-satisfied smile, conveys marvelously the stubborn ingenuousness of the spurious cowboy, his naive confidence in his capacity to master women and life, then the wounds within and the painful infiltration of reality. As for Hoffman, he shows what was not all that clear in *The Graduate:* He is a first-rate actor. He makes Ratso, with his ferret face, his crippled walk, his swindler's ingratiation on top of an ultimate sense of his own dignity, his repressed affections and loyalties, a memorable figure. The two play together in superb counterpoint and make their odd couple explicable and convincing.

The film is less impressive than the leading performances. John Schlesinger has a freshness of vision that bathes the American scene in a distinctive light. But at times his Americanization becomes insistent—need we have had, for example, quite so many pseudo-folk ballads on the sound track? He has a good instinct for American types, but sometimes this spills over into the grotesque. And, on occasion, as in his evocation of New York (and especially at a party featuring Andy Warhol's stock company), his images decline into clichés.

Moreover, he goes wild on what used to be called montage: the dissolution of linear narration into a whirl of images. Such impressionism can, of course, be tremendously effective in conveying states of mind and emotion, and John Schlesinger uses it well to deal with the power of memory and fantasy in the lives of his protagonists. But he uses it too often. At first, this is merely irritating. Then it becomes evident that it is not only self-indulgent but represents an escape from harder problems of characterization and structure. If only Schlesinger's directorial self-discipline had matched his luminous sense of scene and his extraordinary skill in handling actors, this would have been a far more considerable film.

GOODBYE, COLUMBUS

ROBERT HATCH

It puzzles me that Hollywood films of social comment like *Goodbye, Columbus* (or like *The Graduate* and *Pretty Poison*), which strive so hard for accuracy of detail and exactness of nuance, nevertheless come off the screen as Pop-art distortions of contemporary life. In part it may be the color, which is not used creatively, as in stage lighting, but is an approximation of natural hues just sufficiently awry to call persistent attention to its dyes. (The "color" in black and white films, supplied from the viewer's memory bank, is always superior to prismatic nature faking.)

But beyond that, I think, is a nervousness on the part of the proprietors that impels them to tick off their sociological data with the insistence of a television commercial making its sales points. *Goodbye, Columbus* seems to pause for an instant each time an item is scored, as though the director (Larry Peerce) had an ear cocked for the appropriate audience response. It is not a very obtrusive mannerism, but cumulatively it bends a dramatic performance toward a pitchman's demonstration.

In the dramatization of Philip Roth's story, the social medium is, of course, Jewish upward mobility and the items proliferate: Bennington is good but Radcliffe is better; food is for stuffing; rich women have golden hair and raucous voices; their daughters have their noses fixed; a proliferation of telephones is a sign of domestic elegance; men are wolves at work and slobs at home, and so on. Since the intent is satire within the "family," the signal flashers are, I think without exception, gently (and not always so gently) pejorative. Somewhat to my surprise, no mention was made of medicine as a prestigious career.

Much of this is funny, but much of it is self-conscious and gives the picture a case of the gulps. For all that, it is a much better than average movie. There is a lot of humanity in it and it is particularly well served by Richard Benjamin and Ali MacGraw in the poor boy-rich girl core of the story. Benjamin, playing what I assume to be Roth's alter ego, is quietly impressive as the bright, quick-witted but awkward young man who is fascinated, a little overawed and yearning toward a world he despises—and thus in the end more cruel than all those others he sees as the tramplers. *Goodbye, Columbus* is an adaptation of one of Roth's finest works, and much of the virtue comes through.

Moreover, the picture is evidence, I think, that anti-Semitism is at last behind us. Even five years ago, I would guess, it would have sent B'nai B'rith marching through the streets—now there seems no poison in it. Some day a similar picture will be made about the blacks, and we will know that another corner of tolerance and understanding has been turned. But not yet awhile.

BLUNTED IRONIES

JOHN SIMON

Social comment of a sort is provided in *Goodbye, Columbus,* Larry Peerce's incompetent film version of Philip Roth's novella. Incompetent and vulgar, to be exact. On the one hand, the already sufficiently horrid, petty-bourgeois parvenu, Jewish milieu of the story is underlined and overstressed in its horridness to the nth degree; on the other hand, Neil and Brenda's affair is suffused with color so glowing, framed by surroundings so pastoral, that, at the very least, it seems intended to sell Doeskin toilet tissues on TV.

For all its attitudes of daring, the film boggles at any number of things. The various characterizing references to Mary McCarthy are omitted as, presumably, too literate for the average viewer. Omitted as too disturbing for the viewer are things like Neil's and Brenda's anti-Semitism; thus the bit on the telephone, when Brenda asks Neil how she will recognize him at the Boston station ("'I'll be disguised as an orthodox Jew.' 'Me too,' she said."), is cut from Arnold Shulman's allegedly ever-so-faithful script. It is a curious phenomenon that so-called courageous films are almost always made by bunglers, cowards or phonies, or all three in one.

Emblematic is the treatment of Harriet, Brenda's sister-in-law. Whereas in the story she is just like Brenda, only bosomier; in the film, she is a horsy, ungainly creature. Whereas in the story her conversation is subtly unnerving with its dignified banality, in the film, she merely chortles and acts equine.

Even the very point of the story, Brenda's deliberate abandoning of the diaphragm where her mother will find it, gets fudged over and submerged in near-incomprehensibility. Not made clear is the ghastly sense of guilt and belonging that subverts Brenda's seeming emancipation: the horror of the family that has not released her from its tentacles, and of her own weakness in not being able to extricate herself. The fact that the hotel in Boston is made into some sinister dive instead of the standard Sheraton it should have been; that Brenda is shown from the beginning of the last scene outraged and angry, as if some Higher Morality were propelling her; that Father and Mother Patimkin's letters are not reproduced in their disheartening entirety—all suggest a belated moral awakening rather than a surrender to dehumanizing conventionality.

Peerce's direction is steadily obvious, sometimes pseudopoetic, often coy. The sex scenes in particular become one big cute giggle, though here Richard Benjamin's otherwise more than adequate Neil is also to blame. A typical Peerce touch is the opening shot of the film in which a pretty girl emerging from the country club's swimming pool loses the top of her bikini—what has this to do with the *nouveau riche* ambiance and theme of the film? Again, a hammy rear-view closeup of Neil's and Brenda's profiles nuzzling each other luminously in the narrow gap between the two dark backs of their beach chairs is actually repeated, lest we miss its cleverness. And so on, leapfrogging from blatancy to blatancy. But Peerce is fortunate in most of his performers, especially in Jack

Klugman as Patimkin; and in his discovery, Ali MacGraw, he has a very lucky find: an ex-model who, unlike most ex-models, actually is an actress.

Miss MacGraw, and for this Peerce may deserve some directorial credit, gives a delicately balanced performance, her Brenda emerging tough and unfeeling at times, tomboyish and silly at others, considerably yet not repellently narcissistic all along. There is inchoate feeling and vestigial thought, and also, at the right moments, something touching and pitiable. It is a graceful, nicely shaded piece of acting, enhanced by the fact that it comes from a young woman not merely lovely, but actually gifted with a kind of thinking man's loveliness. The updating of the movie, and such things as turning Brenda into a Cliffie of the late Sixties when she is clearly a Wellesleyite of the Fifties, are unfortunate—they frequently dull Roth's sharpness of observation; but Ali MacGraw exudes a pervasive authenticity that almost puts everything back into focus.

IF . . .

STALKY GOES MAOIST

ARTHUR SCHLESINGER, JR.

This is a deceptive film. It starts on a note of total conventionality. We are back in the familiar world of the English public school. It is the beginning of winter term. A new boy timidly asks directions. The student head of the house barks orders. Masters read lessons in chapel. We are shown what George Orwell described in his essay on "Boys' Weeklies" as "the usual paraphernalia—lockup, roll call, house matches, fagging, prefects, cosy teas round the study fire, etc., etc." Is this to be nothing more than *Stalky & Co.* revisited?

The camera moves restlessly about the school, flashing briefly on a variety of characters and scenes. After a time the elements of a plot appear. It seems at the start no more than the traditional public school confrontation: authority in the person of the head of the house and his three prefects vs. mischief in the person of three dissidents, latter-day versions of Stalky, McTurk, and Beetle.

Yet, within the stereotypes one begins to detect another note, aberrant, eerie, even sinister. The homosexual theme, implicit in such stories since *Tom Brown's Schooldays*, becomes explicit. The fagging system seems on the surface more genial; but, on provocation, the hazing turns vicious. The rebellious three drink vodka in their study underneath photographs of Che, Mao, and Lumumba. The headmaster, a brisk, modern type, delivers hopeful platitudes about bridging the generation gap.

Gradually the pace accelerates. The boys skip a school rugger match to go into town where they steal a motorcycle and meet a girl. The senior prefects decide they have become a disgrace to the house and subject them to brutal canings. Like characters out of Orwell's boys' weeklies, the rebels swear a blood oath. Then the film begins to take off, almost in the manner of Jean-Luc Godard. Tormented beyond endurance by imbecile and arbitrary authority, the three, joined by a younger student and a girl, seize arms and revolt against the school. "I understand you. Listen to reason and trust me," the headmaster calls out to them before they shoot him down.

If . . . is a brilliant and disturbing film. The director, Lindsay Anderson, sees the school, with its structure of irrational power, as a microcosm of society. The prefects are the old ruling group, continuing to give nineteenth-century orders in a new world of aspiration and anger. The headmaster is a voice of contemporary liberalism, complacent and ineffectual. The rebels are the young anywhere, eventually driven mad by the irrationality and inhumanity of the system. Unlike *Uptight*, however, *If . . .* bestows no maudlin blessing on revolutionary violence. Its mood is clinical rather than sentimental, and it is infinitely more powerful for that reason.

Lindsay Anderson has done a superb job. If the first half hour seems amorphous and inconsequential, every scene turns out to be justified as the film gathers momentum and begins the startling transition from the conventions of public-school drama to the terror of guerrilla warfare. I must confess that I do not understand why some passages are in color, some in sepia, some in black and white; here Mr. Anderson perhaps becomes a little too subtle. Still this is the most interesting film so far this year.

SCHOOL DAYS, SCHOOL DAYS

PAULINE KAEL

From the advance rave quotes, I gather that many reviewers believe that *If . . .* will be a great success with youth and that it is a masterpiece. One may suspect that in some cases the evaluation is based on the prediction. I think *If . . .* will be a success, but I think it's far from a masterpiece, and I should like to make this distinction, because so many people are beginning to treat "youth" as the ultimate judge—as a collective Tolstoyan clean old peasant. They want to be on the side of youth; they're afraid of youth. (And this is not irrelevant to the subject of *If . . .*) If they can be pushed by clever publicity into thinking "youth" will respond to a movie, they are then instrumental in *getting* "youth" to respond to it. Movie companies are using computerized demographic studies and market research to figure out how to promote movies. Here, taken from *Variety*, is the report on the technique adjudged most suitable for *If . . .* by the same new "scientific" group at Paramount Pictures (a subsidiary of Gulf & Western) who worked out how to sell Zeffirelli's *Romeo and Juliet*. The report predicted that *If . . .* will repeat its British success in the United States "*if* it is given the same kind of intensive marketing support that made it such a hit in its première engagement in London," and described the key element as "a very extensive screening program for critics, writers, radio and TV commentators, educators, and members of government," continuing, "We went out of our way to pursue every means of reaching the public through newspaper editorials, radio and television panels or discussions, magazine features and lectures before important opinion-making groups. The outpouring of 'breaks' in all communication media was phenomenal and most unusual in that [the film] was treated as a news event away from the usual coverage of motion pictures." It's easy to recognize the standard advertising campaign aimed at the mass audience—the big ads and the appearances of stars and movie-makers on the TV talk shows—but we are still novices when it comes to an advertising campaign that feeds the appetite of the media for something new and exciting, and we may not spot techniques directed at the selective, educated audience. Obviously, these techniques couldn't work if the film didn't have something in it for people to react to, but if it does, the publicity people can build up a general impression of urgent, clamorous response. It's no accident when all those rave reviews come out before a picture has opened; the early reviewers get the taste of triumph as they rush to be the first to jump on the bandwagon. And when this atmosphere of consensus about the importance of a picture is built up, anybody who doesn't go along begins to seem "out of it"—"not with it." *If . . .* has been so well sold that people were discussing it in the *Village Voice* weeks before it opened; that's real marketing, and it means that the whole underground press has been alerted by now. "Youth" will "discover" another movie; in a flash forward, one can already hear the discussions on WBAI. Once this process has begun to work and the publicity has caught on, the film *is* important; people want to see it because they are hearing about it wherever they go. The publicity men have manufactured "news," and the mass media don't want to be scooped and left behind.

The joke about all the rave quotes from the networks and *Cue* and *Life* and the *Ladies' Home Journal* and *Playboy* and *Look* ("I'll be talking about *If . . .* forever") and the rest is that the hero of *If . . .* is firing a machine gun at everything they represent. They are turning "youth" on to armed revolt, and the market-research people and the press are so eager to sell to "youth" that they'd probably include a machine gun with the admission ticket if it were economically feasible. This may be one of the contradictions in capitalism that Marx did not foresee: The conglomerates that control the mass media are now selling "youth" the violent overthrow of the Establishment for the suicidally simple reason that they can find and develop a demand for it.

If . . . deals with a schoolboys' revolt on the model of Jean Vigo's 1933 film *Zero for Conduct*. I think it will have psychological appeal here because it's a revolt of the privileged and provides a basically psychological rationale for student revolution. The battle cry is for freedom and noncomformity and an end to stupidity, rigidity, hypocrisy, and cruelty. The violence is thus given a psychological meaning and justification: It's to explode the repressive system, to liberate men from all the dull nastiness that the corrupt school represents. And because this kind of psychological rationale for student revolt is probably close to how students at American high schools and colleges feel, and because hatred and disgust for the old system provide a simpler, more basic justification than political and social and economic issues do, I think they'll respond. Lindsay Anderson, the director of *If . . .*, gives the rebels a cause.

If . . . may have a potential appeal for young people, but I rather doubt whether it would reach much of an audience without a brilliant selling job. It has a bleak, pseudo-documentary solemnity that is about as attractive to Americans as blood pudding. Anderson's movies—*This Sporting Life* and *If . . .*—draw their considerable power from what one can only assume is unconscious and semiconscious material. Anderson is a major talent (partly because he isn't interested in doing anything minor), but to be successful in the theater or in movies it is not enough to be talented; one must have a certain kind of talent. We may admire sequences in an Anderson film, but his talent really isn't likable, and even his best sequences are often baffling—heavy with multiple meanings that he doesn't appear to think need sorting out. Yet though the material may be staggeringly private, if disguised, the manner of the presentation is coldly realistic and precise; the style is so controlled one might assume the content was, too. At first, and for a considerable stretch, *If . . .* appears to be a clinical exposé of the horrible organized bedlam inflicted on English boys in the name of a gentleman's education. The film is especially fixated on the cruelties that the students perpetrate against each other, and one may suppose that all this lingering attention to scenes of juvenile sadism and flogging and homoeroticism and the allusions to the rot and collapse of the British upper classes are in the service of reform. The detailed (and I think obsessively dwelt-on) material about the school deceives one about where the movie is heading.

In *Zero for Conduct,* the schoolmasters and the other adults were presented non-realistically, the way the derisive, imaginative children perceived them—the principal a bearded dwarf in a top hat (in 1933 the beard meant the opposite of what beards mean now), another school official a tall, skinny spy sneaking around. Though to Americans the film might seem marvelously innocent and poetic, a charming satiric fantasy, with the black flag of anarchism that a child raises on the roof no more than an emblem of youth's desire for liberty, the film was taken much more seriously in France, and was banned there until after the Liberation. The rebellion of children is, in a sense, the first—the primary—rebellion, and is the model for future rebellions, as the school is children's first experience of an *institution.* Vigo's school was like a prison. (Political rebels—especially, the bomb-throwing kind—spent their lives in and out of prisons, and Vigo's father had actually spent part of his childhood in a children's prison.) The words that the child who instigates the revolt speaks to the teacher tormenting him ("*Monsieur le professeur, je vous dis merde!*"), which sound like what every schoolboy on occasion longs to say to his teachers, had a more specifically dangerous meaning in France. Vigo's father, the almost legendary anarchist leader Almereyda, had been one of the instigators of the mutiny of the French Army during the First World War—the only historical example of an army's mutinying in the face of the enemy. The words "*Je vous dis merde*" had been Almereyda's challenge to the government in the headlines of his newspaper, *La Guerre Sociale*. (His name was itself an anagram of "*y a* [*de*] *la merde*.") When *Zero for Conduct* was attacked in France as violent, perverse, and obscene, there was no doubt that, as André Bazin said, "for Vigo the school is nothing less than society itself." Anderson's model for *If . . .* is a key film both aesthetically and politically, and Anderson's school, following the same plan, seems meant as a mirror of society, and his conscious aim in all that stuff about rigidity and sadism and the rot of the upper classes seems to be to demonstrate that our society drives us to violence as the only solution—that it is the only pure act that can come out of all this. Anderson's adults are grotesques, but, unlike Vigo's, they are presented literally, and may even be intended to be taken realistically, as proof of the effects of stultifying traditions. They will probably be taken by most adults in the audience as evidence of conditions that must be improved, and by at least some students as evidence that the only thing to do is blow everyone up—after all, killing them isn't like killing real people, because they don't seem to have any honest emotions. *If . . .* is intended to be a revolutionary epic, and there are so many strong, coldly repellent scenes and such a powerful (even if possibly displaced) sense of anger that sequences that individually fail to move us accumulate steadily until the sheer grinding tendentiousness may make the climax pass for inevitable.

Vigo's vision was "poetic" partly because of its consistency and our instant recognition of its meanings. We responded immediately to the juvenile conspirators, who were not the innocent children seen by adults whose own childhood has become a sentimental memory but, rather, children seen by a director so young and so close in temperament to childhood that they seemed to be children as they saw themselves. The movie could leap along and we could make the connections, and the Surreal touches were intensifications of vision that reawakened our own old feelings. But Anderson's Surreal touches and episodes simply don't work; they just seem to be odd things happening, and one's reaction is "Huh?" I rather doubt whether one can successfully use Surreal distortions in such a humorless, tight style. Vigo, like Buñuel and Godard, could be wildly funny, and could do startling, imaginative things and make them seem perfectly natural. Anderson doesn't have the right tone; he's a scourge, not a poet, and the picture is clogged by all the difficult, ambitious things he attempts and flubs. Yet the visual style provides a kind of unity (despite the changes from color film to black and white, which I assume were the results of accident and economy—I assume that when the light wasn't adequate for using color film, they went on shooting with black and white), and Anderson's tone of cold, seething anger unifies the film, too. But we don't really know—immediately and intuitively—why he is showing us what he is showing us. This kind of picture should hold together emotionally and intellectually much better than it does, yet Anderson precludes such criticism by setting up as the No. 1 target the disgusting, hypocritical headmaster, who is calling for reason when he gets it—*ping!*—right in the middle of the forehead.

The basic inconsistency—the true craziness—of Anderson's vision of youthful revolution is that he is full of bile about youth. Vigo's children were united by the high spirits that were bursting out of repression (they saw one of the teachers, who had kept *his* high spirits, as a clown, and an ally), but Anderson devotes most of his energy to the meanness of the students, and it is really not a rebellion of the young that he shows us but a rebellion of a self-chosen few—three boys (and a girl picked up along the way) who set fire to the school on Speech Day and start sniping at those who flee the fire, including the rest of the young. Anderson's concept of destroying the prison is to kill the inmates. The conspirators are cleaning out the whole mess, apparently—killing everybody, because nobody's fit to live. The last shot is a glamorous, approving closeup of the hero as he fires away, like Robert Taylor aiming at "the Japs" at the end of *Bataan*. Anderson has dehumanized the other people as shamefully as Hollywood dehumanized "the Japs" during the war years, and has set up these few as the judges and purifiers of humanity. It's as crazy, in its way, as it would be to make a movie hero of that demented boy at the University of Texas who climbed to the top of a tower and fired at everyone in sight, and yet because these kids *are* students at school and are firing away I think they will be taken as youth driven to clean out the dead wood.

Anderson may think he has made a movie about revolutionary youth and freedom, and I guess that's what David Sherwin thinks he was putting into the script, but though they may think it's there, it isn't. We can read the signals, all right—the poster of Che and the hero's forbidden mustache and his playing the "Missa Luba"—but are we to believe the signals or the style of the film, which is constricted and charged with inconsistent, ambivalent feelings? We could tell what *Zero for Conduct* stood for because the movie was free and liberating, but the material about the revolt *feels* added to *If . . .* because we haven't sensed a movement toward freedom. Anderson is skillful at scenes of sadism, but when he wants to suggest that his nonconformist heroes have some of the joy of life that the others haven't, he becomes as banal as a TV director and shows them speeding lyrically through the green countryside on a stolen motorcycle. And, because one of his arguments against the school is the homoerotic atmosphere, he apparently feels it is necessary to show that his hero has "healthy" appetites—and does so by presenting him in a sexual scrimmage with a girl who is harder and tougher than the boys. The ways in which Anderson tries to illustrate the desire for freedom are so mechanical and carry so little conviction that I think one may conclude that the heroes are shooting because he needs to discharge his rage—which may be closer to why the boy in Texas was shooting than it is to a revolution. Anderson seems to have lost sight of what was so apparent in Vigo's view, and what was so funny in it—that school is a *child's* mirror of society. Vigo's vision was a comic metaphor; Anderson's movie has no wings, and his literal-mindedness about the school leads to the climax of shooting up the people in the school. Vigo did not confuse the children's view with "reality." Anderson does, and what makes the film such a can of wriggly worms is that his confusion will probably be the basis of its appeal. It's so convenient for older students to use a child's experience of institutions and to take the school for the Establishment. The conglomerates and the mass media may go on playing their dangerous turning-on games as long as the clowns and academics and liberal institutions, rather than the real centers of power, are the targets.

THEY SHOOT HORSES, DON'T THEY?

MARATHON '32

STEFAN KANFER

The mirrored chandelier whirls, the trio blares "Brother, Can You Spare a Dime?," and the master of ceremonies booms, "Yow-sah, yowsah, yowsah." The place is the Aragon Ballroom in Los Angeles, the time is the Depression, and the event is an extravagance of sadomasochism known as the Marathon Dance.

They Shoot Horses, Don't They? is a strenuous attempt to make that marathon a metaphor for man's fate. The contestants are the populace of a wasted nation. One girl, Ruby (Bonnie Bedelia), is pregnant. Gloria (Jane Fonda) is a brassbound bitch from the Dust Bowl. Robert (Michael Sarrazin) is an open-faced kid from a farm. Sailor (Red Buttons) is a Navy veteran whose ship has gone out. The man running the marathon—and carrying the movie—is a dime-store Barnum named Rocky (Gig Young). The son of an itinerant faith healer, Rocky has read the book on corruption and added footnotes of his own. Disgusted at what people—including himself—will do for money, he articulates the film's message: "There can only be one winner, folks, but isn't that the American way?"

Ironies like that are easy to manufacture, and Scenarists James Poe and Robert E. Thompson operate an assembly line. Ruby tunelessly chants "The Best Things in Life Are Free," then crawls for the pennies people throw her way. A Harlow-eyed blonde (Susannah York) is in the contest not for the $1,500 prize, but for a chance to be seen by a movie talent scout who might elevate her to bearable unreality. When the marathon begins to drag, Rocky dresses the participants in track suits and has them race around the floor—an event that literally causes the ancient mariner's heart to break.

At this melodramatic point, the film achieves its peak. Sailor's face empurples, his lips work and bubble, his body goes limp. "Walk, you son of a bitch, walk!" screams Gloria, carrying a corpse on her back, defying Rocky, circumstances, the Depression—and finally life itself in a racking finish that leaves the spectator as weary, and in a sense, as degraded as the participants. But it is precisely because of Gloria's inexhaustible drive that the film buckles. The dancers stay up for more than a thousand hours. The hall becomes a human zoo where legs, spines and, finally, minds fail. Rocky extends a typically cynical offer: Why don't Gloria and her new partner Robert get married out there on the floor? They can get divorced afterward, can't they? After all, warns the M.C., "I may not know a winner when I see one, but I sure know a loser."

Gloria arbitrarily accepts Rocky's put-down as her epitaph. Out on the boardwalk and out of the marathon, she aims a pistol at her temple. Then, for the first time, her temerity falters. "Help me," she begs Robert, and Robert obligingly turns the attempted suicide into a murder. The farm boy's explanation to the police: "They shoot horses, don't they?" Yes, they do—but only when the animal is broken. As Fonda plays the part, Gloria is a born survivor, a cork of a woman who would bob to the surface of a sewer or an ocean.

Devoid of motivation and imprisoned in the dance hall, the movie hungers for some message from the outside world. The contestants are soon reduced to figures without a landscape, whose despair is often expressed but seldom reasoned. Even Director Sydney Pollack seems to sense the claustrophobic atmosphere—and he restively punctuates the non-happenings with slow-motion scenes and rapid flash-forwards. Seldom effective and much too mannered, they serve only to bring the wrong kind of poverty to the project.

Still, as a footnote to American history, *They Shoot Horses, Don't They?* is invaluable. The entire cast—particularly Young and Fonda—understands the era when existence seemed one long bread line. The penciled eyebrows, marcelled coiffures and bright, hopeful faces change by degrees into ghastly masks; the bodies seem to pull against a gravity that wants them six feet underground. The music goes round and round, and so do the actors, in a coruscating dance of death. It is a pity that the picture is not left to them. The filmmakers should have known better than to cling to undimensional symbolism and stylistic conceits. They shoot movies, don't they?

DAMNATION WITH A DIFFERENCE

JOHN SIMON

They Shoot Horses, Don't They? is made from Horace McCoy's underground "classic" of 1935. The reel McCoy is, unfortunately, not quite the real McCoy, which itself fell short of a true work of art. Edmund Wilson, while conceding that it was "a subject with possibilities" and "worth reading," also noted the lack of characterization and motivation in the novel. But, in a sense, it was just this spare, straightforward, journalistic account of a monstrous Depression phenomenon, the dance marathon, that made the short book so unsettling: wholesale human degradation as the most matter-of-fact thing in the world. What weighs on this film is the passage of time: McCoy wrote his novel without the knowledge that he was creating a symbolic microcosm embodying universal hopelessness. The French existentialists were not hovering over his shoulders as they are over those of the filmmakers.

Nevertheless, the chief weaknesses of the film are like two or three bad sections of a tangerine, and can easily be spotted and mentally removed. They include a slow-motion prologue, or prelude, reminiscent of Sidney Lumet at his *Pawnbroker*ish worst, in which a boy witnesses the shooting of a glorious white stallion for no very convincing reason; some flash-forwards of Robert Syverton's trial for the shooting of his dancing partner Gloria—scenes shot in spooky ocean green and easily mistakable for flashbacks; and a bit of montage whereby the dying Gloria is seen collapsing no longer on a shabby pier but, in slow motion, in that meadow where the proud steed was killed. The sad thing about these blemishes is that the director, Sydney Pollack, is fully aware of their faultiness, and first made the film without these fatal embellishments. The original version of the film, without any of these elements, was screened for audiences in Palo Alto and San Francisco and elicited so much laughter in the wrong places—notably when Gloria produces a gun from her pocketbook in the last scene—that the additional material was put in to foretell disaster and forestall guffaws.

But, alas, the guffaws are not entirely the fault of cloddish spectators; both in the book and in the film there is something incredible about this ending. In the movie, Gloria is so dynamic, resourceful and clever that we cannot see her as the loser Rocky, the marathon's shady entrepreneur, recognizes in her. And though Pollack and his screenwriter, Robert E. Thompson, have labored to stick in grim little details to justify this suicide, to me the dosage does not seem lethal enough. I am not even persuaded that the strong-willed Gloria would need the bland Robert to act as her executioner.

Here the fault lies partly in the movie Gloria's greater attractiveness and less pronounced death wish than her fictional prototype's, and partly in Michael Sarrazin's not being a good enough actor to convey how one may be swept into this deathly compact at the cost of one's own life. I think of an actor like Gérard Philipe in this part, of the Mishkin-like quality he would have brought to it; this might easily have compensated for the insufficiency of characterization which the film in part inherits from the book.

To be sure, the movie does supply Gloria with a reasonably adequate background, as it also provides Rocky, a character largely created by the filmmakers, with a plausible past and interestingly complex personality springing from it. The other figures have to be taken at face value, which in all but Robert's case is not a serious loss. Rather more disturbing is the fact that in the film, as already implied, the marathon tries too hard to be emblematic of the world without quite being able to carry off the allegory. Thus the film makes the marathon's management corrupt in several additional and unconvincing ways, but even this is less of a problem than the sometimes top-heavy dialogue, as in the case of that line McCoy relished enough to make it the title of his book. It makes a good title, but it is a poor line.

Yet, for me, these faults fade beside the solid achievements of the film. There is, first of all, the dazzlingly authentic atmosphere: the mendaciously optimistic music nudging on a dance that looks progressively less like dancing and more like chronic somnambulism, as if some sinister narcosis from another planet were infecting our world. And there is the hideous parasitic life that swirls around these staggering corpses: the management, the employees, the audiences. And the garish, pathetic, hysterical backstage activity—or merely leaden inactivity—during the brief rest periods of which many dare not avail themselves lest they never rise again to shuffle on. The sleazy dance emporium is recreated in all its tawdriness, the costumes are painfully accurate, the false gaiety enough to make a tin angel weep. Yet through this jiggling morass there runs a thread of life, of gallows humor, of sheer defiant tenacity, toward a paltry but touching heroism.

Not the least remarkable thing about *They Shoot Horses, Don't They?* is the photography by Philip A. Lathrop. There were considerable problems to contend with. Though shot in color, the film had to have the shoddy look of a godforsaken ballroom jutting out into the Pacific, and Lathrop accordingly underexposed and overdeveloped the film, getting a grainy texture and somber coloration—predominantly purplish brown of an unwholesome, almost macabre quality. And because the camera had to keep whirling along with the dancers, no ground-level lights, only overhead ones, could be used. It all works very well, despite the difficulties, and when Lathrop's camera seems to collide head-on with some of those overhead light beams, the result is not only glaringly realistic, it is almost hallucinatory.

The director, Sydney Pollack, and Lathrop keep the camera chasing after the dancers to good effect, particularly in the brutal elimination sprints. These grueling footraces around the ballroom, with the couples holding hands while the band plays rousing music, automatically eliminate the last three pairs to cross the finish line. Even during the regular dancing one partner has to support the other while he or she sleeps; here one or the other virtually has to carry the partner through lap after punishing lap, while the camera spins, lurches, staggers along. These scenes bristle with horror, and when Sailor, an overage contestant, is dying of a heart attack, the film expresses his agonizing vision by going into slow motion. What results is spooky, deathly, diabolic—perhaps a cross between Holbein and Dante.

But all kinds of scenes are managed with quiet brilliance. Scenes on the dance floor when nothing much is happening beyond the monotonous, lethargic roundelay, or when exacerbated contestants pick fights or just pick away at their partners; scenes in the rest area, backstage, with people often too tired to rest properly, crumpled up in bizarre positions, or bickering, or snatching at pitifully inadequate remedies, or having hysterics; scenes in Rocky's, the entrepreneur-MC's office, where everything from seedy skulduggery to sterile lovemaking takes place. And even such very minor characters who say next to nothing, like Turkey, Rocky's fat, cigar-smoking assistant (Al Lewis), or the 67-year-old woman who sponsors Robert and Gloria because they are Number 67 (Madge Kennedy) are vividly conceived in terms of appearance and mannerisms, but are not caricatured or condescended to.

For such things we must be grateful to Pollack's direction and Robert E. Thompson's screenplay (though James Poe gets top screen-writing credit, his contributions do not survive in the final version). Pollack and Thompson have created two especially memorable characters: Gloria, the girl with the deathwish worn on her sleeve, and Rocky, the low-grade, hardened showman, are both absorbing and rich in surprises. At every turning of the film they reveal something further of themselves—sometimes unexpectedly better or worse than we would have thought, sometimes thoroughly fulfilling our aroused expectations. And both are played very nearly to perfection.

As Gloria, that fine little actress, Jane Fonda, graduates into a fine big actress. If there is one thing wrong with the performance, it is the vestige of a Vassar accent; other than that, it is solid, untricky acting, squeezing all the juice out of the part but not chewing up its rind. What impressed me most is that I did not really recognize Miss Fonda—and I don't mean the frizzed hair and other tricks of make-up, good as they are. I mean that the actress here gives an antipodal performance: There is none of the glitter, kittenishness, or jollity that have been her specialties in the past. But even her hardness has (unlike in *Spirits of the Dead*) a lining of humanity, and there is something about her very toughness that repeatedly moves us. And there are even fortuitous benefits: Miss

Fonda has fascinatingly long, spatulate fingers—hands that are bony and poignant without being aristocratic or beautiful. They show up splendidly in the two-shots on her partner's shoulders and appear to be the hands of both Death and the Maiden in one.

As Rocky, Gig Young, that ex-matinee-idol-that-failed, makes a spirited comeback. The character emerges sleazy enough, yet not without a hardboiled charm, corrupt but with moments of solidity and even sympathy. His reminiscences of childhood are neither too sarcastic nor too touching; they are aimed at understanding, not empathy. He is not afraid of overplaying the two-bit MC aspect of his role, as overplayed it must be; but he keeps the other aspects in firm control and handles the transitions effortlessly. Young has just the right good looks gone partly to seed, and the properly flexible voice that turns oily in the limelight and greedy in the shadows.

Other roles are very neatly managed, too, both individually and in the here all-important ensembles. Especially imposing are Susannah York and Bonnie Bedelia, two actresses I have previously been less than keen, and sometimes downright down, on. Miss York plays a semi-refined, semi-absurd would-be actress, strenuously emulating Jean Harlow, and trying to attract the eye of producers who might wander into the marathon's audience. She does it with a judicious balance of preposterousness and pathos, poise and desperation: The superficiality and flightiness of the character are kept as much to the fore as the naked need for affection, even if only from a vulgar audience, or, lower yet, from sordidly quick sex with another girl's partner. The hysterical scene in the shower is sensibly played much more for the sickness and horror of it than for vulnerability and heartbreak. It emerges, with Gig Young's strong collaboration, as a shattering and humane scene devoid of false heroism or histrionics.

As for Bonnie Bedelia, she is an actress whose appeal lies in some kind of fundamental ordinariness, which she usually epitomizes for other people's delectation, not mine. But here, as a famished, several months pregnant Okie wife, in the contest mostly for the food (her husband, by the way, is played with fine, fanatic, dumb-animal anger by Bruce Dern), she manages to be honestly gripping: naive, confused, downtrodden, yet willingly, tenaciously dancing, plodding, hanging on. When she smilingly sings, out of the pit of her hopelessness, a mendaciously cheerful pop song and a few coins are tossed at her by the audience, the screen fills up with that dauntlessness and endurance that is the countertheme of this dirge with dancing.

Deserving of note, too, are the performances of Allyn Ann McLerie and Red Buttons as overage contestants who nevertheless defy mortality. For in this rock-bottom marathon there are no runners gloriously expiring as they announce the victory of a Miltiades, only obscure human beings dragging themselves to exhaustion or death to proclaim obscurely the persistence of the human spirit.

Praise must go also to the make-up department, headed by another McCoy, Frank. It is an awesome sight to see these contestants grow feeble, haggard, ghostly before our eyes, becoming images of shuffling death. Time and all its creeping ravages, so powerfully conveyed by the acting, are as brilliantly evoked by the mutations of make-up.

Hovering over all this is the banal music of the period, suggestively yet unostentatiously chosen and arranged by John Green who, in his previous avatar as Johnny Green, also wrote many of the catchy tunes. The music reflects, exalts, mocks, and finally provides an aural epitaph for these dancing damned. As for Harry Horner's setting, it is a shrewd replica of an old Los Angeles ballroom that could easily double as one of the lower rings of Dante's Inferno.

But, but, but. There remain the flaws I discussed in my last column, and the ultimate incredibility of Gloria's suicide—at least as presented on the screen. Sydney Pollack says that the last straw is supposed to be the accidental ripping of Gloria's last pair of stockings, and I concede that such an absurdly anticlimactic minor mishap will drive the exasperated person over the brink. But either because the incident is not etched sharply enough, or because too much time (including the seemingly liberating emergence of Gloria and Robert from the ballroom onto the boardwalk) intervenes between it and the shooting, Gloria's death remains unconvincing.

I suppose this is partly due also to her not being made into enough of a loser in other episodes of the film, and to Jane Fonda's deep, vital attractiveness, which even the dark triumphs of make-up, costuming and performance cannot quite overshadow. Still, although *They Shoot Horses, Don't They?* does not, as a whole, reach the domain of art, many of its aspects and an aura that lingers on establish it as a true and eminent cinematic achievement.

II:

ADVANCE OBIT.

1969 may have been to the movies what 1955 was to Detroit. Tooled up for headier chrome and heavier chassis, the automobile manufacturers found themselves undone by a persistent little German bug. Hollywood's Volkswagen was *Easy Rider*, made for under half a million—and expected to gross over forty million. The tendency toward profitable small movies had, of course, been building for well over a year, but *Easy Rider* crystallized it—and in the new sociology of 1969, the fat musicals, the absurd million-dollars-up-front contracts for stars, the big budget bombs appeared to be more than a business disaster. They were a moral waste.

An alteration in audience attitude, inconveniently coupled with a tight money policy, attacked the major studios with more force than the blacklist, more even than television. Viewers began to sue for alienation of affectations. It is now no longer possible to tell whether, if there is a twenty-first century, there will be a Twenty First Century-Fox. It is only known that the overupholstered studio couch is doomed, and with it the overupholstered studio film, and, with them, the overupholstered studio itself.

S.K.

Hollywood: Myth, Fact and Trouble

JOSEPH MORGENSTERN

In *The Decline and Fall of Practically Everybody*, Will Cuppy once explained why the Great Pyramid still stands. "It is not in the nature of a pyramid to fall down," he wrote. "It probably could not fall down if it tried." Six seemingly solid monuments to the movie business still stand in Hollywood, the last of the major studios producing theatrical films with their own vast facilities. Shaken ruthlessly by television and foreign competition, they have not fallen down. But now, aided by incompetence and abetted by cultural changes they can't comprehend, several may finally prove they weren't such Great Pyramids after all.

Four of the six studios responsible for 65 to 70 per cent of all the business done by feature films in the United States are in serious trouble. The fifth, Warner Bros.-Seven Arts, has been turning a good profit on phonograph records and medium-size features (*Bonnie and Clyde; Rachel, Rachel; Bullitt*) and is merging with Kinney National Service, Inc., which also runs parking lots and funeral parlors. The sixth, Columbia, has a costly turkey in *Mackenna's Gold*, but is still riding high for the moment on *Funny Girl* and *Oliver!* Both these musicals are fine entertainment made by uncommonly gifted artists, so the lesson would seem clear: To succeed, a studio need only make good movies.

That, however, is just what the studios can't do with any consistency. It doesn't matter if they're run by traditional showmen like Darryl F. Zanuck of Fox, or conglomerated, computerized, systematizing and maximizing magnates like Charles G. Bluhdorn of Gulf & Western, which owns Paramount. These leaders of the leisure industry know how to make money on trash for television, among other waste products of their factories. When it comes to something better, though, they seem to have lost the Midas touch. Studio press agents and a willing press peddle so much nonsense about the popularity of movies with the movie generation that one fact of the matter is almost obscured: The American feature-film business as a whole is a losing proposition with a shrinking share of the national population as its audience.

In public, the nation's major movie producers are determined optimists. Their spokesman, Motion Picture Association of America president Jack Valenti, points to climbing grosses and growing international markets. He says that "the general level of quality in the movie business is higher than it's been in a long time, and it's on an ascending curve." But grosses inevitably climb with inflation and a growing population, and the exportation of increasing numbers of conventional, predictable American films to Asia or Latin America doesn't necessarily warm the hearts of those who want movies to change and mature with the times.

In private, the producers and studio chiefs are running scared. What scares them most at the moment is that they can't seem to give the paying public enough of what it wants. The public, in Hollywood's private language, means kids in their late teens and early 20s; nobody talks of retrieving the lost audience of over-30s from television-watching, reading, or whatever old folks do at night. And Hollywood today is terrorized by the mercurial tastes of restless children.

What do the kids want? How should Hollywood know? The sad, vulgar men who slapped together *The Impossible Years* had no idea of what sex means to adolescents. The brain-weary propagandists who made *Che!* into an asthmatic hoodlum had no idea what their hero means to young revolutionaries. What do the kids want? At every studio, audience-survey specialists are staring into their crystal computers to find out. But it takes eighteen months or more to get a movie out, and the tastes of a sensation-hungry public can't be projected forward eighteen days. For the moment, it seems certain that someone out there is buying a lot of tickets to a lot of cheaply made (mostly in Europe), independently produced quasi-skin flicks. Such popular delectations as *I Am Curious (Yellow)* have lured the peepers away from their peepshows in Times Square and other urban tenderloins to the art houses of the nation. Donald Rugoff, the head of a leading New York City art-house chain, likens the current situation to "a whore moving out of her neighborhood—you never noticed her as long as she stayed where she belonged."

The studios would love to turn madam, to match the independents at their own sleazy game. But they don't dare. The independents have little to lose. The publicly owned major studios must stay clear of censorship and stay in favor with their constituency of some 13,800 U.S. theaters. The studios inaugurated a ratings system last year, hoping to head off government censorship with industry self-censorship, but it isn't working well. And the backlash to permissiveness is here. The Pastore hearings into violence on TV have frightened the networks, on which the feature-film business heavily depends, while police in cities and towns all over the country are closing movie houses, seizing prints, even jailing projectionists and managers for showing alleged pornography. Senate Republican Leader Everett Dirksen introduced an anti-obscenity bill intended to circumvent recent liberal decisions of the Supreme Court. Even the complexion of the Supreme Court can change quickly, as the aftermath of the Fortas case has shown.

Since sleazy little pictures are too risky for whole production programs to depend on, the studios often swing to the other extreme: relatively antiseptic, big-budget, wide-screen, reserved-seat spectacles made on the theory that people will pay to see what they can't get for free on TV. It's not a bad theory except when the movies are bad, which they frequently are. And even if the movies aren't bad entertainment they're usually bad financial risks. To show a profit after distributors and exhibitors take their cuts, a movie must gross at least twice what it costs to make. Expensive pictures, those budgeted at $5 million to $6 million, say, have an insidious habit of escalating into very expensive pictures that can't possibly make back their costs of $8 million, $12 million—even $18 million in the notorious instance of *Dr. Dolittle.*

Why do costs escalate so? One factor is labor. "We've got the whole American standard of living to contend with," says Valenti. Another factor is management. "The movie companies have lost control of their product," says Louis F. Polk, Jr., the 39-year-old

Harvard-trained financial expert who six months ago took over as president of embattled M-G-M.* "They don't develop their own actors any more, don't develop directors, don't develop writers. Instead of using packagers, they're at the packagers' mercy."

Common sense would dictate a way out of this box: Provide compelling alternatives to the cheap trash and the dear slush; make interesting movies at reasonable prices. Once again, though, that's just what the studios don't know how to do. Even if the people running them knew how to judge the worth of a script, which most of them can't; even if they knew where to look beyond best-selling books and shows for original, inexpensive scripts, which most of them don't, the system within which they operate today militates inexorably against reasonably priced movies or reasonably priced anything.

Bigness makes for bigger bigness. Agents, producers, actors and unions work together in a consortium of greed while babbling all the while about creativity. If Michelangelo had talked about creativity as much as people in Hollywood do, he would never have found time to build the scaffold to get up to the Sistine ceiling. Distributors and theater owners who rarely go to movies themselves still insist on expensive stars, even though stars alone can't sell tickets and never could, even at the height of the star system. What sold tickets then was habit and lack of competition. And the major studios really want to make expensive movies. They're impressed by the prices they themselves pay, and they're mesmerized by the few great successes that saved whole companies, as *The Sound of Music* did for 20th Century–Fox. Hollywood was crazy from the start, but in the old days it could afford to be. Today the world is changing fast, and Hollywood, the world's great provider of myths, is falling victim to some myths of its own.

MYTH—Hollywood is still the technical capital of the movie world.

FACT—The physical plant is badly worn. Lights and cameras are antique. Few Hollywood sound stages are soundproof; a small fortune is lost every day on takes spoiled by airplane noise. American producers run away to Europe not only because of taxes but because equipment and working conditions are better, overhead is lower by at least half. "We should continue to have a studio," says

* A few months later in 1969 James T. Aubrey was named President and Chief Executive Officer of M-G-M.

Herbert F. Solow, 38, the new production chief at M-G-M. "Unfortunately this studio was built 45 years ago and so were all the others in town. There are technical advances in so many other industries, but I don't know that there are many here."

MYTH—Studio chiefs run the studios.

FACT—Sometimes they do. Sometimes it's the producer-packagers, sometimes the agents. Sometimes the agents don't know who's in charge. "Because of the conglomerates, no one knows any more who controls Hollywood," says one powerful agent. "Nobody is what he's supposed to be."

MYTH—The big money in feature films is made by those who make features.

FACT—The filmmakers are mostly babes in the woods. There's much bigger money in distribution, which is the major studios' stranglehold on feature production. In 1950 the Supreme Court ordered the studios to divest themselves of their theater chains. But they still distribute films that they and other producers make, and charge some 35 per cent of a film's gross earnings for doing so. The studios say this is a reasonable charge for getting the right prints to the right theaters at the right time. Many independent producers say it's highway robbery, but travel the same highway repeatedly because they know of no other route. Norman Lear, a successful producer in partnership with Bud Yorkin, says, "We know less about the distribution business than any manufacturer knows about his trade."

MYTH—The movie business is a business.

FACT—It's a crap game with unmarked dice. "You think I'd invest my own money in a studio as a regulation business that makes a product that can be sold?" asks the producer of *The Graduate*, Lawrence Turman. "Not me!"

MYTH—Movies are the studios' greatest asset.

FACT—Real estate is. M-G-M owns 1,850 acres in Ventura County, 140 in Culver City. Fox owns 2,738 acres of Malibu ranch, 74 acres a gemstone's throw from Beverly Hills; Warner Bros. has 105 acres, Paramount 54, Columbia 53 and Universal 420, including a mountain. Land is the bedrock of the studios' asset structures. Land makes them alluring to conglomerate managements. But the facilities sitting on that land give the major studios their major and perhaps incurable headache. They've got to keep grinding out movies that nobody wants just to fill the sound stages, pay the taxes, reduce the overhead. In their present form the studios are as likely to succeed as dinosaurs. What was once an unthinkable thought in Hollywood is now perfectly thinkable. If the studios collapsed tomorrow, no one but the stockholders would miss them.

A production firm can always rent equipment and sound stages. Avco-Embassy has no studio but it produced *The Graduate* and *The Lion in Winter*. Output is growing among such new outfits as National General, Commonwealth-United and the TV network feature-production arms, ABC's Palomar Pictures and CBS's Cinema Center Films. United Artists has no studio, yet this giant of its field, established in 1919 to combat restrictive distribution practices of that time and now a subsidiary of Transamerica Corporation, produced the Beatles pictures and the James Bond pictures and continues to make scads of money under shrewd management.

At one time studios were absolute necessities for making entertainment movies. Now, with changing concepts of entertainment, almost anyone can make them. All it takes is a good idea, three people, some film and some rented equipment. Studios have become a convenience at best; at worst they're anathema to many serious moviemakers. When M-G-M's Solow says, "It's not our business to promote the culture of our country or make art films, it's to make money for the studio," he is taking a sensible businessman's position. But there are people to whom moviemaking means more than making money for a movie studio, and their work is beginning to reach the mass audience whenever they can break the distribution stranglehold.

Right now, in theaters all over the country, movies are playing that were made entirely outside the Hollywood establishment. These aren't underground films, but features such as *Faces, Greetings, The Wedding Party,* the Norman Mailer and Andy Warhol movies; and increasingly popular feature-length documentaries like *The Endless Summer, Salesman, Monterey Pop, A Face of War, Warrendale, High School.* If you measure importance solely by cold cash earned, most of these movies possess pipsqueak proportions. *The Sound of Music* is still safe. But the amazing thing about them is that they exist at all, that so many individuals were able to make so many motion pictures entirely on their own. Together they constitute the vanguard of a revolution in American film production.

They were shot quickly and easily with lightweight, portable 16-mm. equipment. Not one of them cost as much as $100,000. They were made outside the union structure. "Until now," says one practicing member of the Directors' Guild of America, "this was a police state patrolled by the unions." These films got national attention before they got national distribution. *Faces* made a big stir at a succession of film festivals. Most of the others made debuts at dinky theaters rented for the occasion. Just the same, they were reviewed by influential newspapers and magazines with all the respect and space once reserved for star-studded multimillion-dollar world premières. The line between professional and amateur production has begun to be drawn with invisible ink.

This is not to suggest that 16-mm. features and documentaries are driving Hollywood out of business. The lesson of these minor-league movies with major-league appeal is not being lost on Hollywood. The incipient revolution outside the industry has produced the beginnings of crucial change from within. Hollywood has embarked on a belated but promising research program to modernize its cameras and lights. It has finally recognized the need to pool its resources in cooperative studios. "What's cheering me up is that the new leadership coming up recognizes the problems," Valenti says. "I can't tell you when these dinosauric vestiges of the old Hollywood are going to disappear, but I know it's going to happen." And in two recent cases, dramatic union concessions have made it possible for feature films to be produced at reasonable costs under reasonable working conditions.

In New York, an ex-TV commercial director named Barry Brown used an eight- or nine-man crew, instead of the usual 35 or 40, on United Artists' *The Way We Live Now,* which was shot in 35-mm. color for an astonishingly low $350,000. And Francis Ford Coppola, who directed *You're a Big Boy Now* and *Finian's Rainbow,* produced and directed *The Rain People* for under $1 million for Warner Bros.-Seven Arts with a crew of nine or ten technicians, traveling cross-country and housing the entire production in a couple of trucks and a mobile home. (Coppola, who is 30, has recently joined filmmakers Haskell Wexler and John Korty in building a small production facility of their own in San Francisco "in order to control our own means of production." Next, the three may actually buy a theater as a showcase for their films.)

There's no guarantee that little movies will be better than big ones, but the prospects for American filmmakers have finally started to brighten. The big fish are being chomped on by a lively new school of little fish. Low production costs, small crews and reduced risks could mean the return to a system in which talented people control their movies, and not the other way around.

THE STUDIO by John Gregory Dunne

STANLEY KAUFFMANN

The Studio resembles earlier "documentaries" that have peered close at the pores of film people, but with two big differences. Most previous books and articles of this kind, like Lillian Ross's *Picture*, have followed the fate of one film; Dunne has sliced the matter laterally by following the activities of a studio (20th Century-Fox) for a year, thus cutting across the fates of a number of pictures. And Dunne's account includes the studio's latter-day involvement with television.

His motives, as he describes them, are a bit factitious; he sounds as if he thought he had invented the idea of exploring Hollywood and its relation to our culture. But he observes shrewdly, listens sharply, and writes without fuss. We see various films at various stages: from proposal of ideas to world premières. The sums of money that get mentioned at every stage are, to mortals, like astronaut distances compared with earth distances. (Not new in films. D. W. Griffith spent nearly $100,000 on an outdoor stage for an Al Jolson picture; Jolson took one look at his screen tests and fled.) The nerves, the sycophancy, the sense of technical proficiency and creative poverty, Dunne skewers them all.

The chief trouble with the book is that, although it is new, we feel we've read most of it before. Only some nouns and figures have been changed. The dialogue about revamping a sci-fi TV serial might have applied to a Saturday-afternoon serial 30 years ago. The staff producer may be disappearing, as executives hire a producer along with his package; but the gavottes and fandangos within the production unit have not altered much.

One can always accuse a reporter like Dunne of looking for the seamy or ludicrous side, but, after all, he is writing about men who, with their magnificent offices and conferences and cables, came up in a year with such gems as *Dr. Dolittle, The Boston Strangler, The Secret Life of an American Wife*, and *Star!*

Two highlights. Christopher Plummer got $300,000 *not* to be in *Dr. Dolittle*. Rex Harrison said yes, then he said no, which was when they signed Plummer, then Harrison said yes again, which was when they had to pay off Plummer. Second, out of all the quotable dialogue, one passage by a Hollywood agent lingers:

> You fail upward here. A guy makes a ten-million-dollar bomb, the big thing is not that he's made a bomb, but that he put together a ten-million-dollar picture. Next time out, they give him a twelve-million-dollar picture.

Seems that one old adage needs to be changed: You're as good as your last picture's budget. If only it had been true in Griffith's day.

PAINT YOUR WAGON

SOMEBODY ELSE'S SUCCESS

Pauline Kael

Paint Your Wagon is not the sort of movie that people who read movie criticism are likely to go to, but it's one of the three or four most expensive musical films ever made, and I don't think it should just be ignored. It's probably one of the last of its breed—the super-gigantic blockbuster musicals, such as *Camelot* (fifteen million), *Sweet Charity* (eight million), *Star!* (fourteen million), and *Doctor Dolittle* (eighteen million), that have finally broken the back of the American movie industry. There is almost no way—short of a miracle—that it can recover its costs, and although there are several other movies of this kind waiting to be released or to be completed, and at least one of them is even *more* expensive, it is highly unlikely that any new ones will be scheduled for production in the years to come, or, perhaps, ever.

The movie companies have gone on bringing out these Edsels; this one cost twenty million, give or take a few, and the company makes a valiant attempt to turn its release into an event. Everybody goes through the motions, and just about everybody expects the picture to come down the ramp and sink. It won't be the critics' fault, though they'll get blamed, and there will be more of those high-level everybody-commiserating-with-everybody-else discussions about how you just can't tell what people want anymore. The director, Joshua Logan, did no better or worse than he usually does—he must have been hired for what he can do, and this is it. The stars—Lee Marvin, Jean Seberg, and Clint Eastwood—have never pretended to be musical-comedy stars, and they must have been hired for what *they* can do: Marvin to overact and cavort energetically, Jean Seberg to be lovely, Eastwood to be sensitive in that deadpan way that is supposed to have mysterious power at the box office. The financial failure won't be the fault of Frederick Loewe, some of whose music is very pleasant, or even of André Previn, whose additional music isn't. Nor can it be blamed on Paddy Chayefsky, even though he did the adaptation in short scenes that never give one a chance to get involved with the characters; he did what he can do. (Remember when Eddie Fisher wanted Chayefsky brought in to work on the script of *Cleopatra?* The bad jokes of yesterday come home to roost. But not to crow.) And, maybe, though we're getting warmer, it won't really even be the fault of Alan Jay Lerner, who produced the movie and did the screenplay and lyrics. In a certain sense, they're all responsible, but what they've all done is part of a rotting system in which mediocrity and skyrocketing costs work together to turn out films that would have a hard time making money even if they were good. If the pictures were good and lost money, there would be some glory in it, but it's financially disastrous and inglorious, too, to make these big movies in which the themes are modernized and the elements jiggled around until finally nothing fits together right and even the good bits of the original show you started with are shot to hell. *Paint Your Wagon* plays it so safe that it has been directed by a man whose qualification is having directed *Camelot,* which was also a failure, but *in the same financial class.* Here he is, making another big musical with stars who can neither sing nor dance; their qualification is that two of them appeared a year earlier on the lists of top box-office stars. The major studios are collapsing, but they're not being toppled over by competitors; they're so enervated that they're sinking of their budgetary weight.

The studios looked at the profits on a few big musicals and thought big musicals were a safe investment and tied up enormous sums of money in them—so much of a studio's total investment that two or three flops can actually mean that the studio changes hands. But to be successful a musical must give you a joyous feeling—a sense that it's good to be alive, a communion in the simple pleasures and the common emotions. Maybe those who made *The Sound of Music* got by with it because of their shamelessness. It was such a cornball enterprise that they threw in everything: the opening mountaintop exaltation out of Leni Riefenstahl, the draperies cut up for clothing out of *Gone with the Wind*—what did it matter? Ever since, the industry has been trying to calculate what made that picture a hit, trying to repeat the success. But the moviemakers are full of shame, and the pictures sicken from it. The musical is a stylized form for releasing and celebrating emotions through song and dance. When Fred Astaire sang a bit of verse to Ginger and then reached out his hand and whirled her into the dance, that dance and their whole series of dances together were the most exquisite courtship rites the screen has ever known. Astaire's happiness was contagious; it's obvious that it takes a performer who wants to give us something to make us happy that way. When Harve Presnell suddenly turns up in *Paint Your Wagon* and sings "They Call the Wind Maria," the movie comes to life for a minute, because he belongs here; he can *sing*, and he stands and breathes like a singer, with some pride in what he's doing. How can we watch Clint Eastwood in a musical? When he walks around in the great outdoors of a gigantic movie and sings "I Talk to the Trees," in his toneless, light little voice, he hardly seems to be in the movie. He's controlled in such an uninteresting way; it's not an actor's control, which enables one to release something—it's the kind of control that keeps one from releasing anything. We could stand the deadpan reserve of Nelson Eddy's nonacting because he gave of himself when he sang, but Eastwood doesn't give of himself *ever*, and a musical with a withdrawn hero is almost a contradiction in terms. His singing isn't bad in a rhythm number like "Gold Fever," but as the amiably nameless Pardner of No Name City he's only slightly more animated than as the Man with No Name of the Italian Westerns, and now he lacks even his wooden menace. We wait for him to shoot somebody, because that's all he can do, and he doesn't do it. He's a nowhere man, woodenly proper. Jean Seberg has become a pale, lovely, dimpled movie queen—a synthesis of Bibi Andersson and Stella Stevens, and with that worn, somewhat used look, like Ava Gardner's, which makes her more humanly beautiful than in her French films. But she's just barely alive in a musical: She can't sing or dance; she can hardly *move*. Her eyes are as coolly blank toward Eastwood as toward everyone else; why should we care if these two get together? They are so devoid of romance or passion they're like the unpeople at the end of *1984*. And so Lee Marvin comes on comical, as if he were something left over from *Cat Ballou*, and he works at it, doing double takes and backfalls and W. C. Fields imitations—because somebody has to give this show some charge—and he works so frenetically that it kills some of the quieter things he does rather well, such as his handling of "Wand'rin' Star." There's a stock bit involving a farmer boy's triple initiation into liquor, smoking, and sex that has a nice, warm, corny feeling; Logan is good at this kind of humor, as he demonstrated in *Bus Stop*. But the movie is a road show and it's meant to be *sustained* rousing, lusty Americana of the *Oklahoma!* and *Seven Brides for Seven Brothers* variety, so at intervals it stimulates epic joy by throwing in a men's choir and turning up the sound. You come out smashed from the noise of it.

One of the reasons each blockbuster musical is such a gamble is that we need to build up familiarity with a voice and have our expectations satisfied from movie to movie, as we did with Astaire's dances. The dubbed voices (like Jean Seberg's) and the nondescript voices, like Eastwood's, don't carry over; the producers have spent twenty million dollars, and they haven't even developed a singing star for *another* picture. Their methods are practically suicidal; they make each picture as if it were the last. And therefore, because of the way they work and the financial pressures, the company needs a general, not an artist, and it wants a man with a broad "popular" approach. So it settles for a compromise figure. Logan tries hard, but there's no beauty of feeling when he does "pictorial" scenes, such as the miners coming from miles around to stare at a woman. A fortune has been spent constructing a goldmining camp, yet the contrast between that transient, womanless life and what the heroine wants is fumbled, and so the big theme is lost and only the big scale remains. Logan doesn't aim for coarse effects, but his handling is coarse, and so there are crude, stupid scenes, such as Lee Marvin tearing open Jean Seberg's blouse just after she's been shown suckling an infant. Logan is looking for laughs, and so he caricatures people—like the farming family—at the expense of the remnants of the theme. A picture like this involves one emotionally in the moviemaking process, because one can see why they're doing just about every damn thing they're doing. They don't use the original plot because the thin little story about a young girl and a Mexican boy didn't sound very "in," so it becomes a *ménage à trois* instead—a "now" plot. Because they're afraid that the movie might be considered an operetta, they cast cool non-singers, like Eastwood and Seberg. Because they want to sound hip, the lyrics use rhymes like "Californy" and "horny." One can't help feeling sympathetic to all the effort and anxiety, but all the problems they're trying to solve are *business* problems. Broadway composers forage around for some old movie that can be made into a musical, and that's essentially what Lerner and Loewe are trying to do, too; though they reverse the procedure, and though *Paint Your Wagon* is their own old property, they're trying to revamp it into a new commodity.

So many people in the movie business, as on Broadway, are trying to pump new revenue out of a few old songs or jokes or a piece of an old plot. But if a show can't be done the way it was written in the first place—if it has to be brought up to date—isn't that because it wasn't really very good in the first place? Wouldn't it be better to start fresh? And not just for the public but for the "artists"? If they have so few ideas that they've got to hoard the old ones and try to mold them into new shapes, are they still artists, or are they now just tired businessmen trying to get additional capital out of old investments of talent and effort? In the climax of *Paint Your Wagon,* No Name City collapses because the heroes have tunnelled under it to catch the gold dust that falls between the floorboards of the saloons. The studios are collapsing the same way on the Hollywood moviemakers who have been scrounging around for old gold dust. They take their old work off the shelf and try to get it rewritten to make it "youth-oriented"; they come out with a leering family picture that won't appeal to youth, and—what's worse—it doesn't honestly represent anybody anymore. Nobody believes in it; everybody just hopes that the beads on Lee Marvin will have magic, or that John Truscott's gold-rush hippie costumes will sweep the nation and save everything. At the high-level conferences, they'll say, "If only we hadn't had all that production trouble, if it hadn't rained, if only we'd finished sooner, when the hippie movement was still big . . ." They'll explain the bind they're in by saying, "We got it out too late." They'll be wrong, because they couldn't have made it with this picture last year or the year before or five years ago. There was never a right time for a picture that shifts around trying to find the secret of somebody else's success, yet that's the only kind of big picture the businessmen who now control the major studios really believe in.

III:

AUTEURISMS

"Ultimately, the auteur theory is not so much a theory as an attitude, a table of values that converts film history into directorial autobiography."

—ANDREW SARRIS

S.J. Perelman once compared scenario writing to stuffing a pillow with kapok. Even that simile is generous. The sleeper, after all, does not believe that the pillow made up the stuffing as it went along. Yet for half a century some credulous viewers believed that actors more or less improvised their lines to fit the situation. And for over a decade that notion has enjoyed the intellectual imprimatur of the auteurists—enthusiasts or worshipers of the director who, they insist, is the true, the only author of a film. In the neologists' hands, writers thus become sketchmen, actors chessmen, and history an anthology of personality quirks.

And yet . . . and yet . . . the auteurists' estate is continually renewed by works unified by a single vision. In 1969, the auteurs were, as always, few but potent. Their "autobiographies" proved sufficient to carry their detractors and champions for yet another round.

S.K.

INTIMATE LIGHTING

Andrew Sarris

Ivan Passer's *Intimate Lighting* is clearly designed to elicit the warm laughter of rueful recognition. And it succeeds admirably in its intention. What we have here basically is the old story of the city mouse visiting his country cousin, and the country is a realm where, in Wordsworth's phrase, incident serves as event. In this instance, a young cellist with the Prague symphony visits an old classmate, now a provincial music teacher in the groves of musical academe. The cellist arrives with his mistress, comely, cosmopolitan, ironic, easily amused. The country house is crowded with three generations of a rural violinist's family, the adults all too fat from ease and frustration. First paradoxical counterpoint: The violinist, having aimed higher, has sunk lower. Parents, wife, children, house, community all dissolve in the morning mists before the never-forgotten promise of Prague. The music on the soundtrack spurs the two men on toward their drunken dream of fraternity and sublimity, but the middle-aged realities bring them back to the boredom they must learn to endure as mortal human beings.

If Passer's films (*Intimate Lighting* and *A Boring Afternoon*) now seem somewhat richer and mellower than Forman's, it is because Forman remains a miniaturist, a director who reduces his subjects in his lens to the proper scale for satiric inquiry and symbolic evocation. Forman himself remains outside the spectacle so as to function with scrupulously scientific detachment. Passer, by contrast, passes through the lens into the landscape of his characters. The comic confrontations, so grotesquely pointed in Forman's films, taper off in Passer's films into gentle incomprehension, ambiguous smiles, and generous silences. The warm laughter of the audience arises not from the fatuousness of the awkward, the witless, the literal, and the maladroit, but rather from the civilized love that bathes all the characters in the marvelous glow of their own irreducible uniqueness, however haltingly they may choose to express it. The druggist who belabors the obvious with the same imperturbable confidence with which he mangles Mozart on the violin; the unspeakably ugly half-wit who tries to sweet-talk a city girl with his paralyzing stammer; the farm women who inspect the girl on their way home from the fields; even the chickens that infest the garage of the glum violinist: all attest to Passer's awareness of a social structure marked by its unjust contradictions, and yet mollified by its unspoken kindnesses. And Passer's sensibility, so harshly, uncomprisingly dialectical in *A Boring Afternoon* with its pitched battle in a barroom between philistia and intelligentsia, is more understanding in the more mature half-light of *Intimate Lighting*, a testament to nuance and style and mise-en-scene from a country that may never enjoy such artistic luxuries again in our lifetime.

LA FEMME INFIDÈLE

ANDREW SARRIS

Claude Chabrol's *La Femme Infidèle* is the most brilliantly expressive exercise in visual style I have seen on the screen all year. Every cut and change of camera set-up, every camera movement, every color composition, every grin and grimace tells us something new about that most belabored of all classes: the bourgeoisie. Chabrol's attitude, as always, is both satirical and sentimental, but the mood is more disconcertingly mixed than ever before. Indeed, the film may be almost too controlled and too concise for its own good from the point of view of audience appreciation. Even I, certified Chabrol champion that I am, felt at times that my breathing was being affected by the relentless beauty of the film, particularly in the first half-hour of lateral camera movements denoting the velvety confinement of a man and a woman and a child in horribly-humorously-materialistically connubial bliss.

The plot is slight even by the standards devised by Vittorio De Sica when he observed that adultery was the only drama of the middle class. Charles (Michel Bouquet) is living in a suburban fool's paradise in Versailles with his wife Hélène (Stéphane Audran) and his precocious little boy Michel (Stéphane Di Napolo). Gradually Charles begins suspecting his wife of having an affair with someone in Paris. He hires a detective (Serge Bento) who has done work for the insurance firm Charles manages in his commuter's Paris. The detective confirms the husband's suspicions with the name and picture of the lover Victor Pergala (Maurice Ronet), a dilettante writer with private means and a bachelor's pad in

Neuilly. Charles pays a call on Victor, and calms the nervous philanderer by pretending to be a swinging and hence understanding husband, a role that takes its toll in pain from this neurotically constant husband. Charles finally and fittingly cracks when he sees a monstrously pop-enlarged Zippo lighter he had given his wife for their third wedding anniversary now reposing in all its sacred ridiculousness on Victor's bedroom dresser, a breach more of property than of propriety. Charles then murders Victor impulsively but decorously with a handy objet d'art, and disposes of the body, the blood, the clues and fingerprints, less like a criminal of passion than a good housekeeper. When he lugs Victor's body wrapped in white sheets to the trunk of the car, Charles resembles an overdutiful husband taking out the laundry, and when he dumps the body into a swamp and waits for the bulky white shroud to sink (a rather obvious tribute to Alfred Hitchcock's *Psycho*) he resembles nothing so much as a husband taking out the garbage. He returns home after his hard day's work, and without anything ever being acknowledged explicitly, the wife eventually learns of the murder and fully accepts it as an act of love by her husband. The police come and Charles looks back at his wife and son steadfastly posing in a loving home-and-garden tableau. As the camera tracks back from this tableau in a receding motion of physical separation, it zooms forward in an optically contradictory expression of emotional union. Chabrol picked up this technical trick from Hitchcock's belltower stairway scene in *Vertigo*, but Chabrol gave it his own newer and richer meaning.

La Femme Infidèle is not the kind of film that gives an audience a rooting interest in the characters. Michel Bouquet's cuckolded husband is nowhere near the scale of Emil Jannings's Professor in *The Blue Angel* or Raimu's Baker in *The Baker's Wife* or Ake Gronberg's Circus Impresario in *The Naked Night*. Bouquet's white-collar-and-vest persona is dedicated to an avoidance of the very sordidness his more passionate predecessors wallowed in with such gusto. Charles does not murder Victor out of sexual or even emotional jealousy, but rather out of a predatory instinct for the preservation of order and property, an instinct that never lurks too far beneath the surface of bourgeois complacency. Bouquet's performance is never too moving, the personality of his character never too engaging. Charles seems too comfortable in the role of the professional put-upon, or perhaps too emotionally lazy to play any other role. He is at his best when he is momentarily at cross-purposes with his environment, particularly in a go-go nightclub sequence in which Charles makes one last pathetic attempt to restore conjugal contact with his wife only to find himself more strenuously separated. The go-go atmosphere, however pallidly Parisian, is rendered for the very first time from the fixed point of view of the dully disenchanted audience at the scene. By contrast, most previous go-go scenes have been filmed at kinky angles and from multiple viewpoints and in jazzily edited shot sequences, all more appropriate for manipulative advertising than psychological narrative. Chabrol is never manipulative and never condescending. He himself, like most of us, is bourgeois to the bone, and what he hates about being bourgeois he feels also, and very deeply. Thus he is not merely involved with his characters; he freely implicates himself in their crimes and sins. There is something undeniably enchanting in their false paradise, and something undeniably empty as well. Viewers who insist on feeling comfortably superior to the characters on the screen will be disappointed by *La Femme Infidèle,* a film in which everything and everyone is sublimely uncomfortable under the gay, passive, ultimately hideous mask of superficiality. When Stéphane Audran's coolly wistful wife resigns herself to the loss of her lover by reclining on a sea-blue coverlet, it is appropriate that one of her possessions should be more emotionally (and chromatically) expressive than her own personality. The transference of feeling from people to things is the most crucial process of capitalism.

STOLEN KISSES

TEN YEARS OF TRUFFAUT

JOSEPH MORGENSTERN

By almost any standards but those he has already set, François Truffaut has an enormous new success in *Stolen Kisses*. It's certainly an entertaining movie, bringing us up to date on the adventures of Antoine Doinel, the wayward kid we first met a decade ago in *The 400 Blows*. Instead of finding Antoine where we left him, frozen by the camera on a chilly beach with his future in grave doubt, we find him ten years or so later in an army prison, about to be drummed out of the corps for general misfittedness and with his future in grave doubt. He's still the same wayward kid, it would seem, still worshiping Balzac, still trying to find a suit that will fit him on the rack of contemporary society, and he's still played by the same fantastically talented actor, Jean-Pierre Léaud, who's still somewhere between wizened man and unwisened boy.

Antoine's situation, or his lack of one, makes him a soul brother to Ben Braddock of *The Graduate*, and you're constantly struck by parallels between the two films. But there are important differences, too. Unlike Ben, who's a product of prosperity, Antoine has probably been forced to scratch for his bread since his reform-school days. If Ben tries to flee affluence with his lovely young middle-classmate, it's understandable that Antoine should be in hot pursuit of a girl who can induct him into the *bonne bourgeoisie* and, worse yet, may even manage to keep him there. Unlike Ben, who can't seem to do anything but buzz around in his little red car, Antoine is willing to try anything once and is soon bungling the works as an apprentice detective.

Unlike *The Graduate*'s Mrs. Robinson, who was a pure predator, Antoine's older woman, Madame Tabard, is sweet, tender, subtle, beautiful, gentle, generous, wise and anything else you could want an older woman to be except young. She is elegantly played by Delphine Seyrig, who was the icy centerpiece of *Last Year at Marienbad*, and when she turns on the charm in her big seduction scene there's nothing that Antoine—or we—can do to resist her. But we were pushovers to begin with. We, after all, have known Antoine much longer than she has. We know what a wonderful kid he is and we wish him everything good in life, including her. Partly because we're old pals, because we're the ones Antoine was really talking to in that unforgettable interview with the school psychiatrist near the end of *The 400 Blows*, we follow his new exploits with uncommon interest.

This is not to say that Truffaut's very real successes in *Stolen Kisses* are unearned. A good, gentle man, he has filmed a good, gentle and often hilarious tribute to love in all its forms: heterosexual love, homosexual love, imperfect love lived haphazardly, perfect love pledged by a funny figment of every romantic's imagination, physical love that is a way, as a detective tells Antoine, "of compensating for death, of proving you exist." Truffaut even gives us a superb comic monologue on the absence of love, as Madame Tabard's husband (Michael Lonsdale) hires a gumshoe to find out why people loathe him.

By no stretch of any romantic's imagination, though, is *Stolen Kisses* a great film, even if it's having a great success in Paris and will probably do just as well here. The direction and performances turn uncomfortably coy on occasion, and so does the generally fine writing, with such determined paeans of praise to humanity as the description of someone's father's dying words: "People are terrific." Truffaut ends his two main seduction scenes before the body-contact sports begin, and that's a refreshing departure from current convention, but it would still have been edifying, in at least one of the two scenes, to see how Antoine actually behaves in the process of compensating for death.

Léaud is such a phenomenon in his own right that his return to the role of Antoine evokes almost unmanageable nostalgia for those who saw him and suffered with him in *The 400 Blows*. But his return to the role may also obscure the fact that he's been around a lot in the past few years—it's not like the forthcoming film version of *The Wanderer,* in which Brigitte Fossey makes her first screen appearance since her magical infancy in *Forbidden Games* seventeen years ago. And Léaud has done much better work in Godard's *Masculine Feminine* and *La Chinoise.*

Truffaut encourages us in our nostalgia, and a little nostalgia is a dangerous thing. He takes the title of his film from a sweet and scratchy Charles Trenet record that plays off-screen as the story begins. What's left? asks Trenet in his wistful tenor. What's left of our love, of our beautiful bygone days? His refrain is a beguiling compendium of romantic clichés, a French counterpart to early Lorenz Hart lyrics: memories of a little village hideaway, wind-blown hair, stolen kisses, and nothing left now but a photograph, "an old photo out of my youth." It must have been great fun for Truffaut to pour a few drops of this heady old wine from a brand-new bottle. But the danger of using such a song is that it invites us to think back on some bygone days of our own: not the days when we were smooching with those wind-blown girls in those windy little villages, but when we were sitting in the movies and being enraptured by the beauty and the revolutionary promises of Truffaut, Godard and all the other young French filmmakers of the New Wave.

What's so profoundly troubling about *Stolen Kisses* has less to do with what it is—charming, entertaining, wry, witty, all the things a nice movie should be—than with what it isn't, and what Truffaut isn't, or doesn't seem to want to be any more. He is indeed a good and gentle man, but he was so much more than that so very few years ago. In *The 400 Blows* he was outrageously audacious, too busy with detail and action to be bothered with mock poetry or the picturesque, and he was strongly antisocial in what was basically his autobiography. He was a defiant iconoclast in *Shoot the Piano Player,* and in his great *Jules and Jim* he was a true poet distilling the elixir of youth from a first novel by a septuagenarian.

Stolen Kisses is also autobiographical, in spirit if not in literal detail. On that score you must commend Truffaut for his honesty while deploring his bourgeois fate. On the strength of Antoine's acceptance of social necessities, and on the strength of the conventionally entertaining film that Truffaut/Antoine has made about finding his place in the adult world, there's little reason to doubt that Antoine will stay in the middle class with the girl of his dreams and live prosperously ever after.

Must such brilliant careers as Truffaut's be conventionalized and thereby destroyed so quickly by public acclaim? The evidence isn't heartening, although there are exceptions. Truffaut seems trapped, at least for the moment, in repeating past glories. He also seems trapped by a penchant for filming minor novels he read when he was younger: *Fahrenheit 451*, *The Bride Wore Black*. Another New Waver, Claude Chabrol, is likewise being praised to artistic death for repeating himself with such fancy junk as *Les Biches*. The flabbergasting invention of Louis Malle's *Zazie* has yielded to the blithe amusements of *Viva Maria* and *The Thief of Paris*. Alain Resnais, however, has changed and grown since *Hiroshima Mon Amour*, while Jean-Luc Godard remains a prodigy of energy and revolutionary inspiration to everyone who makes modern movies.

Godard calls his young characters in *Masculine Feminine* the children of Marx and Coca-Cola. Well, movie fans my age, which is pretty much the same age as Godard's and Truffaut's, are the children of Jean-Luc and François and we're all too young to die of recapitulation. It's not a case of asking Truffaut to play Godard and race around the world making fragments of brilliant, eccentric, generally unpopular films. It's only a case of asking Truffaut to play Truffaut, who's also an international treasure, who has such strikingly different gifts from Godard's: unabashed tenderness, ruefulness, generosity, a more accessible sense of humor, plus that dazzling daring he seems to have laid aside in his premature middle age.

Stolen Kisses is a conventional, fragrant and undeniably charming film; a rose by any other name than Truffaut's would smell sweeter still. You can even defend Truffaut's choice of that sweetly nostalgic song that's so much older than Antoine's memories could possibly be. Maybe the director meant the music to remind us that whatever we do in the present instantly becomes the past; we manufacture our nostalgia from moment to moment. Ten years from today Antoine may be looking back on a whole new past and Truffaut may be using the same Trenet record to comment on it. In the here and now, though, the film also functions as a dirge to its own sweet self, and here we sit being charmed by it all as if we, and Truffaut, were in our damned dotage. What's left?

ALIVE AND WELL IN PARIS

Hollis Alpert

Ten years ago, François Truffaut rode the crest of the French *nouvelle vague* with his *The 400 Blows,* starring a then fourteen-year-old boy, Jean-Pierre Léaud, as the delinquent adolescent, Antoine. The last freeze-frame of that film is still retained in many a memory, so much so that freezing a frame for impact, dramatic effect, and poignance has become a virtual cliché in movies and television. But, for those who remained haunted by the lost, frightened face of Antoine, who may have wondered what his fate would be, the news is good. He is alive and well and in Paris—the present-day Paris of Truffaut's latest film, *Stolen Kisses.* And for those who have been waiting, as well, for Truffaut to reassert himself as one of the younger greats of our day, the news is equally good. He is in top form and in rare good spirits. He has made a film that has the airy, almost inconsequential ingredients of a soufflé, and, like the soufflé of a master chef, it amazes and delights.

Truffaut, after making one of the film masterworks of the Sixties, *Jules and Jim,* did not exactly go into a decline, but he sort of muddled around. His best film after that was a short segment in *Love at Twenty* (also featuring Léaud). His work was polished in *The Soft Skin,* the story of a middle-aged man's tragic affair, but it was really just another tragic affair. He made *Fahrenheit 451* under Universal's auspices in London, but working under these circumstances was presumably not congenial for him; the film came out constrained, rather dull, almost pompously literary. He went next into his Hitchcock phase. Cinematic expertise appeared to be what he was after. So he interviewed the suspense king at length, and compiled from tapes a voluminous account of their conversations. Fascinating stuff, but distinctly worshipful.

His *The Bride Wore Black* was neither good Hitchcock nor good Truffaut. The suspense was desultory, the mystery not very mysterious. The intelligence was there, and some self-consciousness. In a way, the film was cause for alarm, for it seemed that Truffaut was seeking commercial answers to a talented director's dilemma: how to be good, how to be true, and at the same time attract a wide, international audience. With *Stolen Kisses* he has abandoned the search and, at the same time, found the answer. By returning to Antoine he returned to himself. Having tested and tried commercial methods, Hitchcock techniques, he has now found that the improvisatory informality of *The 400 Blows* can work well for a variety of purposes and subjects. In a way, it is the new traditionalism.

Thus, there is nothing that seems particularly startling or flamboyant about *Stolen Kisses;* the director's hand doesn't show as it does in Lester's *Petulia,* for instance. Yet, the technique Truffaut uses could have been disastrous if mishandled. Like a soufflé, the insubstantial story could have fallen flat. On the other hand, he must have known he had exactly the right actor in Léaud. This young man takes filmmaking seriously. He went behind the cameras for a while, serving as an assistant to Truffaut, Godard, and other directors. In 1965, at age twenty, he starred in Godard's *Masculine Feminine,* and he has been seen frequently since. *Stolen Kisses* should establish for him a continuing demand.

Léaud's "methody" manner of working would probably give pause to Lee Strasberg. In fact, he confesses to not having read the script before beginning shooting. This was by Truffaut's design, too, for he wanted Léaud to experience the film more or less like life, with its surprises, risks, and occasional rewards. As Antoine, Léaud is a young Army conscriptee, anxious to get back to living and to begin loving. He fakes a discharge for reasons of mental instability, and heads immediately for Pigalle and the first prostitute he can find, who, it turns out, isn't to his taste, or vice versa.

Antoine's problems (after that sad beginning in *The 400 Blows*) aren't very weighty, given all the awesome problems at large in the world today. He wants a girl and he wants a job. He wants to get going, but isn't sure of the direction. He does, of course, clearly reflect some current young French attitudes: a distaste of the Establishment, for one thing. He is naively idealistic and naively cynical at the same time. Truffaut views him sympathetically and tolerantly, but hardly with solemnity. Antoine becomes a hotel night clerk and, after goofing quickly at that, becomes a trainee detective for a large private detective agency. Here Truffaut appears to be laughing ruefully at his Hitchcock phase. Being a private detective can be a nutty job, particularly in Paris with its wealth of *types*.

Among those who appear in the agency office are a homosexual seeking the whereabouts of a lover who has gotten married, and Monsieur Tabard, who is trying to discover why people dislike him so. The answer is apparent—he's just not likable—but Antoine is assigned to the case, masquerading as a stock boy in Tabard's shoe emporium on the Champs Elysées. It isn't long before he betrays his duty and his client by falling in love with Tabard's svelte wife (Delphine Seyrig), who returns his affection briefly by sending Antoine two expensive ties and visiting his room for a quick fling. There is more to Antoine's youthful odyssey, all of it surprising, bubbly, occasionally shocking, as when an elder detective suddenly keels over, dead, in the middle of a routine phone call. There is Antoine's charming girl friend, Christine (Claude Jade), and the mysterious stranger who follows Christine unobtrusively and finally reveals to her his rationale for so doing.

By then, Antoine is a TV repairman, and fully as inefficient as most TV repairmen. But he has made his temporary peace with Christine. The two are seated on a bench talking companionably. The mysterious stranger approaches and declares himself to Christine. He's in love with her, totally and forever. The two young people find this revelation so surprising as to be almost incomprehensible. The fellow's out of another world.

What Truffaut was after and has found was the fantasy in reality. What people do, how they reveal themselves, the strange ways in which they wiggle through the maze of modern metropolitan life—all this can be the stuff of a film. But it must be caught on the wing, so to speak. Too much preparation, a too carefully defined script plan, and the essence of this kind of thing can be lost. Not only Léaud—all the actors were encouraged to interpret their scenes in their own ways. Harry Max as the old detective contributes a gem; Claude Jade has a sweet, unprofessional freshness; Delphine Seyrig makes of herself a fading beauty alert to hasty romantic adventure. And, behind them, Truffaut, alert to the gesture, the glance, the sudden expression. But never intrusive. Only on reflection does *Stolen Kisses* become a remarkable film.

FILMS: ASPECTS OF LOVE

ROBERT KOTLOWITZ

François Truffaut's *Stolen Kisses* is a thing of lyrical shreds and patches, made by a wandering minstrel who knows how to sing a pretty tune. At its least, this new film is a lightly hokey improvisation that is somewhat askew for its opening sixty minutes or so, as though Truffaut couldn't make up his mind exactly where he wanted to take it. It meanders along, its narrative not quite in focus, following its young hero without the slightest urgency as life does him in in unimportant and not-too-painful ways. (He is an apprentice in a private-detective agency, having arrived there after failing as a soldier and a hotel clerk, and it's clear that he's never going to be exactly a sensation as a private eye, either.) But *Stolen Kisses* is also something more, an unembarrassed tribute to the good, disturbing emotions that can be aroused by love. All of this —the best of the movie—is in the final half-hour and every minute of it is sweet with Truffaut's feeling for people and his awareness of the kind of happiness they can sometimes bring each other.

Jean-Pierre Léaud is the hero—Antoine Doinel, the young boy of *400 Blows* grown up. ("Antoine Doinel," he repeats to himself in front of the bathroom mirror, testing the reality of his existence. Antoine Doinel, Antoine Doinel, over and over again. Then he starts on his girl friend's name and ends with the name of his fantasy-mistress, who happens to be the neglected wife of one of his clients.) Spunky, enthusiastic, intelligent, Léaud is also one of the most resourceful actors on the screen today, one of the few in whom a talent for comedy and other matters coexist, so that he is able to play whole scenes on varying levels, mercurially changing emotional direction with no loss of balance. It is he—and Delphine Seyrig as the wife—who give *Stolen Kisses* its most attractive quality, a kind of offhand, humane knowledgeability about love.

In the film's climactic scene, one of the most affecting and comic Truffaut has ever done, Miss Seyrig lectures the hero in his garret apartment on the reasons why he should permit her to seduce him into an affair that will last perhaps an hour-and-a-half. (It will be over, she promises him, right after breakfast.) She is not really completely confident of herself, a little shy of being rejected by the cowering figure in bed, who actually idolizes her and cannot believe his luck. As she talks to him, a flickering smile of hope lights up her face. No absolutes, she tells the young man; they will deal with love and love alone, just for the moment. It is a speech every young man dreams of hearing once—and deserves to—from a woman who looks like Delphine Seyrig.

A little later, the young man and his girl friend—the girl he wants to marry—are approached in a public park by a portentous figure who has been trailing the girl friend all over Paris. He makes a declaration of love, of absolute, definitive, final love. The hero and his girl friend think the man is a little crazy and so, I think, does Truffaut, who in *Stolen Kisses* makes another one of his practically irresistible gestures on behalf of grace and shared tenderness, in defiance of all absolutes.

THE GURU

ROBERT KOTLOWITZ

Although *The Guru* treads with the same delicate step on territory opened up decades ago by E. M. Forster, it still has its own flavor, which is perfumed, witty, and lightly mocking. These are not the right ingredients for a smash hit at the box office, but mixed with intelligence and taste by R. Prawer Jhabvala and James Ivory, who together wrote the screenplay, and directed by Mr. Ivory, they make a captivating movie. Like the River Ganges, it starts on its way slowly but the diffident pace turns out to be a kind of trap for the audience. Mr. Ivory set the trap once before in his last film, *Shakespeare Wallah*. Jokes make their own quiet way; character is respected; little is stated and nothing emphasized or underlined.

The film is about a young English pop singer named Tom Pickle who visits India to study the sitar with Ustad Zafar Khan. Khan is the Guru, Pickle the disciple. There are also other English people clamoring at the gates of Eastern enlightenment. One, Jenny, forces herself upon the Khan household, even though she is practically devoid of musical talent. Both Jenny and Tom, as the story tells it, learn a certain amount about playing the sitar; they also learn a certain amount about themselves and about the lives of Indian mystics.

That is the whole story. But while the narrative may seem thin, a great deal happens. Khan, for example, has not one but two wives and his disciples have a chance to stay with both. An old-fashioned seduction and murder scene is played out at a music festival set in a maharaja's palace. It is entirely the product of Jenny's fevered English imagination, and it is very beautiful. Tom Pickle's manager arrives from London, pockets stuffed with unsigned contracts, to haul his questing young singer back to the fleshpots. The Guru, it turns out, has his own Guru, whom he visits for guidance. Gurus are like mothers-in-law: half their influence on their disciples comes from nagging; the Guru's Guru takes one look at him and tells him he's getting fat.

Michael York plays the likable and perhaps too reticent Westerner, Tom Pickle. Rita Tushingham is Jenny. The casting of these two is not quite right. York is fairly inscrutable and carries a constant Liverpudlian cool with him, like an umbrella. She, on the other hand, wears the face of comic British weltschmerz, ready to dissolve into tears at any moment. But they are surrounded by dozens of gifted Indians. Utpal Dutt is their Guru, Nana Palsikar his Guru, while the spirited Aparna Sen, languishing by the waters of Benares, plays the Guru's second wife. Convent-educated, hungry for companionship, and somewhat petulant, she is unforgettable as a young woman who wants to waltz on rooftops and taste a little of the life she dreams about in her remote unhappy situation.

HERE'S YOUR LIFE

TRUE AND OTHERWISE

Stanley Kauffmann

The very first shot (after the titles): a glimpse—not more than a second—of the hero's face. Then a fast cut to the house in the woods toward which he was turning his head. So small an unconventionality, that opening, yet so radical. Immediately there's a thrill of expectation that this film is in the hands of a director with a vision of his own, and the expectation is quickly confirmed. The film is quiet, visually lovely, done with an ingenuity that enriches its materials instead of distracting us. It's the first feature by a 37-year-old Swede named Jan Troell, a former schoolteacher who has made some shorts for children. Troell directed, photographed, and edited, and he is co-author of the script (based on a novel by Eyvind Johnson) with the Swedish critic Bengst Forslund.

Here's Your Life it's called, and that's exactly what it's about, in two senses. Here are the formative events of young Olof's life in northern Sweden from age 14 to 18, during the years of World War One, and here now is life waiting for him at the end of those formative years. The story is quite ordinary: Olof's first jobs, in a lumber camp, in a country movie theater, as projectionist for a traveling movie show, in a railroad yard; his first sex experiences; his first intellectual and Marxist political experiences. But Troell knows as well as we do that the materials are familiar, knows that his deep engagement with them is apt but insufficient, that he must treat them with art to make them both fresh and endearingly familiar. He succeeds generally well in this, and he does more: He composes a little poem on his country. He is a Swede making a film about Sweden, about the north of Sweden—hard, with men companionable against the cold, with those specially delightful summers that come around in cold regions. It was Lewis Mumford, I think, who said that we can no longer be nationalists but that we must not stop being regionalists. Troell is singing this region through the story of young Olof.

Some outstanding Swedish actors appear in relatively small roles. Per Oscarsson, who was tremendous as the hero of *Hunger*, is a railroad worker. Gunnar Björnstrand, a Bergman stalwart, is the theater owner. Ake Fridell and Ulf Palme and Ulla Sjöblom, all familiar faces if not names, are the touring impresario, a sawyer, a carnival lady of generous virtue. Their parts are all minor, except Miss Sjöblom's, and they are all fine; and the fact that they are *in* those small parts gives the picture an added aura of integrity. Only Eddie Axberg, the Olof, is merely adequate. Troell clearly wanted a credible working-class boy and not a charm-bomb, but, with Axberg, credibility is about all he got.

As for what happens to Olof, Troell traces it delicately—with deft, significant ellipses, with humor, and with some superb photography. Some random samples: A grizzled lumberjack skips along gracefully over logs in a river, and a double image of him appears just behind him, embodying his grace as a separate entity and somehow prefiguring his death. When shy Olof teaches a shy girl how to ride a bike, the sound-track repeats the soppy violin-piano music of the movie-house pit duo—which they had played for a torrid vamp movie. In one unearthly shot, a sled bearing a casket slips along under a sky as completely white as the ground below. And on the old film battlefield of the bed, Troell manages to devise one fresh strategy: The woman and the boy sit on opposite sides dressing in the morning; we see them past the footboard, separated but connected by it.

Not all of the film is successful. There are too many freeze-frames—a device that by now has become the June-moon of poetic filmmaking. There is a flashback in color (the rest is black and white) about a minor character's wife, which is overemphasized by the color and overlong. The character of the carnival woman, though well played, goes past the familiar into the stock. And there seem to be a few wisps and loose ends. (What happened with the railway strike?) The picture has obviously been condensed. *The International Film Guide 1968* says that *Here's Your Life* runs 167 minutes, "the longest Swedish film ever made." The version being shown here runs 110 minutes. Perhaps it was Troell himself who condensed it, and I'm not necessarily regretting it, because a film needs to be a considerable masterwork to justify 167 minutes' running time. But whoever did it left some threads hanging.

Let none of this discourage you from seeing the picture. As is, it's a gentle, humane work by a newcomer of outstanding versatility and gifts. His attitude toward artistic tradition is the one I admire most: He follows no rule just because it exists, he breaks no rule just because it exists. He comes from somewhere, artistically speaking, but he insists on coming from there, not staying.

Since he finished *Here's Your Life* in 1966, Troell has made a second feature, *Eeny, Meeny, Miny Moe*—with Per Oscarsson as a schoolteacher—which won the Berlin Festival prize in 1968. I hope we can see it soon.

RED BEARD

Stanley Kauffmann

No picture by Akira Kurosawa can go unnoticed. *Red Beard* was shown at the New York Film Festival in 1965 and, I believe, has since played in the US only at some Japanese-language theaters on the West Coast. Now it is generally released, and there's no mystery about why it was delayed. It runs three hours, and the script is dreadful. Imagine that Frank G. Slaughter had been hired to write a monster installment of a Japanese *Dr. Kildare*, about a 19th-century rural hospital run by a gruff old humanitarian doctor nicknamed Red Beard whose example alters and inspires a rebellious young intern. Add only that Toshiro Mifune plays the older doctor and that Mifune fans demand a scene in which he wins a physical fight against great odds. Here he uses fisticuffs, not swordplay, to disable eight ruffians—or was it 80?—in a brothel, where he has gone on a house call.

Still I recommend *Red Beard* heartily, though within limits. It may bore the general public, not film specialists. The latter will have the chance to see yet again the mastery of Kurosawa, a man who knows infallibly in every split-second of a film (and there are plenty of split-seconds here) where his camera ought to be looking and how to get it there; how to create an environment through which his narrative runs like a stream through a landscape; how to help his actors—particularly Mifune and Yuzo Kayama as the young doctor—into the very breath of their characters.

The bog is that script. If ever I saw a refutation of the thesis that style is everything in art, it's *Red Beard*. Throughout, I was conscious of great talent being lavished on hokum, like Toscanini conducting "The Stars and Stripes Forever" (which at least is short). But, on every score except script selection, makers and students of film can learn wonderfully from it.

PIERROT LE FOU

FUGUE FOR SWEETHEARTS

JOSEPH MORGENSTERN

Jean-Luc Godard's *Pierrot Le Fou* is a trying movie—not trying for us but for the lovers in it, a hung-up rationalist and a strung-out sensualist. They try so hard to touch, to merge, to be constant in an inconstant world. They make such an unholy mess of trying to be whole.

Completed in 1965 and only now finding its way into commercial distribution in the United States, *Pierrot* is less successful artistically than several Godard films that followed it: *Masculine Feminine, La Chinoise* and *Weekend*. It's much more than historically interesting, though, this funny little fugue for soured sweethearts that sends Jean-Paul Belmondo and Anna Karina from the whore-frost of Paris to the futile warmth of an azure coast. You can see Godard trying out scenes and themes he would develop in the future, but you can also see what a great entertainer he could have been if our pleasure alone had been his pleasure.

In one casually brilliant sequence Belmondo, as an intellectual gone to seed in television, goes to a ritzy Parisian cocktail party where everybody talks in commercial slogans. In another scene Miss Karina, as the baby-sitter for whom Belmondo forsakes his wife and kids, sings a wonderful song by Duhamel and Bassiak, "I Never Told You I'd Always Love You," and you're swept by the same sheer pleasure you felt when Jeanne Moreau sang "Le Tourbillion" in François Truffaut's *Jules and Jim*.

Godard makes much of music in *Pierrot*. He throws in a hilarious set piece in which Raymond Devos, as an obsessive romantic, sits on a pier and rambles on and on about a Dooley Wilsonesque song they're always playing in his head. Miss Karina does another little music-hall turn on a beach. These moments of acute pleasure, in which people who can't reach each other almost do, foreshadow Veronique using words as concrete music in *La Chinoise*, and the fragile magnificence of Paul Gégauff playing Mozart to the villagers in *Weekend*.

Yet pleasure cannot carry the day, not even in a film photographed by Raoul Coutard, a man who could find beauty in a hippopotamus's behind. While Coutard's camera is carrying on shamelessly with sea, sun, sand and other inveiglements, Godard's script, based loosely on Lionel White's novel *Obsession*, keeps insisting that sweet dreams and true romance are no longer possible.

Godard clutters his simple story, just as we clutter our lives, with the lurid bric-a-brac of cheap fiction and gangster movies —a murder plot, arms traffic, bleeding corpses, some unintentionally feeble slapstick, a reprise of the water torture in *Le Petit Soldat*, a quick look at the vehicular violence that grows into a leitmotif of *Weekend*. He stops the whole film, as he's done in every film since, for a desperate comic protest against the United States role in Vietnam. He stops it again for a witty story about the man in the moon and Lenin and Coke which prefigures the "children of Marx and Coca-Cola" theme of *Masculine Feminine*.

Having bestowed the dubious gift of speech on Pierrot and Pierrette, the stock comedy characters of French pantomime, he uses them to explore the subject that interests him most—the conflict between words, which misrepresent by being too specific, and feelings, which misrepresent by being too simplistic. "You speak to me with words and I answer you with feelings," Miss Karina tells Belmondo in despair over his penchant for analyzing the juice out of life.

She has him dead to rights. He's the fellow who feels that his eyes and ears are unrelated sensors, that "there's no unity" to the creature he likes to call himself. But she's no more whole than he is, no more at home in their hopeless dream of a perfect life on a tropical isle. When Belmondo, doing a great imitation of Michel Simon, talks wistfully about writing a book that would describe life itself—not just the words and emotions of life but the spaces and sounds of it, the essence of it—that's Godard talking about his own hopeless dream, a movie he'd like to make that would *be* rather than have movement, color, thought, sound, life. He won't make it, of course, because it can't be made. But that's just his point. It's no more possible for us to achieve a unity of perception these days than it is for a phoenix to rise from the counter of a chicken-in-parts store.

THE RED AND THE WHITE

PEOPLE WITH ROOM

PENELOPE GILLIATT

Tamara Karsavina, the great Diaghilev ballerina, once said that she thought Russian dancing owed a lot to the scale of Russia. Sitting at the time in her minute drawing room in Hampstead—she married an Englishman—and aged over seventy, she suddenly bounced up, put out her tongue at the room, and did a wonderful leap across to the opposite wall. "In Russia," she said as she went, "you feel you have a terrific amount of space to cover." I remembered that beautiful and un-English leap when I saw Miklós Jancsó's *The Roundup*, in 1966, and again when I saw his new film, *The Red and the White*. He comes from Hungary, the land of huge plains. The draftsmanship of his films (one thinks of them that way, as if the montage had been planned first in black-ink drawings, like Eisenstein's) replies to the space he was born to, and his scenarios are peculiarly about figures dwarfed by their setting. As with the matter that he found in the 1848 Kossuth rebellion for *The Roundup*, the situations of Reds and Whites in his new film keep coming back to the image of men accustomed to ranging across enormous territories who suddenly find themselves trapped in buildings and smashing themselves against them, like caught birds mistaking windowpanes for air.

The Red and the White is set in 1918, in central Russia, where it was shot. The civil war is going on, with Hungarians joining Russian Reds against the counterrevolutionaries. Jancsó and his cameraman, Tamás Somló, used Cinemascope, and for once it belongs organically instead of striking one as a feat of headless technology. The new loping screen shapes don't often seem to have much to do with people, partly because this isn't the way a real eye sees anything, and they almost never become a necessity of the material, but *The Red and the White* makes Cinemascope the only apt proportion. It expresses feelings in the characters' bones. As the soldiers are physically on the screen, so they are psychically in the story: small and unsuitable figures trying to fill impossible distances, serving life sentences in the upright cells of self while new names for brotherhood prompt hopes of merging with the world.

The film begins with a map, and then a slow-motion shot of Cossacks. There is no sound of hoofs—only a trumpet. We are on the upper Volga. Red soldiers are being rounded up and shot. Some of them escape and gather around a Hungarian commander in an abandoned monastery where the Reds' prisoners, in their turn, are lined up for execution. Each time it happens, to Red or White, the people to be shot are fleeced of their shirts and boots. The Romanoff symbol of subjection remains potent to the Soviets. If one therefore gets muddled about which side is which, I think that this serves Jancsó's implicit point about the fogged and dual nature of the things he photographs so distinctly. The Reds' monastery, a sanctuary full of sun, turns out to be infinitely more dangerous than the plain. The Whites have surrounded it, and they trail the Red commander to the bell tower. There is an amazing and terrible moment when he suddenly leaps sidewise to kill himself. He simply jumps out of the camera frame, and there is no more of him except a thud.

The White commander tries to sort out the Russian Reds from the Hungarians. The Magyars are told that it isn't their war. The Russians—skinned, as usual, of shirts and boots—are told they have fifteen minutes to escape. Everything resembles its opposite: The order of release is snapped out like a prison judgment; the Reds have the same fighting habits as the Whites. In the eye of the hurricane of change, there is immobility. *The Red and the White* is a profoundly anti-dialectical film. The narrative is not a progression but a repetition: Events and rhythms recur, and history has no engine. The characters are haring across Asia, and at the same time their feet are stuck in mud. The objective gets lost, as it does in nightmare, and there is only motion, interspersed with scenes that suddenly have an eerie tranquility although they are splashed with blood. The aims of revolution and counterrevolution merge and disappear. There is a running theme in the film about attempts to force distinctions that aren't real: Hungarian Reds sorted out from Russians, only to be treated exactly the same; nurses told to separate Reds from Whites, when their ethic is that all wounded men are the same; a rabid White commander cooled down by an adjutant who arranges that the uniformed nurses reminding him of present troubles shall dress up in prerevolutionary muslins and dance with each other in a birch wood. This scene comes up through the action unannounced, with humor and the stab of an epiphany. Among all the shots of half-clothed men being killed and of soldiers racing over ground for their lives, there is suddenly this ridiculously beautiful game of grace through dressing up, with a maddened commander being subdued by a charade of gentleness forced at pistol point. Jancsó's timing and montage—frantic battle stagnating into a scene like this terrified waltz, or the slow-motion gallop at the start—state exactly what his intellect means them to. Nothing could be simpler or swifter than the happenings of war, say many of his shots. No, nothing could be more ambiguous and alluringly suspended, say others. Fugitives swim slowly in water and duck to escape. Oars plop. A man about to be executed stands with his head idly to one side and his hands on his hips, reposed and aloof, as if he had already outlasted the men who are on the point of killing him. He has more time than they, the shot implies —which is inside out, brave, realistically fallacious, made true by his stronger opinion, and very typical of Jancsó. At the end of the picture, all that is left of the revolutionaries is a sword stuck in the ground, to be found and kissed by the next wave of Reds.

The effect is not of a story coming to climax but of an incessant rhythm of thin victories and losses that shuttle because of an obstinate symmetry in the process that Jancsó describes. His intellectual notions have intimately to do with the physical locations he chooses, which are places of double meaning: hospitals that offer no safety, dells illusorily protected by hills that can actually be taken in ten seconds, sanctified shelter that turns into an obscene booby trap, hermetic buildings that are suddenly as open as the plain. He photographs like a man drawing, almost like a mapmaker, and at the same time he imbues this clean, soldierly vision with a very unsoldierly feeling for the complicated. There are no defined people in the film, and this may be what makes it a remote one to watch. Jancsó's attention is fixed on behavior abstracted from personality—behavior clinging with mysterious stubbornness to its reverse at a time when the awful simplicities of civil war are most desperately concerned to assert that good and evil are separable.

Robert Hatch

An American moviegoer is apt to feel physically at home in *The Red and the White*, Miklós Jancsó's Hungarian film of action on a sector of the Russian Civil War. The man-dwarfing sweep of open prairie (more liquid than the American plains), the arced flight of pell-mell horsemen past the emplaced camera, the sudden raids and revolver justice are basic components of the Western. The picture was made in Russia, and it no longer needs saying that Russia is beautiful.

There is about it also something of *The Red Badge of Courage*—the ambiguous currents of battle across disputed territory, the unidentified figures that become familiar by mere coincidence of appearance in successive forays, the unemphatic, almost lazy nemesis of generalized musketry that lets most men survive longer than they expect, but picks off every man in the end.

What may be less familiar is the particular type of sportive cruelty that runs through the picture (as practiced by the White troops, but then the Reds won the victory and the privilege of writing the history). It is not physical cruelty (none of our scalping or trial by fire); the killing itself is quick. But there is a tendency to play cat and mouse with amnesty, to demand ceremonious participation from the condemned, to set men running, and use them as clay pigeons. Everyone concerned seems to understand the rules: If you're caught in any game, you pay a forfeit; in the game of war, you pay with your life. It is not atrocious, perhaps, but with us killing your enemy is pleasure enough; we don't ask him to embellish the moment.

I can't guarantee the narrative clarity of *The Red and the White*. The cutting is very abrupt, the logistics of combat are nonexistent and identification by uniform is not reliable with such impromptu armies as these. Fortunes often change hands so suddenly that it would be ludicrous if it were not so lethal. The only constants are that men are escaping but will not escape and that humane impulses are irrelevant in war.

All this confusion Jancsó intends; it is his understanding of war. What I am less sure he intends is a monotony that falls over his film as it proceeds. It is not so much that situations repeat (war is repetitious and he might well intend to convey that) as that his deployment of actors and cameras falls into a pattern. A group is trapped, its members are ordered to form up, they are closely examined, shifted to and fro in different combinations, disposed of. Then on to the next entrapment: always the same angles, always the same camera sweep, always the same moment of stillness before the denouement. It is as if a single remembered photograph so summed up for Jancsó the whole content of war that it imposed itself on his every statement.

This scene loses by repetition—its meaning is displaced by its formula. What one remembers, rather, are disconnected flashes of personality from persons otherwise unknown. How a man stands as he awaits death, how another rejoices in the exuberance of a good horse. One notes how time lags when a bullet pursues its victim, how death in battle is the most trivial way to die—an unseen root in the path will bring a man down as quickly. And I was struck by the fact that, for Jancsó, there is none of the widely sentimentalized camaraderie of battle; his soldiers rarely make more than the necessary minimum contact.

Perhaps the best scene in the picture is that of a sextet of army nurses waltzing at the command of a dapper officer in a birch forest. It made no sense to me, and I thought it appropriate to war.

THE WILD BUNCH

A WESTERN FOR VILLON

Penelope Gilliatt

Children of 1913, dressed like little Renoirs, laughing at the spectacle of the slow slaughter of a scorpion by ants in the Texas desert. Five bandits, in the clothes of the United States Cavalry, riding into a Texas border town to hold up a railroad cash office. On the roofs, a ring of gunmen, under instructions from a railroad executive to keep order for society, opening fire on the townspeople as well as on the robbers, and getting too drunk with it to stop. The beginning of Sam Peckinpah's *The Wild Bunch* says that nothing is purely what it seems. We see pretty children aesthetically amused by death; we see actions sanctioned by Army uniforms given another moral tone when the uniforms turn out to be a piece of dressing-up; we see the mercenaries of respectability outdoing criminals in crime; we see a simple town becoming a bloodbath that runs with sophisticated evils. Dying bodies crash to the ground in slow motion with deluding grace, and we find ourselves in the position of the children—aesthetes about extinction, without meaning to be. But somewhere under the credits there is a line spoken: "I don't care what you meant to do, it's what you did I don't like." It is the amassing of things like this in the first few minutes that makes you know *The Wild Bunch* is going to be a good, good movie. Its mind turns out to be worth ten times the puffy ethical theses of films like, say, *Judgment at Nuremberg.* It holds first-rate performances by Ernest Borgnine and William Holden, playing tired, scrapping gunslingers of the old West in a new West where the gleanings are thinner and the components of heroism less clear. Better even than these, it has Robert Ryan—one of the very best actors of his generation in America, and someone who would have been playing the big classical parts for years in most other countries—as the railroad executive's underling, an ex-convict who has to obey orders but who will never be brought to heel because he will always sustain an opinion. The exchanges between him and Albert Dekker as his boss—the screenplay is by Walon Green and Sam Peckinpah—are written with again ten times more perception than the dialogue in most of the studiously high-class movies made here, which shove deep-breathing thoughts into the nearest mouth and foist on intimates the sort of point-making arguments that suggest the people have never met before, whereas you feel that Albert Dekker and Robert Ryan have been fighting over the same ground endlessly. It is like listening to characters in Ibsen: when we see them, they are a long way into their lives together. Dekker taunts Ryan about doing the job of killing when he doesn't like it—we have just seen Ryan's eyelid shake at the sound of some shot being fired—and Ryan replies quietly, "What I like and what I need are two different things." Open trouble erupts between them. Ryan sees Dekker getting paid for farming out much dirtier jobs than he himself went to jail for and he says so. Goaded, the clumsy bull played by Dekker only yells that he wants the whole wild bunch brought back before the month is out with their heads over a saddle, or else Ryan goes back to the clink. Yet the pillars of society whom Ryan can call on to help him to catch the thieves and bounty-hunters are the true dregs of mercenaries. They are scared, distractible, incurious, craven, any man's men. They stand knee-high to the criminals they are hunting. The chase takes us over the border into Mexico, where Villa is fighting a rotted government while the United States and Germany quietly stand by and weigh up the political benefits to themselves of providing arms. In a desperately poor border town, where Mexican women slung with ammunition are feeding their babies and making tacos, feasting bigwigs of the Mexican bandit army in cahoots with German emissaries tell the wild bunch that they are interested in finding soldiers "who do not share the sentiments of the American government." They want an ammunition train exploded. By the end of the film, most of them are dead and no one has won, least of all the Mexican people whose town has been razed in a foreigners' battle. Ryan and a shrewd old man survive. To do what? "Drift around here. Stay out of jail." Ryan sits on the ground, propped against a wall, holding his horse by the reins. Civilians stream out of the town gates with their dead and their cattle and their pigs, and a Mexican soldier hops out on one leg. Apart from Peckinpah's simple technical control and the cut of his script, which is a knife that never slips off the bone, there is an angry quality to his mind.

MASTERY OF THE "DIRTY WESTERN"

RICHARD SCHICKEL

The Wild Bunch is the first masterpiece in the new tradition of the "dirty western." I doubt if it can even be tolerated, let alone appreciated, without some understanding of the new set of feelings about the frontier that it *consciously* summarizes.

The old "clean" western is, as a rule, no more firmly located in time than a dream. Indeed, it has generally been considered the dream work of the American collective unconscious, referring us endlessly to a lost Eden that we probably never inhabited, a land whose inhabitants, when they killed one another, usually did so for an understandable reason. Death in Eden was a convention rather than a stinking reality.

Not so in *The Wild Bunch*. Its simple story, of an aging, morally moronic bandit gang in fruitless search of one last major robbery, is mainly a convention to get us from the terrible massacre that follows one botched job in reel one to the even more terrible (and quite suicidal) one that concludes the film. It is only in these moments of mass death that the film is, ironically, completely alive, only in them that Director Sam Peckinpah's enormous talent seems completely committed and fully extended—so much so that I am sure that they rank among the greatest action sequences ever made. Moreover, they make a vicious, very contemporary point: When death comes in wholesale lots, when there is no way even of counting the bodies, then there is no way of feeling anything about it except a strange, sick exultation. We are here arrived at a point far beyond good guys *vs.* bad guys; we are, as the saying goes, beyond good and evil.

Well, this sort of thing—without Peckinpah's intensity of realization—has become increasingly familiar in the dirty westerns of this decade, and a lot of people, myself included, have regarded them at best as an attempt to de-mythologize our history, and at worst as part of the general escalation of sensationalism in popular culture. There is, however, a good deal more than that going on in *The Wild Bunch.*

The Bunch does not live in never-never land. They ride through the teens of this century, at a point when Frederick Jackson Turner and the other historians had officially closed our frontier, and the Bunch is feeling it—so much so that they attempt to ride right out of our history and into Mexico's, where they are not yet anachronisms. Such careful location of the movie's time and place strikes me as the key to its success. For while the physical closing of the frontier is now some 70 years past, the date of its psychological closing is much more recent—say about five years ago—and we are still hating it. In the mid-'60's it became generally obvious that we were finally and irrevocably an urban nation, that such a nation required a radical redefinition of its concept of community and individualism so as to eliminate, among other defects, the under class (mostly black) that had supported previous definitions. An acquaintance of mine, lately returned from Vietnam, which could readily be considered a modern attempt to externalize the "frontier" and keep it alive for another generation, tells me that, so far as he can see, there is nothing in civilian life that can support the "imaginative intensity" that ordinary soldiers bring to fighting the war there. Certainly a similar statement could have been made about pioneering. Why else has it ruled our imaginations for so long?

Perhaps these are pretty large statements to pin on a movie. Still, it seems to me that the dirty western has been groping about in our violent past, unconsciously searching for some historical correlative that would help illuminate our present sense of desperate psychological dislocation. In *The Wild Bunch,* Peckinpah has brilliantly concluded this search, helped by co-writer Walon Green, cameraman Lucien Ballard and a cast of old worthies (William Holden, Robert Ryan, *et al.*) and new one (Jaime Sanchez, Warren

Oates). The promise of *Ride the High Country,* in which, as early as 1961, he rather wistfully explored similar terrain, has finally been fulfilled in what may someday emerge as one of the most important records of the mood of our times and one of the most important American films of the era.

VIOLENT IDYLL

JOHN SIMON

Seemingly the most debated film of the summer season is *The Wild Bunch.* One need only glance at any two reviews to get some idea of the critical divergence. To me, Sam Peckinpah's latest western appears neither so good as Vincent Canby would have it, nor so loathsome as Judith Crist proclaims. It is, rather, an important bad film, avoidable by people who want genuine art, but recommended to all those interested in the faltering steps by which the American cinema might titubate into maturity.

There is no doubt that Peckinpah has a nice sense of time and place; that his locations and groupings, as well as the faces and peripheral activities that fill a shot have the right look and feel about them. But he is much less sure about the staging of the main action in a scene, except where seedy debauchery or sudden flare-ups of violence are concerned. He is quite apt to fall into sentimentality and substitute a liquorice stick for his usual wormwood. The dialogue rides high and wide from the awful to the quite acceptable, but the dominant strain runs to things like "Well, why don't you answer me, you damn yellow-livered trash?" Peckinpah is half Indian, and that may have induced our guilt feelings to turn him into an *auteur* before his time; it may also give him a keener understanding of his subject matter.

The Wild Bunch deals with a group of hardened outlaws who, in 1913, find themselves hemmed in on all sides: by the railroads with their bounty hunters, by the vanishing frontier, and by their own advancing years. The plot is fairly typical and not worth detailing; it records the last—ingenious, brutal, heroic—capers of the gang. Reduced to four, they are finally forced by their loyalty to a butchered comrade to take on the entire division of a semi-bandit Mexican general. After wreaking conspicuous slaughter, they are themselves finally riddled to death.

Despite an inventive twist or two, the plot settles all too comfortably into the usual western groove with all the beloved mythic commonplaces. But there are differences. The world of Peckinpah and his co-scenarist Walon Green is predominantly evil; there are no really good people anywhere, only the less bad and the much worse ones. The members of the gang stick together and have a certain code by which their leader, Pike, can, albeit with difficulty, make them behave. The men who hunt them down or exploit their services, on the other hand, are cruel, greedy, generally craven, and have no code whatever. One of the outlaws, Angel, is a Mexican Indian; his village seems to be full of good, exploited people. Yet his girl leaves him to be the mistress of Mapache, the swinish general. Later, it is Angel's own mother who betrays him.

Women are represented as particularly untrustworthy, and, next to women, children. Throughout the film we see kids enjoying the bloodshed and brutality around them and, whenever possible, joining in the fun, if only by torturing animals. Pike is brought down by the combined bullets of a Mexican prostitute and a little Mexican boy, both of whom shoot him in the back. In the case of the children, it may be the example of the adults that is to blame, but corrupt they are, and this is something new in a western. Except for Angel's concern for his villagers (he sacrifices his share of the loot for them), and the dignity of some of these folk, there are no unalloyed positive values in the film—even the gang's solidarity is labile and continually threatened from within. But Pike is idealized, and here the film goes soft. His opposite number, Deke, a former gang member who to save his own skin reluctantly leads the bounty hunters, is a considerably more ambiguous character, yet he too is sentimentalized.

The reverse side of the coin is the turning of the railroad people into absolute rotters, the U.S. Cavalry into bumblers (quite an innovation!), the Mexican soldiery into feckless layabouts, the bounty hunters into scum (this, at any rate, we don't question), and the plain townsfolk into arrant fools. All this is not so offensive here as in *Bonnie and Clyde,* from which much of it derives, because there is less obvious sympathy drummed up for the members of the gang, except perhaps for Pike and Angel; but even in their behalf no easy sociologizing is trotted out.

Pike's motto is, "When you side with a man, you stick with him; otherwise you might as well be some kind of animal." Whereas the unresonant "animal" is not much better than the lush vibrato of "damn yellow-livered trash," such literary weaknesses have a way of being absorbed by the able filmmaking. Yet that, too, is uneven. Take, for instance, the scene where the gang is leaving Angel's village. The entire population lines the main street on both sides, women rush up with sundry farewell goodies, everyone is singing a schmaltzy Mexican song. The camera is on a dolly, the point of view of the departing horsemen, and we are treated to a cordon of picturesque physiognomies, among which we single out the compassionate lineaments of the village elder. We would like to think this is tongue-in-cheek, but no, it is pure treacle.

The film has a good many of these oversimplifications, exaggerations or platitudes along its lengthy way. But then, again, there are powerful images: an ugly, mannish Mexican woman in Mapache's camp, who sits in full military gear suckling an infant; chickens scurrying underfoot and underhoof at the damnedest times; Pike trying to mount his horse and falling off because an old leg wound acts up as his men make sarcastic remarks; and, immediately afterward, Pike getting into the saddle and riding defiantly ahead.

This last is truly lovely: Peckinpah is a master of the rear tracking shot, for which he uses a telephoto lens. Here Pike rides on, his shoulders squared against the jibes, the horse and rider jogging up a sandy slope until they suddenly disappear over its edge. The telelens clings to the figure, lovingly flattening out the landscape around and for the rider; the camera seems to bob with him out of sympathy, and a terrible decency pours out of that careworn but gallant back. When the figure vanishes from the image, we feel the stab of loss.

There is an equally fine rear tracking shot following a reverse pan as the four outlaws go forth to liberate Angel from Mapache's hands; here, from the back, the posture and the way of holding his weapon characterizes each man. At this point, the smoke of the campfire makes the image blur and swim before our eyes, and the scene becomes appropriately hallucinatory and ominous. There is a curious, devil-may-care bravado about these four silhouettes pacing and pacing and pacing into the lion's maw.

Lucien Ballard's cinematography is skillful but his colors are insufficient; the blues and beiges predominate, absorbing the flesh tones and virtually excluding the warmer colors of the palette. Jerry Fielding's score is serviceable and unobstreperous but a long shot from, say, Ennio Morricone's for the Italian western *Once Upon a Time in the West*, where the score almost becomes a participant in the action.

With the editing of Louis Lombardo, we are once more brought up against *Bonnie and Clyde*. Even more than that film, *The Wild Bunch* revels in blood-letting; not since baroque poetry and mannerist painting have there been such human fountains, blood spurting from them in manifold jets. They are photographed either in slow motion or, conversely, in a quick montage of single-frame or very short takes. The result is, first, that a great deal of horror sneaks in subliminally, making it more bearable but still present; secondly, that much of the dying takes on a balletic quality which, again, makes it easier on the eye, though ultimately more appalling. Indeed, there is too much gore in the film.

The objection requires reflecting upon. Can one remonstrate with the frequency of refrains in a ballad? Can one cavil at the number of holes in travertine? The gore is of the essence. But cannot the essence be defective? By the use of slow motion, Peckinpah makes these deaths look rather like the similarly decelerated performances of shot putters or high jumpers in Riefenstahl's and Ichikawa's great films of the Berlin and Tokyo Olympiads.

The man whose face is suddenly bathed in crimson perspiration and who sinuously gravitates to the dust is a twin of the pole vaulter who has just cleared or not cleared an improbably high crossbar. The gun arcing away from him is the now useless pole, and he the winning or defeated athlete-hero hitting the sandlot. Win or lose is unimportant; what matters is the nobility of the sport. But killing and dying for sport should not look Olympic or Olympian: The gods who kill us for their sport should not get off the hook so cheaply.

But was it not so in Homer? Doesn't the *Iliad* chronicle, catalogue, itemize deaths and the details of dying? True, but those are for us the least worthy parts of the poem—and hasn't the epic as a genre bitten the dust precisely because it depended overmuch on war and violence and unlikely derring-do? Is not the epic as such an infantile form of art in both senses: a primitive art form and one appealing to puerile minds? The film, to the extent that it wants to achieve maturity, must outgrow the western.

There are no particularly noteworthy performances in *The Wild Bunch* (though Jaime Sanchez as Angel is winning without becoming sticky) nor particularly bad ones. The right kind of face and appropriate stance become the performance (William Holden, for instance, does not look Pike enough). But that is a kind of shorthand, not art: It is much more closely related to traffic signs than to metaphors.

PUTNEY SWOPE

PUTNEY'S COMPLAINT

ARTHUR KNIGHT

Packing them in at a small New York cinema these past few weeks is a wildly offbeat little movie with the improbable title, *Putney Swope*. No small factor in swelling the attendance has been an all-out poster campaign that graphically gives the finger to Madison Avenue, which is what the film is all about. (The posters are on sale inside the theater at $1.50 a copy.) But the picture itself is not to be discounted, because, in addition to jabbing away at such relatively easy targets as Madison Avenue morals and television commercials, it also gets in some telling blows at Black Power demagogues, their lackeys, and their satellites. Curiously, the large Negro contingent in the theater the night I caught the show seemed to enjoy this aspect at least as much as they enjoyed the hilarious TV parodies.

It is no secret that far more can be accomplished with humor than with the most trenchant argument, and Robert Downey, who wrote and directed *Putney Swope* (and also spoke Putney's lines), is a very funny man. A product of New York's "underground" scene, he works with a free-wheeling, irreverent, even scatological impudence to undermine whatever aspect of whatever establishment he chooses for his attacks. Unfortunately, for all his zest and gusto and sense of fun, there is also a lack of precision, an inability (or unwillingness) to focus upon one subject and explore fully its comic implications. He scatters laughs like buckshot over material that demands first-class marksmanship.

Putney, the only Negro board member of a large advertising

agency, is elected chairman upon the death of the firm's founder. (All the other board members had voted for him because each thought that nobody else would.) Switching the company name to Truth and Soul, Inc., he promptly replaces his white confreres with black soul brothers, casts his commercials with Negro performers, and uses whites only in the most menial capacities both in the office and at home. But money corrupts, and as the agency grows more successful, Putney forgets such earlier principles as refusing to handle whiskey, cigarette, or war toys accounts. He grabs the money, makes deals, and ultimately, in Fidel Castro garb, takes off, leaving the shambles of an agency to his black brothers—whose unbridled greed promptly destroys the remaining assets.

Black comedy, if you will, but Downey plays it for the easy laugh and the clever, if obvious, sight gag rather than for the mordant humor beneath the surface. And it is here that Downey betrays his underground origins. The film, photographed by Gerald Cotts in rich black and white (with color inserts for the TV commercials), looks marvelous; the music, by Charlie Cuva, is always apposite; and the cast, headed by Arnold Johnson and Laura Greene, is generally at least equal to the demands made upon it. But in Downey's no-holds-barred approach to his material, there is a lack of discipline, a lack of self-control that gradually works against the entire picture. A line that is funny is repeated until it grates. Running gags, such as the one involving the white office boy who must use the service elevator, slow to a walk when they recur without variation or fresh point. But if *Putney Swope* is neither as incisive nor as consistently amusing as one might wish, there is still verve and audacity in its view of what might happen should blacks inherit the white power structure.

MUKEL SWINK

Penelope Gilliatt

Robert Downey's *Putney Swope* has a good title. For some reason, it made me think of "mukel swink"—words that come up in the Middle English Mystery Plays. "A man of mukel swink." A man of much toil. The wretched Putney Swope, played by Arnold Johnson, is a worn-out-looking black expected to be an energizing force because of his color. He gets elected head of an advertising agency, called Truth and Soul, Inc., by the sort of mistake that can hoist nonentities to high political office. Black or white, everyone at the board table votes for him because everyone thinks no one else will. An even more worn-out-looking white, called Nathan, drooping like a highbred rose in a smoke-filled room, tells him hopelessly that it's a terrible job. Other men at the table say patronizingly that he'll make a great chairman if he stays in line. "The changes I'm going to make will be minimal," Putney says honestly, flushed with a version of the modern statesman's special sense of powerfulness when he is going to do as little as possible. "I'm not going to rock this boat." Some phantasmic revolutionary spirit then kicks in him for a second, and he says wildly that he's going to *sink* the boat. He is seen next in African robes, elocuting a rhetorical slogan that goes, "You can't change nothing with rhetoric and slogans." Growingly muddled but clinging to spryness, he throws his weight around in the agency. Blackboards seen in the background at meetings show the way his mind is working. He will do his exhausted damnedest to keep things exactly as they are by giving them more calming labels if the public shows signs of fret. With Worth-It Life Insurance and Lucky Airlines, he seems on to something.

"Mr. Swope," says a white yes-man, playing bravely with Mr. Swope's own pencil to show strength of character, "I do exactly the same job as everyone else, and I don't get paid as much. That doesn't seem fair." "If I gave you a raise," says Swope, "I'd have to give everybody else a raise and we'd be back where we started." The white says he hadn't ever thought of it that way. "And *that*," says Swope, clinching it, "is why you get less money. Because you don't *think*." There are one or two sweet passages of false logic in the film—scraps of dialogue that might have caught the ear of Waugh, who knew as much as any wit of our century about both the ancient, sanctioned skills of casuistry and the modern forms of success-with-the-boss by voluntary missings of the point. Swope's effect on his employees is like the effect of Waugh's Lord Copper, the newspaper magnate who surrounded himself with voices to say "Definitely, Lord Copper" when they meant "Yes," and "Up to a point, Lord Copper" when they meant "No," the difference being that Swope's air of freebooting command is slightly cockeyed and seems bluffed. You feel he probably stays awake a lot at night worrying in secret. Seen occasionally in the film in revolutionary circumstances, with fellow blacks gunning for change by this man who has simply been landed in a very staid seat, he fumbles along in the same old way, and grasps sometimes at a spot of radical farce to cheer himself up. He makes a commercial that shows a black girl in a gold lamé minidress prancing around a tenement. "You can't eat an air-conditioner," says the ad gaily before plugging "a new experience in 'lectric fans." Miss Redneck of New Jersey ("Five foot four, with blond hair and matching collar and cuffs"), who works in a restaurant and majored in philosophy, is asked to tell TV audiences in twenty-five words or less what her philosophy is. The distraught girl, thinking strenuously, forgets she is in a pie commercial and says, "Confidentially"—I like "confidentially"—"I think that every person of all race, color, and creed should get a piece of the action." She needs a lot of prompts to say "a piece of the pie."

Putney Swope jibs at form. Wild jokes come up and disappear without a trace, like the arms of jocular swimmers signaling hello far, far out from the beach. Some of the cock-a-hoop inventions work; some don't. Downey has a very special sense of humor, but it wouldn't be anywhere near right to say that he is funny only when he knows where to stop. Sometimes, though not always, he is funniest exactly when he does go too far and piles it on insanely. In one of his earlier films, for instance, there was a brief scene with a big naked lady, a gorilla, and Beethoven's Ninth Symphony; any two of them, one thinks solemnly, wouldn't have been up to much, but the fact that Downey did pile all three on top of one another went too far in a fine way. There are things in this new film that do the same, and others that go too far in a wan way. (I don't necessarily mean the cheeky bits or the lewd bits. A startled reply that a black in a breakfast-cereal commercial makes to the sales gobbledygook on the commentary cracks me up. Downey anticipates trouble from quibblers, anyway. "*Gourmet* magazine calls Putney's ads tasteless," says the film. One of Swope's own aides says severely that he is confusing obscenity with originality. "Your mother had a creative idea when she bore you, and you had to go and blow that," he says witheringly.) The scenes that one withdraws from aren't even exactly definable as the moments when Downey falls into the Surrealists' old trap of trying too hard, for he doesn't seem to be trying particularly hard at all. The feeling of the film is more like being in the company of a crackerjack talker who makes way-out puns and lunges—some deadening, some brilliant, with a germ of fool's sageness here and there, and also with the very special appeal of buffoonery. The buffoon is a man who hasn't a notion what you're thinking of him. In American comedy writing, trained for so long by Broadway and by TV laugh shows to fit in with audience response like man and wife, there is a liberating sort of funniness about a humor that is unlivable with, that stays quite deaf to others and drops its old socks all over the floor. When I was seeing the film for a second time, at an afternoon show, midweek in the rain, with an audience of blacks and whites who were handing out laughs enraptured by the kicks at cant whenever they worked, it was like being at a party invaded by a cheerful, impossible boozer who alternately bores offended people into the ground and revives them by the sheer intentness of his ambition to swipe enough of the nobs' cocktail canapés to see him through another starving week. Some of Downey's film is lousy. Some of it has a peculiar surreal opportunism and rudeness to his hosts—to the party, to the payers, to the American economy—that work blissfully. The film comes out politically as a wit's mishmash of élitist-Communist-nihilist, which probably suits the mood of a good many audiences in America at the moment. It is sophisticated, anti-capitalist, heedless, distractible, with a Geiger-counter ear for cruelties hallowed by custom (a man carrying a huge metal object is sent down thirty-odd stories to take the freight elevator—the innovation being that he is white and the order comes from a black). Downey's monkey-on-a-stick humor, paced to a new upper crust of the quick-witted but non-competitive, and inaccessible to anyone not in the know, expresses something specific about this moment and this place's mood. "Things Are Changing," says a placard in Swope's office. No, says the film, things aren't, and they won't, not by a long chalk —not if we only shuffle places and keep the armchairs the same. And, along with saying that, the film sends itself up for saying anything at all, and simply enjoys—for instance—its idea of a character called Sister Basilica, a nice chain-smoking nun who is eager to impress the agency by introducing a child orphan called Billy. "If you want to be his pal," she announces, "all you have to do is fill in the necessary papers." "Why don't you just adopt me and get it over with?" says the awful, scathing child to the fawning grownups, going on to leave them with a line aimed at the hearts of all of them and shooting home the film's underlying thought about how to sort out the mayhem of bigotry and phony dissent it describes. "Whatever you do," says the kid, with nasty shrewdness, "don't do it out of guilt."

PUTNEY'S PUTDOWN OF CRASS CONSUMERISM

RICHARD SCHICKEL

I tried my best to cop out on Robert Downey's *Putney Swope.* It is the first of his films to get a full-scale, above-ground release and therefore the first to expose to general view the talents of a very rare mole: an undergrounder with a sense of humor and an ability to make us laugh at his work—intentionally.

Frankly, on first viewing, I wasn't at all certain the great world was ready for Mr. Downey, because his stuff is often rough, crude, vulgar—in a word (whose meaning is no longer clear to me), tasteless. Nor did I think that he's put it all together yet. His gift for surrealistic social comment is not matched by complete technical mastery and a sure sense of when a joke is over.

But a couple of things have happened since *Putney Swope* was released. To begin with, in an almost unprecedented gesture of contempt, one critic, who rates movies by awarding them up to four stars, granted none at all to *Putney*. It seemed to me that any picture getting zilch on a scoreboard that automatically gives a couple of twinklers to your average Vincent Price chiller couldn't be all bad. Then, circumstances obliged me to see the picture a second time, in an audience composed of young theater people. Their uncomplicated delight in it opened my eyes to the simple fact that its virtues far outweigh its defects.

The latter are mostly structural. The premise is that the black hero accidentally becomes head of a powerful ad agency, which he promptly renames Truth and Soul (or TS for short) and from which he fires all but a few token white staffers in order to replace them with a complete range of dark militants. This is no more than a thin clothesline on which he closely pegs a dizzying succession of one-liners, blackouts, quick satirical sketches and simple shockers. Ideas, situations and characters come in and out of focus too often, too quickly, too carelessly. The film never develops the richness, the rhythms, the cumulative momentum one senses could have been there had a little more time and discipline gone into its making (though budgetary limitations surely account for the former defect).

Still, as Putney says upon accepting the TS presidency, "I don't believe in rocking the boat, I believe in sinking it." So does Downey, who has Putney and colleagues doing their damnedest to punch holes in most of the basic premises that keep us afloat. Chief among them is consumerism. In the commercials they make for such clients as Ethereal Cereal, Lucky Airlines and Face Off (a pimple cream for adolescents) they replace the usual euphemisms and evasions of ad land with blunt promises of visceral satisfactions (on Lucky Airlines, for instance, the hostesses cease to be just sex symbols). In short, innuendos become full-scale promises to fulfill the desperate needs we hope the purchase of goods and services will fulfill. It may not be soulful, but it is truthful—not just about the cynicism with which we are often manipulated but about the feebleness of our most common definition of happiness.

Downey claims his sociopolitical beliefs may be summed up as "paranoid anarchy," and he flails about at other institutions besides consumerism with a fine, impartial fervor. The intellectuals get it in his first sequence, when a McLuhanesque media-guru descends on Manhattan, his helicopter flying the skull and crossbones and the Stars and Bars, while he is dressed in his true colors (Hell's Angels garb, with his club name—Mensa—scrawled across his jacket). The politicians? Well, he imagines the President of the U.S. as a midget, one of whose advisers endlessly mutters bad jokes in his ear, another of whom is a tycoon-pothead-anti-Semite. The blacks themselves? They end up by selling out, as corrupted as anyone else by proximity to cash and power.

It's all, as *Mad Comics* would have it, "humor in the jugular vein," a vein which perhaps suits our time somewhat better than the Wildean or Shavian modes. It has the raucous truth of a cry from the balcony or the bleachers—the kind of Bronx jeer that has long been the specialty of the archetypal American democrat, a man who sometimes misses certain subtleties but has always managed to hang on pretty well to the basic truths. There's vigor in this vulgarity, health in these hee-haws, the strength of wind to blow away those disinfectant perfumes with which we have attempted to hide some of the bad odors our society has been giving off lately. *Putney Swope* is a kind of *Laugh-In* for adults.

MEDIUM COOL

JOHN SIMON

Medium Cool impresses me as a landmark in the new American cinema—more for its intentions than for its achievement, yet in a field so technically hypertrophied and artistically backward as the American film, *Medium Cool* deserves credit for striking out, at long last, in the right direction. Of course, in art as in life, good intentions are only good for paving stones on the most ominous of speedways, but Haskell Wexler's film has much more than that to recommend it. For *Medium Cool* is not just one of your '30s politically oriented dramas, which meant your politics Left and your esthetics left behind. Wexler, who has done very fine cinematography for several otherwise inconsiderable films, functioned here as scriptwriter, director, cinematographer, co-producer, and almost brought off this minor miracle—major, when you add that he also had to contend with the powers at Paramount Pictures.

The plot concerns the awakening of a hardboiled, monomaniacal TV cameraman to the facts, rather than the photographs, of life. The scene is Chicago, just before and during the 1968 Democratic convention. Wexler, anticipating trouble, wrote a loose story outline that he then adapted to and fused with his documentary footage. The blending does not jell so smoothly as in *I Am Curious*, and the plot sometimes looks like a slightly smudgy glass case for the display of the *cinéma-vérité*. But the basic idea is sound, and individual scenes work very well, one or two of them brilliantly.

The three major mistakes are the beginning, in which the callousness of a TV cameraman and sound recorder team on the site of a fatal auto accident is exaggerated; the end, where another such accident, this time involving the film's principals, is dragged in by that hyphen linking *cinéma* to *vérité,* so as to round off the film and all too neatly match the national tragedy with a personal one; and, near the end, the heroine's search for her missing son.

That last scene is crucial and necessary: It provides the unifying thread on which all the documentary shots are strung. Yet there is something uncomfortably arbitrary about a young mother in a canary yellow dress wandering in and out of gray-green melees and mayhem looking for a boy whose disappearance whispers "Device!" into your ear. Still, the photography is, under adverse conditions, so powerful, and the sights so grippingly grisly, that we cannot but show some indulgence even here. The fact that Wexler is an artist more than a polemist is demonstrated by his having shot hours and hours' worth of riot footage, but included only a chaste minimum, as severely pared down as if Aristotle had been looking over his shoulder at the movieola.

Two further flaws trouble me in *Medium Cool.* One is the vestigial Pirandellianism that crops up here and there, a remnant of an earlier layer of the film's development. Thus during a tense confrontation at the '68 Democratic Convention between demonstrators and the National Guard, an off-screen voice yells, "Look out, Haskell, it's real!" referring, presumably, to mace or some such nonlaughing gaseous matter. Again, we see Haskell Wexler and his camera shooting the fatal accident with which the film closes. And in an early sequence, there is a cocktail party attended by John, the TV cameraman hero, and his group. Seen wandering forlornly through the room, in the same yellow dress and dazed manner as at the end of the picture, is Eileen, the heroine. But she could be here only as John's date, and at this point the two haven't even met. Those, and a proleptic announcement of their crash, which John and Eileen hear over their car radio, are the only instances where the device is used, and they are too much or not enough: Drink deep or not at all from the Pirandellian spring!

The film also uses another device: the *hommage*—a built-in tribute to a film, filmmaker, or actor—much beloved by the *nouvelle vague* crowd. Because Robert Forster, who plays John, looks rather like a young Jack Palance, John is made into an ex-boxer—as Palance is in real life. A film is announced as about to be shown on the TV channel Eileen and John are watching; it is Godard's *Contempt* (an abomination, by the way), in which Palance and Brigitte Bardot are killed in a concluding car accident. So we get Forster and Verna Bloom (Eileen) in a similar accident at the end of *Medium Cool.* In John's apartment there is a large poster of Belmondo. I doubt that *hommages* ever contribute much to a film; often they are a distinct nuisance. Here they are mildly irritating because they suggest a certain in-group, *cinéaste* snobbery that clashes with the broad political and humanitarian values Wexler is after.

But the virtues of the film are many and considerable, and I shall insist on them even though the critic I most respect despises *Medium Cool,* and the reviewers I reprehend most adore it. There is, first of all, the photography. At least two shots will linger in my mind like favorite lines of poetry. One occurs when John and his earlier girl friend, Ruth (the exceedingly sexy Marianna Hill) walk through a hospital door. The camera shoots through a semi-opaque glass pane, on which the two approaching figures first look like spermatozoa or amoebas, then swiftly recapitulate both ontogeny and phylogeny until, close against the glass, they become recognizable human beings. And it is during the scene that follows—a date that ends with lovemaking—that John and Ruth become identifiable as a specific man and woman.

Later, there is a shot of John racing along the deserted corridors of his TV station trying to find the boss who just fired him (for protesting against turning over footage of demonstrations to the FBI and CIA). It is a low-angle shot and shows John zooming by in weird, distorting perspective while, in the background, someone is mopping the already spic-and-span floors. You wonder which is drearier: a man fighting for a quasi-worthy, dishonest job; or another having to slave away at an honest but worthless one? I may, of course, be reading more into that shot than it meant to convey, but it surely is, and was meant to be, a haunting image of desolation, active and passive.

There are dazzling episodes in *Medium Cool.* A visit by John and his sound man, Gus, to a group of Negro militants congregated in a small ghetto apartment is perhaps the only instance in the American commercial film of racial tension caught root and branch. These blacks are intelligent and confused, decent yet terrifying, sequestered in their righteous indignation. The whites are nervously apologetic or defiantly logical, and neither attitude works. No one in this room is to blame, but an agony, sometimes masquerading as humor, is imposed on all, and merely to speak means to tread on someone's festering feelings.

The nearest thing to this was a scene in *Nothing but a Man*, when a couple of rednecks threatened a young Negro couple; but *this* scene is more disturbing because it is of more widespread application, there is no villain, no suggestion of obvious melodrama like rape, no pathos—only pathology, the pathology of an entire society in an untenable yet not readily remediable situation. The utmost we see is glittering sarcasm, unreachable doggedness, a leering or lowering fanaticism—closeness preceding a storm. It is truly frightening.

The obverse of the coin is a no less effective scene in which John and Gus (excellently played by Peter Bonerz) interview a socialite by the pool of her club. This is staged *cinéma-vérité,* but it has all the earmarks and smudgy fingerprints of reality. It displays the pathetic stratagems of self-delusion with which white ostriches evade Black Panthers. The matron (a splendid cameo by Beverly Younger) talks about the house the family has acquired in Canada for the long hot summer: "It's good for the soul to get away from civilization sometimes, don't you think so?" And the word "soul" sounds just as unconvincing here as in the opposite camp.

Or take the scene where the National Guard is getting riot training. Some of the men are dressed up as hippies—or their idea of hippies—and they are marching on the improvised city hall of an imaginary city, from which a mock mayor tries to con them: Didn't he let them use his swimming pool every Fourth of July? I dare say credit must go chiefly to the situation, a cinematic *objet trouvé* if ever there was one, but Wexler found it and shot it superbly. The relish with which the Guard enacts its adversaries, the brio with which it hurls insults at itself, the abandon with which it wears its bizarre gear, the comic-strip absurdity the "mayor" arrogates to himself—all this raises Pirandellianism to new heights. What makes men who can fight equally well on either side of the fence pick their particular side? Can one change the man just by changing his uniform? Or does he merely have a secret yearning to be his own antithesis—or why else does he put so much conviction into being what he isn't?

There are scenes that do not work. An interview with young pro-

Kennedy students is too obviously staged; a scene in the kitchen of the Ambassador Hotel, re-creating its languid, vaporous life up to and including the moment when dreadful reality, with its first chaotic outriders, erupts on it, is cleverly done and effectively cut off before it goes too far, yet one wonders whether it is in good taste. A roller derby scene, showing the full brutality and sordidness of a sport that the uninformed might presume to be more harmless than several others, is highly impressive while it remains documentary; but when its violence is made to serve as an aphrodisiac for Ruth and John, it begins to look didactic. A scene in a gun clinic, where typical little housewives work out blood-lustily at the pistol range (these are parlous times, folks!) is quite good, yet here, again, a faint aroma of writers and actors obtrudes, although straight reportage might have been even more on target.

But these are all documentary or quasi-documentary scenes; what about the plot sequences? They, too, vary greatly in quality. When Verna Bloom, that totally natural and winning actress, is dispensing Eileen's earthy, sensible, yet not unpoignant femininity, the scenes move forward with assurance. As her pigeon-fancying son, Harold Blankenship, an authentic Appalachian-ghetto ragamuffin, contributes almost as much: He is neither attractive nor winsome, only a bright, scrappy, scheming, believable, and finally likable kid. Three scenes back in Kentucky, involving Harold's father, who may have simply walked out on his family but about whom we variously hear that he is "at Vietnam" or a casualty of that war, are brilliant in their succinct, unsentimentalized yet touching evocation of a crude but not undignified way of life. They tell a prodigious amount with the sparsest means.

Even so, these scenes exhibit the fatal flaw of the movie: trying to tell us too much, and more than that, everything. This forces Wexler into miniscenes that are to do the work of giants. Often they cannot; thus the bedroom sequence between Ruth and John has to carry too great a burden of characterization. Even when such scenes succeed, they are often left painfully dangling, without another plot scene to latch on to until several *cinéma-vérité* ones have gone by. And sometimes, to compensate for plot ellipses, overemphasis is hauled in, as when John watches a TV documentary on the just-murdered Dr. King and exclaims, "Jesus, I love to shoot film!" Clearly, a sort of pun is intended: The TV documentarist's passion is meant to be bracketed with a more lethal frenzy. But how, then, is *Medium Cool* exempt from the same charge? This shorthand, though writ large, does not abide our question.

At other times, Wexler's wit saves the day. A scene with John's smugly self-pitying boss, who, buzzed by his own superior, can switch to instant groveling, is neat, concise satire, fiendishly well played by William Sickinger. Wexler can do equally well with bubbly Truffaut-like sight gags, as when during a car ride through Washington someone notes that "for every man there are 4½ women," and the camera cuts away to four brief consecutive shots of pretty female strollers, and a fifth, of a girl shot from the hips down.

The acting is generally outstanding even in bit parts; in the lead, Robert Forster, owing probably more to good type-casting than to acting skill, comes across credibly as a stolid but awakening consciousness. Perhaps the best performances come from real people, as when a gum-chewing, very young Guardsman and an equally young demonstrator who tries to win him over seem, for a second, to hover on the verge of contact. Here, as in many other scenes, a Hollywood film for the first time faces up to the wretchednesses beneath our prosperity; dares give us a political America, and one whose politics are not suffused with health. I wish I could like *Medium Cool* completely. But intermittently, at least, I can love it.

Andrew Sarris

Medium Cool parades its innocence, clumsiness, and simplemindedness as civic virtues while it confronts the Chicago charivari of 1968 with footage; some documentary, some simulated; stuck together with the band-aid of broken-headed liberalism. Haskell Wexler's first movie proves among other things that good cinematography does not necessarily make good cinema. His preoccupation with pigeons on one occasion is pleasantly diverting, but hardly conducive to coherence. Nor are some wide-angle gymnastics with two boring lovers more than a cameraman's interlude in a movie that is almost all interludes. My feeling is that Wexler exploits Chicago more than he explores or even exhumes it, and he has fallen back on all kinds of Godardian gimmicks to conceal the blatant contrivances of his plot and the unconvincing schematization of his characters. Robert Forster's television photographer is an especially false characterization in that he partakes of both documentary characterization which describes the way people are at any given moment the camera happens to swoop down on them and dramatic characterization which depicts people at the turning points of their lives.

Wexler tries to have it both ways by starting the photographer off as a kind of hard-boiled, cynical *Blow-Up* character who is implicated in the violent orientation of the media. Then suddenly in mid-convention, the erstwhile cynic is radicalized by the realization that the networks have been turning over crowd footage to the FBI and the police. Wexler thus provides us with the drama of conversion without the drudgery of characterization, a form of cheating that is more ludicrous than lamentable. Meanwhile, love blossoms between the redeemed photographer and a young mother (Verna Bloom) out of white Appalachia. The natural playing of the mother and her stoical little boy (Harold Blankenship) provide the best scenes in the movie, but again these scenes are grotesquely inconsistent with the wildly melodramatic contrivance of the boy's running away during the most riotous day of the convention so that Wexler's camera can follow the distraught mother past the demonstrators and the police, footage of which, simulated or not, is curiously ambiguous when compared with the one-sided impression provided by television at the time. To end the film on a proper note of apocalyptic fatality, Wexler fictionalizes an automobile accident that claims the lives of his two protagonists in a straight lift from Jean-Luc Godard's *Contempt.*

But that's the big problem with Chicago. With all the brutality and head-breaking, no one was actually killed as a result of the convention that nominated Hubert Humphrey whereas seven blacks in Miami were slain during the convention that nominated Richard Nixon but there were no photographers present, no upper-middle-class white demonstrators, no cultural emissaries from *Esquire* and the Playboy Club. The slaughter in Miami was a happenstance rather than a happening, and it only goes to prove that social protest is ill-advised without the proper press-agentry. I have already seen several films on Chicago in 1968, but I don't ever expect to see any on the murders in Miami. Fortunately, I have never been in the habit of entrusting my political education to filmmakers, and to a *faux naïf* like Wexler, least of all.

IV:

ON LOCATIONS

Anyone who visits the set of a picture in progress learns that filmmaking is not as excruciating as it seems. It is far worse. Even the large-budget film set is suffused with an ennui unequaled outside an army base. Ennui from actors doing a take for the seventeenth time. Ennui from the grips, whose faces seem beneath, or perhaps beyond, emotion. Ennui from the make-up artists, the stagehands, the bit players, the entourages and geeks, the peripheral members of any film company.

Traditionally, the movie is shot out of sequence, so that even a casual interest in the plot, in the accretion of suspense or character or humor is denied the filmmakers. Under such antitheatrical conditions, how do films get made at all? How does the ethos of a master's film set differ from that of a journeyman's? The following accounts of visits to three filmmakers in action and reaction—along with one punch-line review—supply a partial answer.

S.K.

The Making of THE ANGEL LEVINE

ROBERT KOTLOWITZ

It was merely *Angel Levine* when Bernard Malamud wrote it nearly fifteen years ago, just as it was several other things that have been transformed in its metamorphosis from a short story on the printed page to a new film on the deluxe-color wide screen. For one thing, Manischevitz—"a tailor"—is now Mishkin, also a tailor, and his suffering Jewish figure, which stood at the very center of the story, has now moved aside (slightly on the bias) to make room for Alexander Levine, a black angel who is also a Jew. "He was a large man," Malamud wrote about Levine, "bonily built, with a heavy head covered by a hard derby, which he made no attempt to remove. His eyes seemed sad, but his lips, above which he wore a slight moustache, sought to smile; he was not prepossessing."

In the film, the sad-eyed Levine has become a tough-mouthed militant given to unexpected attacks of sentimentality; he has a girl friend he wants to marry and he likes to lecture her (and Mishkin) in pungent phrases laced by obscenities. Levine is played by Harry Belafonte (whose own company, Belafonte Enterprises, is producing the movie), a well-known, bright-eyed minstrel, gracefully built and clean-cut, who likes to speak in pungent phrases laced by obscenities. Zero Mostel is Mishkin.

"If you want to know why I'm making this picture," Belafonte says, "it's because one night at a dinner party in Hollywood, I listened to Edward G. Robinson talk about being Jewish. He talked for hours about Jewish law, about Jewish life. You've got to hear Eddie talk about those things. Anyway, I knew that I had to be Angel Levine. But I couldn't be the Levine in the story. We had to get some black reality in there. We had to make Levine a hustler, not a social-worker type. Malamud's story is only about Jewish faith. *My* conception is about human faith." Two screenwriters—one black, one Jewish—were hired to do the job Belafonte's way.

"Forget about that wing shit," Belafonte's Angel Levine tells Mishkin when Mishkin expresses some doubts about his authenticity. "Without wings there are no angels," Mishkin modestly replies. "When you die," Levine tells him, "if they let your fat white ass through the pearly gates . . ." Luckily for Mishkin there is a knock at the door at that moment. "What the hell do you think an angel is, Mishkin?" Levine asks. "Some kind of pink-assed, curly-haired drag queen with a bird for a father?" A smart-ass question, no doubt, that will get a laugh, and one Mr. Malamud's angel could not have asked nor his tailor have answered. "To tell the truth, Mr. Levine," Mishkin says in the movie, "I was expecting a little more refinement in the words from an angel. When an angel speaks, it should be more like a professor. You know what I'm saying? The words should be a little higher up."

Poor Mishkin is suffering from those ancient Jewish blues: He is helpless, somewhat fatuous, passive, and a little dumb when it comes to swingers like Levine. Furthermore, he behaves eccentrically, even for a Jew. In the opening scene in the film, for example, Mishkin is shown taking a stroll in Central Park. "Having just finished urinating into the bushes," the script says, "he is in the process of zipping up his fly. He is aware that people have been looking at him." But Mishkin couldn't care less; if Mishkin wants to urinate in public, he urinates in public. Up human faith! Up Jewish reality! Perhaps only Zero Mostel, in whose face the whole world can sometimes be read, can save Mishkin; and perhaps only Jan Kadar, the Czech director of *The Shop on Main Street* who recently arrived as another refugee in our country, can save *The Angel Levine*. He has a sure feeling for the catalytic effect that two opposing characters can have on each other; ideology in itself does not interest him very much; and he is not, without a doubt, a show-business personality out to prove to the world that he is a Deep Thinker.

It is not hard, I discovered, to find Kadar on the set of *The Angel Levine*, up in the Filmways studio in East Harlem where the movie is being shot. He is a small man, quiet, compressed, the steady, nearly silent eye at the center of a hurricane of movie production; well, almost a hurricane. Around him, two or three dozen people do exactly what he asks for—most of the time, anyway—grips, sound technicians, makeup men, apprentices, publicity people, script-girl, cameramen, assistant directors, lighting experts, two of whom crouch on a catwalk overhead in the vast studio, and of course Belafonte—in a gray sweatshirt, gray slacks, gray shoes—and Mostel, wearing a velvet *yarmulke* and a small goatee. Two or three vaguely familiar faces pass by, confusingly. Who are they? A production apprentice explains: They are stand-ins for the stars, ghosts of twinkling reality, unidentifiable as themselves, but tall and good-looking enough to substitute for Belafonte while the lights are being adjusted; or round and wide-eyed, like Mostel; or small, blond, slightly self-absorbed, like Ida Kaminska, who plays Mostel's wife in the movie. They move around aimlessly. Mostel's stand-in wears a *yarmulke*. Miss Kaminska's has an absent-minded air; she smiles at everyone who looks in her direction. Kadar himself is in a tan turtleneck, a cigarette always in his hand, his thick, graying hair swept back in waves. Nearby an interpreter waits; when things get tough, or Kadar gets tired, he calls on her for help.

"I want you to face here, Z," he is saying to Mostel. "Look right at Háry. I will try just one more thing. One possibility." His voice is soft and very calm, like a baby doctor's dealing with patients in need of sweet assurance. They are working on a confrontation scene between Mishkin and the Angel Levine. In it, Levine is coming to realize that Mishkin may never really believe in him, and without Mishkin's belief, he is lost. The camera itself, as it focuses on Belafonte during the scene, will serve as Mishkin for the audience; they will be seeing Levine through Mishkin's eyes. The setting is Mishkin's living room. A menorah sits on the mantel, family photographs hang on the wall, an old radio and a couple of Yiddish books are on the table. It is lower-middle-class, not shabby but worn. To the right is a kitchen, to the left a bedroom half-filled by an enormous double bed in which Mishkin's invalided wife spends most of her time.

Kadar now has Mostel facing in the right direction. As soon as he turns his back on him to work with Belafonte, Mostel drops his sad face and wags his head. Then he opens his sweater to show his suspenders, pulls his pants down to the middle of his buttocks, and, rolling his eyes, strolls over to Kadar's interpreter, who stands just off the set. "Dolling, dolling, be mine," he says in a whisper that can be heard twenty feet away. She smiles tentatively. He blows in her ear. She moves a bit to the left, or tries to, for he is now pinching her on the backside. "Z!" she says. Kadar waves to him over his shoulder. Mostel, bellowing: "I will never believe in anything anymore." Belafonte, facing the camera: "They knew. All along they knew you would never believe. I never had a chance with you. They hustled me, and why? Why?" Mostel: "I will go to my grave cursing God for what he has done to me." He gooses the interpreter, lets his suspenders snap up his pants, and strolls back to Mishkin's living room, making himself comfortable on a stepladder behind the camera. When they actually shoot he will play it from there, feeding the lines to Belafonte.

Belafonte puts on a black leather jacket. He strides back and forth, slamming his fist into his hand while muttering his lines. "All I've ever wanted to do is stay alive . . ." Bang, whop, bang. Kadar puts him into position. The lights are brightened, the camera gets set. Mostel is now at attention on the ladder; a couple of scraggly hairs lick out from beneath his velvet *yarmulke*. Kadar asks for quiet. One bell rings, then three, indicating that a scene is being shot. Everybody stops in their tracks. "Okay," Kadar says. It is take 1532. Mostel: "I can't believe in anything anymore." Belafonte: "All I've ever wanted to do is stay alive." Mostel: "I wake up every morning . . ." Kadar cuts them off. He asks them to do it again. Take 1532 is followed by 1533, then 1534. Kadar quietly tells both Belafonte and Mostel that he wants them to hold a beat on their lines; there must be no hurry.

Mostel: "I can't believe in anything anymore." Take 1535. "Thank you," Kadar says. Take 1536. Kadar: "Oy." Take 1537. "Thank you," Kadar says. An edge has come into Belafonte's voice. He is still pounding his fist. "Why does this mike have to be stuck right up my behind?" he asks. "Mmm," Kadar says. They take a break then, during which Ida Kaminska's stand-in puts on a nightgown and wig and climbs into bed. Technicians fool with the lighting; publicity people tell jokes to the press; a man in a deerstalker's hat and cape stands in a corner trying to make a deal with a visitor for another production. Meanwhile, Kadar rehearses Belafonte. "Mishkin, you must believe in me, or there's nothing left for us." Kadar quickly sets take 1538; the break is over; then 1539 and 1540. As Belafonte speaks his lines, Ida Kaminska's stand-in begins to look pale under the lights; she mops her forehead with a handkerchief. Like Mrs. Mishkin, she seems a little sick herself.

"I want peace in the studio and a little quiet," Kadar calls in a voice that everyone can hear. "Let's have those bells," an assistant director says. "Bells!" the technician calls. Three bells ring. The noise subsides, then flares up momentarily. One bell rings. Kadar, very slowly: "Please, quiet." He turns to an assistant and, in a rising voice edged with anger, he says, "From you I'm asking to make peace here, not to talk." Assistant to crowd: "Okay, okay, lock it up now." Unhappy now, Kadar rehearses Belafonte; for the first time, he speaks the Angel Levine's lines himself. In bed next door, Ida Kaminska's stand-in begins to cough; she seems startled; everyone stares at her balefully. Her eyes close under the lights; she looks peculiar, waxen, as though she has just died. When the coughs die away—not before growing much worse first—Kadar goes back to work. It is slowly becoming clear that he is trying to extract a sense of bewilderment from Belafonte that the performer has only hinted at in the past hour and the many takes they have worked on; but he doesn't say this explicitly—perhaps the word "bewilderment" is not in his vocabulary. He tries to shape it in the air gently with his hands.

"I *never* had a *chance*," Belafonte repeats, more softly this time. "They h-u-s-t-l-e me. Why? WHY?" Then: "I never *had* a chance. They hustle *me*." Obviously, the reading is all wrong. Kadar waits patiently, like Prince Florimund for the Sleeping Beauty, like a lover sure that with patience and a certain gallantry the ultimate reward will finally be his; he is trying to find the magic touch, the releasing gesture, that will free Belafonte to discover his own self in the role, or that part of his self that Kadar wants. The camera rolls again and again: takes 1541, 1542 (Belafonte goes up in his lines here), 1543, 1544, 1545. Mostel, sighing with boredom on his ladder step, delivers the line, "What am I, a dog, an animal in the street?" in a rich, fruity baritone, then suddenly slides up the scale to a practiced falsetto, and meows, "Or just a plain old pussycat?" By now both Mostel and Belafonte are improvising a little, making up a line here where one never existed, changing words there, accenting speeches with goddammits and hells. Kadar, Belafonte, and Mostel confer. It is Mostel's opinion that Belafonte's line, "They knew. I never had a chance," should be read very slowly, with a sense of wonderment. "*They* put me in this goddam fix," he says. "Who's *they* anyway?"

At last, Kadar begins to get his message across. He wants Belafonte's reading to be slower, less angry, more wounded, less unequivocal; he does not want the Angel Levine to act like a Black Panther. He turns to his interpreter and talks to her in Czech. "He says you do it the simplest possible. He says he must feel how you become conscious of the knowledge of what they have done to you." He wants, it seems, a visualization of the process of thought.

But it goes more easily now. Belafonte is eager to do it on-camera, before he loses it. Takes 1546, 1547, 1548, 1549, 1550 follow, then 1551, 1552, 1553. At that point, Kadar says, "Cut now, that was the best." Ida Kaminska's stand-in signals weakly from the bed. She gets the attention of an assistant director. "I stay in bed, yes?" "You stay in bed, yes." Take 1560—made with a hand-held camera—is over by noon. Kadar is very pleased. He has a compliment after each take. "Fine," he says, or, "The best," or, "One of the best." He is easy on the crew now, easy on Belafonte and Mostel, too, who has taken to wandering around the studio crossing his eyes to everyone he passes and sinking mock baskets into trash cans with crumpled sheets of paper. With take 1560 they are finished with the morning's work. "Sometimes," Kadar says, blowing smoke with clearly exquisite pleasure, "sometimes you have a scene like this that is very difficult. Very hard, very crucial." He smiles and turns to his crew. "Thank you very much," he says and calls a break for lunch. It has taken the entire morning to get perhaps ten seconds of usable footage for *The Angel Levine*, an excruciatingly slow pace, unless, of course, you're not in any hurry.

I left the *Angel Levine* company on a rainy night in New York City, on location in front of a tenement building in the East Sixties. Technicians and extras milled around the street, while pretty young East Side girls walked their dogs in the light drizzle. Fake cans piled high with fake garbage littered the gutters. A fake fireplug stood on the sidewalk. In the basement front of the tenement, which stands alone on the block, surrounded by new, white-brick, terraced apartments, was a fabric store, with a sign overhead that read: "Sol Hercz, Draperies, Bedspreads, Plastic Covers, Custom-Fitted." Just as Kadar arrived, flanked by two assistants, the rain began to fall more heavily; Kadar ticked off his instructions quietly under an umbrella. Carpenters set to work building a false pavement over the real one. Lights slowly came on, blinked off, came on again. As soon as they came on for good, Sol Hercz himself—probably as old as Mishkin and certainly less resigned—eagerly climbed the iron fence beside the stairs that led down from the street to his store, and leaning perilously over the stairwell, began to clean his sign so that it would be clearly read in the movie. He looked like a crazy stunt man. "He'll break his goddam neck," someone shouted. But Sol Hercz, in the face of fortune, just this side of fame, was not to be stopped. On he wiped in the rain. Kadar smiled at the scene and continued to give orders. All the lights were on; at eight o'clock at night it was brighter than day, but without modulation, trancelike, or like death itself; the extras crowded around like sleepwalkers. Belafonte moved into the glare, throwing a huge shadow against a lighting truck. The extras closed in, huddled under umbrellas, steaming cups of coffee in their hands. Kadar smiled again and called to Belafonte. "Háry," he said, "this is what I want you to do . . ."

Fellini at Work

Hollis Alpert

I was pleased when, a few days ago, an announcement from United Artists reported that "Fellini's *Satyricon,* a film spectacle based on the bawdy Roman comedy by Petronius," had completed its principal photography in Rome. In movie parlance, this meant that the picture had been wrapped up, the sets struck, and what remained to be done was the arduous process of editing, mixing, laboratory work, dubbing, and looping that would require another several months of intensive supervision on the part of Federico Fellini. I was pleased not only because the announcement meant that in a reasonable time, by Fellini's method of counting, I would be able to see his opus eleven, but because when I visited him in Rome a few months ago he had expressed some doubt as to whether he would ever be able to finish the picture.

At that time, he was in the midst of filming Trimalchio's banquet on a Cinecitta set designed according to his conception of what a rich, vulgar "freedman's" dining hall would have looked like nearly 2,000 years ago. The director, now forty-nine, acknowledged the world over as one of the great modern masters of the cinema, was in full, lively command of a respectful and obviously competent crew of technicians. A young woman, writing for *Life*—and also contracted to a publisher to write a book on the making of the film—hovered near, incessantly jotting shorthand notes on a pad. A "slave" beat just as incessantly and monotonously on some odd-looking cymbals, meant less as a sound-track accompaniment than as atmospheric and vaguely period "music" to help the mood.

And probably the most decadent-looking group of dinner guests ever assembled lolled on large cushions, with huge trays of sweetmeats in front of them, waiting for directions from the master. There, too, were the two principals, Martin Potter as Encolpius and Hiram Keller as Ascyltus, listening to their host—in real life Mario Romagnoli, a restaurateur—regale them with anecdotes.

As was fitting for so storied a banquet, Fellini was spending several weeks on the filming, and he seemed particularly proud of the huge roasted sow—a facsimile made by the production department—that waited on a barrow for its carving by Trimalchio's cook, standing ready with upraised sword. Incense-like smoke from salvers drifted over the scene as an assistant with a clapboard that said merely FELLINI and gave the number of the scene and the take moved in close to the camera, then withdrew. On Fellini's signal, the cook raised the sword and chopped down on the sow's head, which fell away on its ingenious hinge. It took several such cleavings and several camera positions before Fellini was satisfied the sow was properly decapitated, after which it was time for the lunch break.

It was nearly four years since Fellini had last made a feature film, *Giuletta of the Spirits*. He had visited New York for its opening, and, when I happened to encounter him during his visit, he had generously invited me to watch him work, should I ever be in Rome when he was filming. During the interval he had been hospitalized with a long, serious illness; he had begun work on a few tentative projects; he had made a forty-minute segment for a three-part film; and, fully recovered at last, he was doing the film he had long wanted to do, his own interpretation of the *Satyricon*, based on a lengthy script he had evolved with two co-scriptwriters. The producer was Alberto Grimaldi, recently risen to eminence by way of several gory Italian-Spanish Westerns starring Clint Eastwood, and now partnered with United Artists in the production of the Fellini film.

I had expected, when I journeyed from my hotel to the Cinecitta Studios, that I would find Fellini surrounded by friends, hangers-on, and spectators while he worked, for I had heard that he enjoyed working in the midst of controlled chaos, but this was not the case. In fact, a strict control over who could be admitted to the set had been instituted by the British publicity man, a fussy fellow in the employ of United Artists, who informed me that the rigors of the production were such that only one reporter and/or a press photographer could be admitted to the set at any one time, this on Fellini's own instruction. His job, however, was complicated by the fact that Fellini, without notifying him or anyone else, would invite friends, casual acquaintances, or just about anyone who asked him—often actors looking for work—to see him on the set. Just the previous day, a party of fifteen Japanese photographers, flying from Tokyo in a body, had had to be accommodated. They were allowed to click around the set for three hours before they were politely but firmly shooed off.

Busy as he was, Fellini made me welcome. He may have a little trouble with names, but he seldom forgets a face. He remembered mine, ordered a chair to be brought for me, and, once the sow's head was chopped off to his satisfaction, invited me to lunch with him in his private quarters at the studio. The publicity man was ordered to send up a translator, just in case his English, which now and then fails him, needed bolstering. Also present was a sharp-featured Italian woman, who, I gathered, was his secretary. It is sometimes difficult to know just what relationship anyone bears to Fellini; the waiter who served us lunch appeared to be one of his closest friends and sometimes paused to listen with absorption to whatever he said.

What was foremost on his mind at that moment, as it is with other film artists who must equate what they want to do with the resources available, was money. "I don't think this picture will ever be finished," he told me gloomily. "There is not enough money. United Artists is—how do you say it—too cheap. They have given us for this picture *such* a little money, really a mortifyingly small amount, enough to make the credits." He sighed deeply. "Well, *buon appetito*."

The secretary looked uncomfortable; the waiter smiled. The picture would, of course, be finished, but this was Signor Fellini's way of expressing his discontent.

Earlier, I had chatted with Eugene Walter, who serves as Fellini's dialogue director and English coach—this because Fellini often uses English-speaking actors and sometimes needs to have his directions translated. Walter had mentioned that Mrs. Fellini (Giuletta Masina) claimed that "the only time Federico blushes is when he tells the truth. He has the reputation—which he is proud of—of being the biggest liar in Italy. But he respects the truth more than most people." Thus forewarned, I did not take Fellini's complaints about money too seriously either. However, the matter remained on his mind.

"There are rumors of a $3-million budget," he said. "Lies, just lies. It is much, much less."

Though budget considerations seldom have much to do with the artistic quality of a picture, I later checked with a United Artists executive, hoping to clarify the money question. It was almost too much for him. "Financing Italian films has a way of being incredibly complicated," he said. "We made our arrangement with Grimaldi, but the money allotted to Fellini's picture is tied in with others on Grimaldi's schedule. However they choose to interpret it, the picture *will* cost at least $3 million. Our share takes in the rights outside of Italy. All I can say is that we've kept our part of the bargain."

Fellini, in advance, could see the company point of view. "Our own industry hardly exists any more," he said. "So we make pictures with American money, and the one who takes money from the other has, in a sense, to prove he is not a thief. We are good friends, but I think they are a little fearful. They don't trust us. For this reason, maybe, they have given my producer less money than what, in a real way, the picture costs. Grimaldi is a very nice man. Indeed, he's so nice and gentle that I don't see how he can last very long in our jungle."

One wonders how Fellini has lasted, too. Throughout his career he has been embroiled—again because of the Italian film financing practices—with producers and with legal suits over who owned what part of his films. In the case of his monumental *La Dolce Vita*, he wound up with no vested interest in its enormous financial success. Then there is censorship, in Italy and elsewhere. "The picture industry is still so vulgar," he said, "that if the film author tried to oversee what happens to his work he would quickly die of a broken heart. Between censorship, the vulgarity of the advertising, the stupidity of exhibitors, the mutilation, the inept dubbing into other languages—when I finish a picture I just don't want to know what happens to it. Some theaters will present it as a pornographic picture, others will cut out a reel or two in order to cram in more showings. It's better to forget you ever made it."

And now he has another problem, one which enjoined him from even using his title, *The Satyricon*. That was the reason the clapboard had FELLINI as a title. No sooner had he announced his intention of making the Petronius work when another Italian producer registered the title for a quickie of his own. "We're both using the same laboratory, and while waiting for a court ruling we had to give ours another title to avoid foul-ups in the processing. Privately we call ours 'The Fellinicon,' but at the lab it's simply 'Fellini.' If I had my way I would give it the perhaps boring title 'Myths and Legends of Ancient Rome.' For that's what it is." (The title matter apparently has been resolved with "Fellini's Satyricon," and meanwhile the other "Satyricon" has been seized by the Italian censors.)

Pointing out that it would be totally impossible to know what life was really like in ancient Roman times, and that the Petronius work represented only, at most, a 10 per cent fragment of the original, Fellini emphasized that for him the book "serves as a pretext to make fantasy, almost a science fiction. What I was taught at school, during the Fascist period, was stupid and boring. Archaeology adds to the past a theatrical and phony dimension. And then came the movies! Those huge vulgarizations that further destroyed our chances to conceive of the past. I've had to try to clear my mind of all that, to reinvent, freely and virginally, the phantoms of 2,000 years ago. But with such *cheap money*! It's really very difficult."

Not that he was, in any way, attempting to make the bawdy spectacle mentioned by United Artists. "Perhaps I can describe it as a sort of fresco of pagan times. I have had a certain dream. And, now that I've imagined it, my job on the set is to materialize what I have imagined." This was one of the reasons for a more rigorous control of who could visit the set. "I am working differently this time," he said. "A much more detailed script, for one thing. Previously, I allowed room in the scripts not for improvisation necessarily, but for suggestions that would come from what was being filmed. For example: the aristocrat's party in *La Dolce Vita*. We worked in a real castle, we used real aristocrats. I was able to take blood from them, so to speak. I kept myself open for what could arise during the filming of the situation. Here that isn't possible. Every detail must be known in advance. Having to invent what I do not know is very exacting, even dangerous. The concentration required from me is greater."

Even more important to him was fashioning "a pre-Christian

dimension. Put another way, I've tried to do a story in which there is the absence of Christ. Most of Western art, movies included, is pervaded with moral and psychological conceptions brought about by Christianity. But pagan Romans, having no conception of a Christ figure, unaware of the consequent spirituality, morality, dogma, truly existed in another time dimension—which is why I liken this film to science fiction. For those Romans, any debauchery was worth trying. Their cruelty, so extraordinary to us, was casual to them. After all, for an afternoon's pleasure, they would slaughter hundreds of people in the Colosseum. *The Satyricon* is a story of a society with a pre-Christian character. One must find a *virginal* way of placing oneself in such a time, such a dimension."

It had been suggested to him by those eager to interpret his work and place each film in a context with the others, that both a personal and contemporary meaning would be expressed in his new film. Fellini was benignly aware of all this world-wide *auteur* legwork by critics, some of whom saw autobiographical overtones in everything from *Variety Lights* to, of course, *8½*, in which the film-director hero wore a black, floppy hat exactly like Fellini's. "The American critics," he said, "I find the most practical. They do not try to see too much. The French, on the other hand, are the craziest. They sometimes strike me as delirious. But if they say good things I am happy. I don't want to appear morbidly humble, but it sometimes seems to me I am received with too much respect.

"And since an analogy will probably be made between the time of my *Satyricon* film and the present, I will make my own. The picture might suggest that we are living in a post-Christian time, but the analogy is not made in a schematic, cold, intellectual way. At this moment it strikes me that we are out of Christ and that we are waiting for something else that will have to become. It is a free adventure of people open to everything. Encolpius and Ascyltus are two students who are provincials, but half-beatniks, not dissimilar to those we can see in our times on the Spanish Steps; they go from one adventure to another without the slightest remorse, with the natural innocence and splendid vitality of two young animals. Their rebellion, like some of our own young, is translated into terms of absolute ignorance and detachment from the society in which they find themselves.

"But, it is a very chaste picture—the only naked thing in it is the pig you saw this morning. Not that I pretend to have an innocent eye. Yet, one can show the most unheard-of things without becoming obscene. It is the sick eye of the watcher that makes something sick. I must be careful not to pass judgment on, to condemn, the Romans of that time. For it is we who have invented the conscience; we have given a moral value to things, aided by 2,000 years of Christianity—a Christianity which has made of us stuttering babes crying for our mamas, our church, our Pope, our political leaders. I will do my best to paint the pagan world free of the Christian conscience, and, if I am successful, it may have some clarifying value for our time. Perhaps it will even be seen as an allegorical satire of our present-day world."

As in all of Fellini's films, the faces will undoubtedly fascinate. But he has no Mastroiani this time, no Anita Ekberg or Claudia Cardinale to portray his flamboyant symbols of femininity. The only relatively known name in the film is Capucine, who plays the minor role of the debauched Tryphaena. The major parts of Encolpius and Ascyltus, the two young rogues of the Petronius work, have gone, respectively, to young English and American actors. Neither had previously appeared in films, and Hiram Keller, the American, came straight out of the cast of *Hair* on Broadway.

Fellini, in his mood of the moment, claimed he chose unknowns because the financing precluded the use of stars. Otherwise he might have wanted Gert Frobe or Peter Ustinov for Trimalchio. But he is happiest when he feels free to search for his own faces. Ask him why he chose Potter or Keller, and he will simply say he liked their faces. But why an American face and an English face? "Telling a story like this," he said, "it helps me to have foreign people, that is, to have for myself a feeling of their being foreign to me. Not speaking English very well, there is a strangeness between us. I want the audience to have that sense of the people being strange to them, of looking at a kind of people they have never met—almost as though they were Martians."

As for the language of the picture, he claimed that it would begin in the language of the period, Latin, which would then merge into the language of the country of its release. This sounded like a phenomenal dubbing job for each version, and it is more probable that there will be English, Italian, German, and French versions. But Fellini was not yet willing to give away his solution of the language problem. The half-hour or so of rushes he allowed me to view were spoken in English and Italian, were sometimes soundless, and yet were strange, beautiful, and haunting.

We returned to the set for the afternoon's work. Now, with the sow's head slashed off, two slaves rushed forward to bring out its innards. These proved to be not the entrails, but steaming heaps of sausages, goose livers, and little roasted birds. The Petronian specialties were heaped on brass platters and carried in triumph to the already sated and jaded guests, while Trimalchio watched the gourmand activity with plump and self-satisfied solemnity. Fellini, in between takes of the various angles, embraced a friend, joked with a member of the crew, debated with his cameraman, the great Giuseppe Rotunno, while smoke swirled and the cymbals sounded.

With the time for breaking near, I went over to Fellini to say good-bye, and to thank him for the visit. He kept me for a moment.

"As you can see," he said, "it is not a colossal picture. I must work very, very carefully, with the money they have given me." Then he smiled. "But I am happy—because with this one I have the feeling I am making my very first picture. I have no right to lament. I have always done what I wished to do, and I have always been very lucky. My secretary thinks I should tell you not to mention to anyone what I said about the cheap money. But say what you please. But, if you mention the money, add that Fellini said it smiling, but with sadness." He hesitated a moment, as though he had not given the precise direction. "Yes, smiling," he added, "but with very sad eyes."

They were not sad eyes, however. They were the eyes of a man of enormous talent, full of life and expressiveness, of a man hugely enjoying himself at his work.

Che Lives!

Joseph Morgenstern

Like God and Lucifer, Darryl F. Zanuck of 20th Century–Fox and Fidel Castro of twentieth-century Cuba are vying for the immortal remains of Che Guevara. Castro's Cuba put Che in a Latin American pantheon for martyred guerrilla saints after his death in Bolivia last year, and Che's admirers have covered walls all over the world with posters of his darkly handsome face. Now Zanuck's Fox is making its own myth with a movie called *Che!* and studio hagiographers are working toward a time next spring when the movie will be released and Che's followers will find that their posters are actually portraits of Omar Sharif.

The resemblance is real: strong bones, dark eyes, full black mane, mustache and beard. Lucky for the world's downtrodden masses that Che didn't look like Peter Lorre. "Having this facial resemblance," Sharif says, "I'm trying not to do too much more. I'm taking all the craft from the acting, just leaving the bare bones." He sits in his silent hotel room in Ponce, Puerto Rico, high above the shantytown cockcrows and the infants screaming "Mami!" Fox is shooting its *Che!* locations in Puerto Rico because of the island's typical Latin American landscapes and atypical amity toward the United States. Comonwealth status has made Puerto Rico safe for Hollywood's revolutionists.

Sharif is loafing in air-conditioned comfort today, but he spent most of the previous week slogging through mud for guerrilla-warfare sequences. The mud was in a rain forest 90 minutes and 461 mountain curves away from Ponce by car. The curves were counted by a German make-up man who builds a new nose for Jack Palance each morning so Palance will be completely faithful to Fidel Castro. Authenticity is stressed in every detail of production. It declined to rain in the rain forest, but the mud was authentic enough.

There is authentic novelty, too, in a Hollywood studio leaping to do the life story of a dedicated enemy of the United States. (Che died Oct. 8, 1967. An Italian film about him, starring Francisco Rabal, has already been finished. Other directors contemplating Che movies include Italy's Francisco Rosi and England's Tony Richardson.) Whether the Fox production will demonstrate capitalism's internal contradictions or its invincible adaptability is a moot point, but it is difficult to imagine a Cuban film studio say, doing a melodrama called "Rusk!"

Fox's publicity department is nervous about *Che!* and stresses the film's "objectivity." The script, one press agent says, "goes straight down the middle of the road politically." Rather than discuss Che's politics, most of the cast and production people stress such qualities in their hero as idealism, dedication, courage as a jungle fighter, intelligence and incorruptibility. "Che was uncompromising," Sharif says. "He never copped out. Castro did. Once he entered Havana and became the head of Cuba, that was enough for him.

"To say the film is 100 per cent honest is absurd," Sharif states with calm candor. "It's being made by a bunch of capitalists. But I will say, certainly, that the man himself will be sympathetic, as he should be. He was the sort of man everyone would like to have on his side."

Sharif thinks Che was "totally unsentimental," and the actor puts on an impressive display of unsentimentality himself when he discusses the phenomenon of capitalist Fox putting its money on Communist Che. "A whole younger generation is anti-American," says Sharif. "Not anti-American but anti-Establishment American, and Che Guevara is the ultimate anti-Establishment figure. All over the world people have come to believe that this is a correct position to take." Thus do new American movie markets grow.

Che!'s director, Richard Fleischer, is trying for "a documentary feeling throughout the film, with hand-held cameras and long lenses." The script, he says, combines dramatized episodes with straight-to-the-camera interviews in which people give conflicting views of Che. "What I'm trying to do," says Fleischer, "is an objective character study of a very complex man." The director sees no undue haste in the production. "We're dealing with one of the phenomena of our time. As of this moment he's a tremendous symbol for young people all over the world. But I'm not so sure that five years from now anyone will remember him, because there's no residue, no substance to the man. When you analyze it, Che is a big loser."

Fleischer, whose last film was *The Boston Strangler*, shares Sharif's view that Che should be played sympathetically. "If at the end of this thing you have compassion for this man I'll be very happy," he says. "Che was an idealist who died for his ideals, and to me that's a heroic thing. Take the Boston Strangler. He did monstrous things, but he wasn't a monster. You feel sorry for him in the end. I think compassion is one of the most important human qualities."

Jack Palance stands in an army truck puffing a cigar on a sweltering Sunday in downtown Ponce and waits for wheels and cameras to roll. This will be Castro's triumphal entrance into Havana. Street vendors hawk shaved-ice cones tinctured with fruit syrup. A prop man distributes red and black "26 Julio" pennants for the crowd to wave. One precept of crowd photography—and politics—is that people tend to wave whatever is put into their hands.

"C'mon," an assistant director exhorts the crowd through a bullhorn. "C'mon, now—viva!" The crowd vivas, but mildly. Early this morning Fleischer's staff had dressed, bearded, weaponed and cigared 100 townspeople as guerrillas (the cigar bills run to $100 a day: 10-cent Roi Tans, made in the U.S.A.), and hired 300 more townspeople to play townspeople, in hopes that these 400 extras would attract many more hundreds of passersby. So far their hopes are deceived. As triumphal entrances go, this one is on the intimate side. Much will be done with editing and sound, though, to suggest vast throngs. If movies, as Jean-Luc Godard says, are the truth 24 times a second, they can also generate an equal frequency of fibs.

The next shot has Fidel on a podium, haranguing the crowd. Palance gives an enormous, accurate performance, full of bravura and saliva, but the crowd keeps mostly mum except for giggles.

"His mustache is falling off," people whisper. The cameras stop. The mustache is fixed. Palance resumes his litany of anti-Yankee-isms in the peaceful Ponce plaza. The Puerto Ricans still refuse to respond to off-camera cues. Suddenly Palance pounds the podium with his fist. This happens to be characteristic not only of Castro but of Puerto Rico's governor-elect, Luis A. Ferré. The townspeople finally roar their approval. Palance has the crowd in the heel of his hand.

Next day, the company's last in Puerto Rico before returning to Hollywood, *Che!* moves to San Germán, the island's oldest town. Here it will shoot what another press agent calls "some atrocity-type shots" to show how the Batista regime brought about its own downfall. A stunt man dangles, hanged, from the branch of a laurel tree standing in the Plaza Francisco Mariano Quiñones. Two girls in black keen over the corpse. Onlookers wait until Fleischer calls "cut," then applaud gaily. The next shot calls for women in mourning to be clubbed and beaten by Batista troops. Most of the mourners are women from the village and under strict orders to remain out of combat. Those who will take the actual clubbing are stunt men dressed in widow's weeds, rouge and pink bloomers. Cameras roll, troops and mourners collide, rubber clubs and rifle butts fly. The transvestite stunt men hit the pavement as planned, but many village women do, too, swept into the fray by their rampaging emotions. The spectators love this grisly game of oppressor and victim and cheer wildly from the other side of the square. It is a festive day for San Germán.

Robert Hatch

The anti-Castro Cubans in New York have been vociferously picketing Richard Fleischer's "*Che!*" and a small bomb has been tossed into the lobby of one of the theaters where it is being shown. I must suppose that the exiles are expressing discontent with the quality of the picture; the content should scarcely disturb them. As is usual when a big company grapples with a subject it recognizes as controversial, 20th Century–Fox has leaned over backward to be "fair"—leaned so far, in fact, that it lands in a thicket of clichés on the side of law and order. Batista was a terrible fellow and Bolivia lies under military rule, but Castro, and particularly Guevara, are the kind of men who out of vanity and arrogance topple the dominoes of world-sweeping Communist imperialism.

If the thesis is simplistic—if an account of Che's ill-conceived and disastrous foray into Bolivia should do more than suggest that he was trying to drive the happy peasants from their mountain Eden—the narrative is trite and the characterizations are wooden. Che, according to this account, was a once idealistic doctor who, infected by the fever of power, became the Robespierre of the Sierra Maestra, manipulating the weak and stupid Castro, and deserting him when he decided that this puppet could not be used to conquer the Western Hemisphere from a Havana Kremlin. Che brought the missiles to Cuba, but Che also sent the Russians home by his insulting contempt for their reluctance to engage the United States in a nuclear war. Torn between his dependence on this monkish butcher and his disinclination to be incinerated, Castro took to the bottle and the distractions of female company. It plays like a soap-opera reconstruction of the last days of Ivan the Terrible, and I came from the theater wondering if I had somehow missed the news that the feckless Castro had been hounded into squalid exile.

It is true, of course, that Guevara died because he misunderstood the situation into which he plunged. (A voice in the film says that the CIA had no hand in his capture, which stimulated a resounding cry of "Bullshit" from somewhere behind me in the theater.) True that the Bolivian villagers did not rally to his guerrilla band and very probably acted as informers for the military. But did Che threaten and rob and brutalize the people; did he terrorize women and children when the men hid from him in the jungle? If the film had persuaded me that Castro is a fool, it might have taught me that Che became a monster.

But the characterization of Castro is the most grotesque aspect of the picture. It is never a good idea, except commercially, to have a familiar contemporary figure impersonated by an equally well-known actor, and the decision to cast a performer of the abilities of Jack Palance in such a role suggests an element of dollar cynicism in the project. He is, to put it kindly, a less than intuitive actor, and in this case his "disguise" is the sort that sets border alarms ringing. He is about the right size and weight, but his voice is wrong, his gestures are wrong, his facial expressions are wrong, and no amount of cigar chewing or outbursts of "Latin temperament" will produce a suspension of disbelief. Palance looked uncomfortable throughout—he could be seen remembering the Castro trademarks and then dolefully muffing them—and I admired him for his embarrassment. Omar Sharif had an easier time with Che because the appearance and behavior of his man are less well known; it is not his fault that he had to play a stock case of megalomania.

The effect of this film is mischievous and I suspect its motives. Commercial filmmakers are out for box office, and box office is achieved by reinforcing popular assumptions. Guevara's appreciation of the immediate revolutionary potential in Latin America was wrong, and his death provided the revolutionary impulse now spreading in the world with a martyr whose precepts are often perilously inapplicable to the contexts where they are invoked. But tolerance, understanding and justice are not advanced by ignoring the objective conditions behind large political upheavals and ascribing revolution to the private devils of demented leaders.

V:

DOCUMENTARIANS

Nothing But the Truth

The truth, says a lawyer in Strindberg's *Dream Play,* is anything that can be proved by two witnesses. It is also anything that can be photographed by one documentary filmmaker. The portable camera, catching life on the lam, is a powerful persuader. So is the newsreel clip, with its grainy message from the real world. And a public that lives by its Huntleys and Brinkleys, its newspapers and its total-information stations on its car radios has a certain predisposition to accept the documentary's relevance, if not always its objectivity. Yet the public is also surfeited by journalism, and the documentary is still searching for an audience as well as its own elusive identity. Sometimes it calls itself *cinéma vérité,* a term which suffers from pomposity in the translation. Sometimes, with equal pomposity, it calls itself fact film. What's a fact? Who's got a spare one to shoot? Many of these films are laced with propaganda. Others are compromised by the filmmaker's predispositions or the editor's postdispositions. Once in a gratifying while, though, a documentary does just what it sets out to do. It gives us an assortment of not-so-random observations which in the aggregate ring true.

J.M.

SALESMAN

Harold Clurman

In mid-March the 68th Street Playhouse will show a documentary film, *Salesman*, by the Maysles brothers and Charlotte Zwerlin, which has given me greater insight into America than all the Broadway shows I have seen this season. To some it will seem a comedy, to others a tragedy.

Nothing is invented: There is not a word in it which was not actually spoken by the door-to-door Bible salesmen the picture is concerned with and the folk to whom they sell or try to sell their $49.45 Holy Book. Seeing the picture one is ready to agree with Francis Bacon that "The contemplation of things as they are . . . without substitution or imposture is in itself a nobler thing than a whole harvest of invention."

"You can see," says the salesman, as he points to the illustrations in the Book, "how this would be an inspiration in the home," and then explains how to push the three plans of purchase: "Cash, C.O.D. and a Catholic Honor Plan" (so much a month). He continues: "The Bible is still the best seller in the world." The customers are Irish (as are most of the salesmen), Polish, Puerto Rican. They have been recommended by the local Church; the wares to be sold have the imprimatur or blessing of the high clergy. Many of the prospective buyers cannot even afford a dollar a week. The territories covered are New England (seen amid snow) and Florida.

This Bible is a hard sell ("Could you say if this would help the family . . . ? Could you see where this would be of value in the home? A gain to you?"). The sales manager for the company (of porcine countenance) assures his men at a sales convention: "Money is being made in the Bible business. . . . It's a fabulous business. . . . All I can say to people who aren't making the money, it's their fault. . . . The money's out there and go out and get it." One salesman announced he's going to make $35,000 this coming year. To best him another vows to make $50,000. One wants to push his face in. His pals applaud.

At another meeting in Chicago, the designer and theological consultant of the company, Melbourne I. Feltman, Ph.D., tells the assembled flock in an analogy with the Son of God himself that "the good that comes from the selling of the Bible . . . is definitely identified with the Father's business. Some of you, at one time or another, may or may not have had a higher income, but you have never held a higher position of esteem. . . . God grant you an abundant harvest."

In North Miami, Paul Brennan, the salesman on whom the filmmakers have concentrated, tries to find 118th Street in the town of Opa-locka (how terrifyingly hideous the architecture of the vicinity). The streets through which he drives are Sinbad Ave., Arabia Ave., Ali Baba Ave., Sesame St., Sharazad Blvd. He calls this "Muslim Territory." He makes no sale that day and we notice that he has become grim. A fellow salesman hopes to encourage Paul by reminding him of the firm's adage: "It's not the bum territory. It's the bum in the territory."

So it goes. We see them pushing, pushing, pushing, talking, talking, talking, telling jokes, exchanging confidences, making philosophical remarks, all to wear down the customers and lighten the embarrassed silences of indecision or resistance. A strained heartiness shields the salesman's anguish as it does the customers' mixture of discomfiture at not being able to reciprocate and an unconscious desire to mollify the salesman's hurt. Often the salesmen are not only depressed by their lack of luck but by the realization of the degree of unemployment and poverty they encounter as they make their pitch.

The salesmen play poker among themselves, do a lot of kidding, make long-distance calls to their wives at home, reminisce. Paul remembers his father who counseled him "to join the police f*a*rce and get a p*i*nsion." He imitates the brogue of which there is still a remnant in his own speech. One senses a certain contempt for the accent, the admonition and the "Mickie" breed, mixed with a trace of regret at not having done as his father bade him. These fellows like one another, and when Paul finally prepares to quit the business their compassion is not without some foreboding that Paul's fate may some day be their own.

When we last see Paul mute, immobile and grave, his face is a tragic mask. He has experienced defeat. Through the laughter that the film provokes there runs an ever-swelling vein of tragedy. How can these petty people be tragic, purists may ask, remembering Aristotle and his *epigones*. At most they are merely pathetic.

A pox on such aesthetes! The salesmen and their customers are tragic because we can recognize them as kin and they are legion. They are all of us. They are our countrymen caught in the vise of the prevailing religion: utility, business, success—a religion which erodes. We are unable to feel superior. In all of them we catch a glimpse of the presence or potential of something dear. I left the picture in a maze of sentiments and impulses: of suicide, murder, prayer, fraternal embrace.

The film suffers from a certain monotony—it is too long—but that is possibly part of its intended effect and meaning. We are worn out along with its "actors." They are all great, especially Paul Brennan. The stiffly drooping line of his mouth is a study in itself. There is something close to grandeur in his acrid humor, his self-mockery, his realistic perceptiveness, his ultimate stoicism.

The photography and editing are first rate. The producers, I am certain, would like the reviewers to emphasize the film's comedy. I have laid stress on its cutting dreariness, but that does not signify a defect. The combination of all its elements—including the view of its various landscapes—creates its own kind of catharsis. It is a picture for the brave.

GOD AND COUNTRY

JOSEPH MORGENSTERN

The more I think about *Salesman*, a scary film about Bible salesmen by David and Albert Maysles, the more I find myself in the squirmy position of a self-appointed defender of the faith—and not even faith in God, but country. *Salesman* purports to be a purely factual depiction of four dishonest-to-God peddlers selling $50 illustrated Bibles for a living. It's an important film for the questions it raises: not merely esthetic and ethical questions about the documentary genre, but the central question of whether life in these United States is really as bleak as the peddlers and their customers suggest. The evidence in the film is appalling, but I think it's also inadmissible at worst, inconclusive at best.

How appalling is appalling? Enough to make you think God and country both are dead. The salesmen, whom the Maysles brothers followed from door to door and state to state for six weeks, are beneath Babbittry. They know perfectly well what they do, which is to lure children and shame adults into saving their souls with gilt-edged, plastic-and-nylon-bound Bibles, to drive poor silly people more deeply into debt in the name of Christian devotion. If it is holy to be human, these shameless faith heelers, these predatory Christ pushers may be a little bit closer than most to desanctification. And their clientele! Gaunt, grim, passive, inarticulate people (except for one spunky Latin lady) in shirt sleeves, undershirts, hair curlers, shapeless clothes, people living shapeless lives in their shabby, bare bungalows and artificially flowered apartments with the gleaming refrigerators and vacuous TV tubes glomming them at all hours of the day and night.

The only word for it is Arrrrgh! No writer of ungenerous fiction could improve on this movie's discoveries. "The important part is to have [the Bible] blessed," one of the salesmen tells a customer, "because if it's not blessed you will not get the benefit out of it." At a sales meeting in Chicago the men stand up and pledge themselves—Crusaders going forth to Holy War—to earnings of

$35,000, even $50,000, for the coming year. On the road they're wanderers without women (at least on camera) who drag themselves and their wares from motel to motel, who smoke too much and keep the boozing under temporary control. Most towns they hit look exactly alike, except for Opa-locka, Fla., all done up in fake minarets and street names like Ali Baba Avenue. "Is this Opa-locka?" one of the salesmen asks a native on the outskirts. "Well," comes the unforgettable reply from off-camera, "it is and it isn't."

Salesman paints a picture of human existence as transactions —nothing more. "What kind of country do we live in," asks one of the accompanying press releases, "what kind of times are these, when material success as the measure of a man shapes our way of life?" Who's got the answers? Every day I see and read about much more ghastly goings-on than anything the Maysles brothers found, so I'm certainly not going to naysay *Salesman* for its naysaying. But contempt and self-contempt are so much in style at the moment that I do wish people would see this film for what it is—a number of people with a number of things in common trying to play themselves—rather than the gospel truth about the state of the whole Union.

It is a slippery item to define and delimit. Among many other things—fact, fiction, quasi-fact, quasi-fiction—*Salesman* is a reasonably satisfying story about one of the salesmen, Paul Brennan, whose declining sales reflect or lead to a declining faith in himself. We're made to care about Brennan. "Take care of your tires," his wife tells him on the phone, and we know that his hustle has brought him to a dead end. (He reportedly left the business after the film was finished.) But his story can never be completely satisfying because the rules of the documentary form are so rigid. If only a good writer could have been brought in to break Brennan's long silences, to write him a soliloquy in which he tells us that the game isn't fun any more, that it's too late in life for him to be rejected a dozen times a day. It takes a writer's imagination to get at people who don't know how to get at themselves. It takes an actor's training to play one's self on camera. And the characters in *Salesman* don't get any help from anyone.

That's one of the things they've got in common. They're all on camera and don't quite know how to be. They're drab butterflies impaled by a sharp lens. The salesmen have learned to live with the situation, if not to love it, but their customers have another problem. They've got the filmmakers to contend with and they've also got a salesman intimidating them, trying to extract real money from them while the camera whirs and the tape turns.

The customers have other things in common that bear directly on the film's significance or lack of it. They're all white, lower middle-class, Catholic, and they're all people who signified interest in a fancy Bible by leaving their names and addresses at merchandising displays set up in their churches. They have, in effect, selected themselves out of the population, even though they're presented as a random sample. It oughtn't to be surprising, then, that they dress somewhat alike, live and talk somewhat alike. It oughtn't to be surprising that they and the salesmen are a pretty disconsolate bunch. This is, after all, a film about predators and their prey. The salesmen despise the customers, the customers distrust the salesmen. Maybe that's really what is left of American society, just sullen sellers and sad buyers. Maybe the outlook is entirely that bleak and bound to get bleaker. But *Salesman* doesn't prove it.

IN THE YEAR OF THE PIG

PAULINE KAEL

In the Year of the Pig is an assemblage of news footage and interviews that presents an overview of the Vietnam war; Ho Chi Minh is the hero, and the theme is not, as might be expected, the tragic destruction of Vietnam but the triumph of Vietnam over the American colossus. The movie is not a piece of reporting: Emile de Antonio, who gathered the material, has never been to Vietnam; his footage comes from a variety of sources, not specified on the screen but elsewhere acknowledged to include East Germany, Hanoi, the National Liberation Front offices in Prague, Britain, and some American companies (A.B.C., Paramount News, U.P.I., Pathé News, Fox Movietone News), and there is a Russian-staged reenactment of the battle of Dien Bien Phu. But, taking this footage from all over, he has made a strong film that does what American television has failed to do. It provides a historical background and puts the events of the last few years into an intelligible framework. Though the television coverage has often been covertly anti-war, and though watching the Americans behave like the bad guys in Hollywood war movies has undoubtedly helped turn the country against the war, the general effect of years of this has been a numbing one—constant horror but no clear idea of how each day's events fitted in, and growing uncertainty about the meaning of victories and defeats beyond the day's events. We now feel helpless to understand the war; we want to end it, and the fact that we can't demoralizes us. We seem to be powerless. Because this film makes sense out of what's been going on, even if this sense isn't the only sense to be made of it, de Antonio's historical interpretation becomes remarkably persuasive.

The movie does not claim to be "objective" (except in the way that every documentary implicitly claims to be, because it uses photographic records and, despite talk of media sophistication, "seeing is believing"). One could certainly argue that *In the Year of the Pig* (the title, I assume, does not refer only to the Chinese calendar) is merely restoring the balance by showing "the other side"—that if it attempted to be "objective" it would turn into another of those essays in confusion, like the network specials, that balance everything out until they get a collection of the disparate facts and platitudes that are considered "responsible" journalism. However, while the commentators' face-saving gestures and revelations have made us aware of the tacit commitment in that kind of coverage, we may be less conscious of the games being played with this footage. Some of them are obvious, loaded little tricks, like the film's crude beginning (a body in flames, still moving, followed by satiric glimpses of Hubert H. Humphrey, John Foster Dulles, President Johnson), and there are pranks (the insertion of a closeup of a toothy photo of Joseph P. Kennedy, and one of Arthur Schlesinger, Jr., looking like a lewd Dracula). This is schoolboy stuff: de Antonio's judgment is erratic. But in the main line of the narrative he plays a highly sophisticated game, using the pick of the archives and recent interviews, expertly (and often very sensitively) edited, and with unusually good sound-editing.

What de Antonio has done is to present the issues of the war and American policy and the American leaders as Hanoi might see them, and he has done it out of our own mouths. He has gone to what must have been enormous effort to put the film together so that the words of men like Dulles, Dean Rusk, Joe McCarthy, and Wayne Morse and of experts and journalists like Roger Hilsman, Paul Mus, Harrison Salisbury, Jean Lacouture, and David Halberstam tell the story. They provide his polemic, without any additional narration. This makes it more credible—and more of a feat. De Antonio calls the film "political theater," and the counterpoint of words and actions involves so many heavy ironies it becomes too much of a feat. He's almost too clever, and his cleverness debases the subject; the method is a little obscene. But one tends to accept the line of argument, not just because it's a coherent historical view but because emotionally it feeds our current self-hatred.

The Americans make it so easy for de Antonio to build his case. When you listen to Mark Clark and Curtis LeMay, the war really sounds like a racist war. They're war boosters out of the political cartoons of an earlier era; their dialogue would make us laugh at how old-fashioned the satire was if we read it in a Sinclair Lewis novel. When one hears LeMay's vindictive tone as he talks about how every work of man in North Vietnam should be destroyed if that is what it takes to win, and when one hears Mark Clark say of the Vietnamese, "They're willing to die readily, like all Orientals are," it's hard to believe that the war they're engaged in is the same war that's still going on. I saw this film on the afternoon of Monday, November 3rd, and after sitting there and thinking how far away much of it seemed—Eisenhower with President Diem, the dragon lady Mme. Nhu, Dulles and the domino theory, the American leaders explaining how we were going to help the Vietnamese help themselves—I came home to hear President Nixon's speech, which seemed to belong to the same past as the speeches in the movie, though the new rhetoric is smoother and more refined. The continuity of the war that evoked the earlier crude justifications with the war that's still going on, even though hardly anybody believes in the justifications anymore, makes one susceptible to de Antonio's argument. In the context of the movie, even the casual stupidities of American soldiers sound meaningfully racist. When some American soldiers relaxing on a beach say that they miss girls, they're asked what's the matter with the Vietnamese girls, and a silly, grinning boy replies, "They're gooks. You know, slant-eyes. They're no good," and we're revved up to think, "The pig! And our leaders are trying to tell us he's there to keep the Vietnamese free!" In another context, we might simply think that this silly, lonely soldier was trying to find acceptable male slang for not being interested in girls he can't talk to. It might even mean that he wanted *more* than sex. In this context, America is represented by clips of our leaders at their most repellent, of an American soldier who stands by smiling as a helpless, bound prisoner is kicked in the groin, of Mark Clark and Curtis LeMay, and of young George S. Patton III saying of his buddies, "They're a bloody good bunch of killers" (also a line that would sound very different in the context of, say, a Second World War movie). De Antonio finds a soldier who likes defoliation work, because it seems a step toward ending the war; Morley Safer, it may be remembered, interviewed a G.I.

who said that he didn't like "riding the people's gardens down." No doubt there are both kinds, and certainly they're both destructive, whether they like the work or not. But by selecting Americans who do like it, by selecting Curtis LeMay and the others, de Antonio obviously means to suggest a basic rottenness in Americans, and an America that is anti-life. After one watches the movie for a while, the Americans in it begin to look monstrously callow, like clumsy, oversized puppets.

De Antonio has not merely made a protest film documenting the "downward spiral" (as the North Vietnamese Pham Van Dong described it) of American policy, though that is the film's most valuable aspect. He has attempted to foreshadow the fall of the West—and not just in Vietnam—by presenting the Vietnamese as a people solidly behind Ho Chi Minh, who represents their goals and ideals, and as a people who have been ennobled by war and who must win. In his own way, de Antonio seems to support Mark Clark's view of Orientals; the movie suggests that the Vietnamese are willing to die because they are united in a common purpose, and that if they die, their dying still somehow stands for life, while we are dying though we live. The tone of the latter part of the film is almost mystical; the ability of the tiny country to go on fighting against a great power is not presented in practical terms of how much more difficult it is for a super-nation to fight in a divided, decentralized country than to incapacitate a modern, powerful, centralized state but, rather, in terms of our inability to defeat the mystical spirit, the will (and perhaps the destiny?) of Ho Chi Minh's people. It is, in other words, as patriotic and jingoistic and, in its way, as pro-war as American wartime movies used to be about *our* mission and destiny, and in this reversal it is the Americans who have become dehumanized.

A *Vérité* View of HIGH SCHOOL

RICHARD SCHICKEL

There is good nostalgia and—less familiarly—bad nostalgia. It is the latter form of this somewhat suspect emotion that is induced by Frederick Wiseman's *High School*, a wicked, brilliant documentary about life in a lower-middle-class secondary school in Philadelphia. As the dreariness of this educational environment is revealed to us, the upper centers of the brain register the proper feeling of dismay bordering on despair. Deeper down, however, I think almost any public-school graduate may experience the film as I did, with an odd, by no means creditable sense of relief.

There have been such earnest efforts to reform the system in recent years—so many studies, so many experiments with new teaching methods and technologies—that I expected the film might reveal a fundamental change in high schooling as a basic human experience. The social critic in me hoped so. On the other hand, one is after all an "Old Boy" of public education, bound by a certain sentiment to those forms of hazing that nearly everyone has suffered in the process of growing up absurd in this country in this century.

And that is where the relief comes in. For *High School* proves that newer generations have not escaped these old torments. If Mr. Wiseman's example is as typical as I think it is, they not only survive, they flourish in the 1960s. You may be glad to know, for example, that you can still find on your average faculty a petty sadist to manage the hall monitors and that he continues to pad about the corridors passionately checking passes. At a slightly higher level you will still find that assistant principal whose rage for simple-minded discipline can choke off the adolescent hunger for a more subtle form of justice.

Indeed, to me the film's most powerful scene involves such a character's inability even to listen to a student's plausible excuse for an act of minor rebellion, so intent is he on reading his standard lecture on deportment moronically defined. Out of such acorns of experience, presumably, grow the mighty oaks of college anarchy.

One resorts to irony about such matters mainly to keep from blithering in anger. And then one finds oneself reduced to helpless laughter by the nonsensical pedagogy these amateur cops are serving: a serious young English teacher playing Simon and Garfunkel records in an attempt to stir some interest among the kids in poetry; a more traditional-minded colleague earnestly reciting *Casey at the Bat* while her charges register a wide, exquisite range of boredom; a Home Ec teacher putting on a fashion show and trying to teach her student models good posture and good taste and then, a little later, trying to come to grips with her own mild but ingrained prejudice against her black students.

It's funny in a sad sort of way. Then, toward the end of the film, it ceases to be funny at all. First we overhear a halting conversation between an athletic coach and one of his former players, just back from Vietnam. They are discussing other kids from the school who have served, exchanging information on who was killed, who was wounded, who is still intact. Later, at an assembly, a teacher reads a letter written by another graduate just before he went into action over there. Ostensibly it is an attempt to express gratitude for the way the school prepared him for life. Actually, however, like the talk between coach and athlete, it is an unconscious effort to reconcile the disparities between the reality of life and the middle-class fantasy about life propagated by the school. The gap between the two is, finally, too deep for irony, too appalling for laughter.

The school houses an expensive flight simulator and, to the obvious excitement of the student body, boy "astronauts" fly in it for days, eliciting at the end of their adventure congratulatory wires from the real astronauts. I'm sure the PTA and the Board of Education can point to this piece of hardware and prove, as materialistic parents do, that they have "done everything" for their kids. It is the singular merit of Mr. Wiseman's film that it definitively proves this argument just won't wash.

Closely following his *Titicut Follies* and his Emmy Award–winning *Law and Order*, the film also definitively proves his claim to being our most distinguished practitioner of *cinéma vérité*, using the technique not merely to document the lives of pop singers and show folk but to examine seriously the quality of our institutions. As this is written, *High School* has had exactly one theatrical showing, a situation entirely too typical of serious documentaries. It should get vastly more exposure. We need it as much as it needs an audience.

VI:

PERFORMERS AND PERFORMANCES

Of all the ingredients, preservatives, synthetic additives and derivatives that may go into a modern movie, the most nearly traditional and the most readily recognizable is the individual performance—what one character makes of another in public. Peter O'Toole's performance as old Chipping was the strongest element in a new musical version of *Goodbye, Mr. Chips,* but the year provided an even more striking example of a movie that stands or falls on the strength of a single piece of acting. That was *The Loves of Isadora,* and the Society gave Vanessa Redgrave its Best Actress award for her portrayal of Isadora Duncan in it. A news magazine cover story on Barbra Streisand dealt with the style and substance of her work, while another news magazine cover story on John Wayne dealt with a phenomenon who has for forty years stood, rather than fallen, on the strength of himself.

J.M.

THE LOVES OF ISADORA

THE BRILLIANT BIOG OF ISADORA D.

RICHARD SCHICKEL

As I write, a wonderful movie called *The Loves of Isadora* has been hiding out in a couple of West Coast theaters. There have been some technical problems with it, but it has also been delayed for cutting and retitling (it was just plain *Isadora*), since a less than enthusiastic reception at its première last December in Los Angeles appears to have frightened its distributors. They seem to feel that today's youthful audience cannot connect with a character like the late Isadora Duncan, whose life is the film's subject.

What nonsense! Whatever its condition when it opened, Karel Reisz's film—not improved by its new title, but apparently unharmed by the cuts—stands as a touching and delightful work, far more sensitive to the spirit of the subject and her times than most film biographies. Moreover, I should think it would appeal quite directly to a sizable percentage of the young, since so many of them are Isadora's spiritual heirs—gentle, romantic revolutionaries, experimenting at the farther fringes of esthetic experience (where the artistic merges with the visionary), exalting the need for personal freedom, emphasizing the importance of feeling, of sensory experience over discipline and reason. Indeed, if they ever discover her—a sense of history is not one of their strong suits—one could imagine them turning her into a cultural heroine, since she suffered a kind of martyrdom for her avant-garde beliefs.

In any case, hers is a superb story and it has been superbly realized by Reisz and Screenwriters Melvyn Bragg and Clive Exton. They are amazingly true to the major events of her life—the liaisons with stage designer Edward Gordon Craig, the sewing machine heir Paris Singer, and Sergei Essenin, a mad Russian poet; her obsessive desire to establish a school where young children could learn to blend her theories of the free mind and the unfettered body in a new life style; the tragic death of her two children; her journey to postrevolutionary Russia in search of sustaining atmosphere; her last, disastrous tour of her native America, which had tolerated her experiments with dance but would not tolerate the radical lectures on politics and esthetics that now accompanied her appearances; the physical decline and spiritual isolation of her last years. It is all here and the humor of her romantic and artistic excesses and the tragedy of her ending are both handled with impressively understated delicacy.

What is so very good, so unique, about Reisz's direction and Vanessa Redgrave's performance in the title role is that they have resisted patronizing a figure about whom it would have been easy to make cheap fun. They understand that in any era the greatest risk the avant-gardists run is making fools of themselves and that, of necessity, they sometimes must do just that if they are to accomplish their ends. They are sympathetically ironical about that, without losing sight of her as perhaps the most important figure among the first generation of modern dancers. Similarly, they are neither falsely nostalgic nor especially sentimental about her era (roughly the first two decades of this century), in which, it is sometimes convenient to forget, the basic spirit of modernism in all the arts was formed.

As a result of their care and thoughtfulness (and the extraordinary vividness of Isadora's life) they have succeeded in doing something often attempted yet almost never accomplished in the movies. They make us see and feel what it is really like to be an artist. We are light-years, here, from Cornell Wilde as Chopin or Kirk Douglas as Van Gogh. Even better, they manage to give us something of what we expect from written biography, a critical perspective on the personality and accomplishments of the subject.

Reisz, whose direction of films like *Morgan!* seemed to me forced, has here disciplined his talent without loss of liveliness. And Miss Redgrave is simply great as she gives us Isadora the enthusiastically romantic girl; Isadora in her game and wily maturity, amazingly successful in impressing her vision on the public; and, finally, Isadora betrayed by age, by her own excesses and by a fickle and unfeeling world, becoming a parody of her previous selves. One rarely encounters successful attempts at such a range in the movies and, indeed, one searches memory in vain for any actress who has, in a single film, made us feel the several ages of woman as intensely as Miss Redgrave does here. There are fine supporting performances but the picture belongs to her and to the director who created the world she so magnificently fills.

STANLEY KAUFFMANN

Karel Reisz's film about Isadora Duncan, originally called *Isadora,* opened in Los Angeles in December 1968 to qualify for Academy Award nomination, with a running time of about three hours and with an intermission. After some adverse notice, it was cut to 150 minutes without intermission. It is now released in a 130-minute version with its title amplified to the above. I have seen only this last version. I'm told by a critic who has seen all three versions that the structure has been drastically changed. Whether this was done with Reisz's help, consent, abstention, or disapproval, I cannot say; but I emphasize that my comments pertain only to the third version. Whether those earlier versions were better or worse in total effect, they may have covered some omissions that I note.

The producers of a film usually have control of the film, and often they change it against its director's wishes. When a critic says that "Director Jones has done thus and such," he knows he may be speaking figuratively, that Jones may not be responsible for all defects or all virtues, that the phrase "Director Jones" is a convenience meaning "Jones and those who changed his work." A director protests publicly against alteration at his peril; protest doesn't brighten his chances of future employment.

So here is *The Loves of Isadora,* the work of Karel Reisz *and* the producers Robert and Raymond Hakim *and* some unidentified Universal executives. What hath this conglomerate wrought? On the basis of what is left, the first thing to note is the structural resemblance to *Lola Montes.* This is the story of a celebrated theatrical woman's life with heavy emphasis on her love affairs, told in flashback with frequent returns to the "present," where it ends. Second, the dialogue by Melvyn Bragg, Clive Exton and Margaret

Drabble is of torturous banality. Third, Isadora is largely absent.

No one could gather from this film that Isadora was an important artist ("She was the greatest American gift to the art of dance," said Michel Fokine), a symbol of general cultural forces in explosion and a lasting influence on the dance. The film, as presented, focuses on her men and her egocentricities, with just enough Greek tunics and esthetic asseveration to make her a sort of arty nut, thus justifying to herself and us her bohemian behavior. The result is one more picture about a temperamental star who has lots of lovers—artists and millionaires—and ends up broke. As a dancer, as an artist, this Isadora is about as interesting as Garbo's ballerina in *Grand Hotel.*

What did ancient Greece mean in the life of this Isadora? Well, I think I remember a few fast flashes of some temples in an early montage and a glimpse of the Elgin Marbles in the British Museum. So much for the entire esthetic base of her life. What is shown of her relation to the dance of her time? Nothing. She never sees another dance or meets another dancer. So much—to name just one significant example—for her influence on Fokine. What of her friendship with Duse, her integration with the stirrings of modern consciousness in all the arts? Nothing. Anyone who wants to find out what Isadora was like—both as amorist and artist—would do much better to read the six pages about her in Dos Passos' *The Big Money.*

And anyone who has been trying to cling to some shreds of regard for Reisz had better skip this picture. (I'm speaking only of elements that must be his work.) He made his feature debut in 1960 with *Saturday Night and Sunday Morning,* which was crisp and forceful. Then followed a re-make of *Night Must Fall,* so complete a disaster that I couldn't even hold it against him; it seemed more an aberration than a failure. *Morgan!* was just enough of a disaster so that Reisz had to take responsibility for its diffuseness. In what is left of *Isadora,* the scenes as shot—and surely no one else did the shooting—match the banality of the dialogue. All Reisz's concepts are hard-ticket, movie-spectacle clichés. Take, for instance, Isadora's first stage appearance, in a San Francisco saloon: sure enough, we get the stale argument with the manager and the inter-cut shots of gaping ruffians with beer mugs. (Those ruffians are possibly the busiest actors in films. Seemingly the same rough faces are overcome by talent and beauty in Arizona and Australia and South Africa. Julie Andrews conquered them last in London's East End in *Star!*)

The clichés thunder on. When the lights fail during a dance recital for soldiers of the new Soviet Union, the good-hearted fellows break into song as Isadora holds a lamp aloft for them. All that differentiates the scene from Jeanette MacDonald solacing the troops is the absence of a soprano obbligato. The *idea* of the scene, from the directorial view, is sheer Romberg. When Isadora dances in Boston, the outrage of the audience is inter-cut with the fulminations of a street-evangelist outside in a style that might have been thought offensively mechanical at RKO in 1935. This sequence is a unit; I doubt that it has been much changed by other hands; and it comes from Reisz, author of the best text on the subject, *The Technique of Film Editing.* There is scarcely a trace anywhere in the film of the intelligence or imagination that might once have been expected of him. Oh, yes, there's a lot of mist in some of the lawn scenes. Possibly it was left over from those *Tom Jones* lawns and just drifted in.

James Fox is brisk and personable as James Fox in a moustache. He's called Gordon Craig, but there's no need to fuss about that. (The script doesn't even get its amorous facts straight; Craig was not Isadora's first lover.) Jason Robards, who is Isadora's millionaire, is miscast yet again in a genteel part and is yet again dull in it. Anywhere but a saloon he is uninteresting. As with Isadora, the emphasis with Sergei Essenin, played by Ivan Tchenko, is on outrageous behavior, with little conviction of the truly great artist at the center, in whom the outrage was peripheral. John Fraser has nice peevish devotion as Isadora's latter-day aide; and there is a funny scene in which Ina De La Haye plays a shocked Russian teacher.

This brings us to Vanessa Redgrave, the Isadora, and the subject of egomania, its curses and blessings. Only an egomaniac could have agreed to show us how Isadora danced—a number of times, too. Miss Redgrave, who cannot really dance at all, boldly attempts to recreate the genius of a great, unique dancer. It's a good deal more hazardous than, say, Richard Burton trying to recreate Edwin Booth's genius in *Prince of Players.*

On the other hand, egomania is probably essential to extraordinary acting talent. If we ignore the contradiction between Miss

Redgrave's dancing and what everyone says about it, then what there is of legitimacy in the film comes from her acting. Take such a familiar scene as the one in which they place a newborn baby on the pillow next to the mother. With her freshening imagination, with the uniqueness that she has in *her* art, Miss Redgrave makes the scene new, as if it were the first time we had ever seen it on the screen. When she drives through a tunnel and feels memory and foreboding, the shadow of death really seems to touch her. In her 1927 turban, she moves around the Riviera like an exiled queen with a rag or two left of her court. In these scenes she provides the best job of *voice* aging I have heard since Peggy Ashcroft got old in *Edward, My Son* on Broadway; and, throughout, she has fair success with her American accent.

What we get from her—as she is allowed—is a gawky, beautiful Californian girl, brimming over with *fin-de-siècle* dedication to Beauty, a term she uses indiscriminately for art and sex. Insofar as this describes Isadora Duncan, which is not very far, Miss Redgrave has created the character.

"She was afraid of nothing; she was a great dancer." Dos Passos' statement is simple, beautiful, complete. There was a film to be made of Isadora's life, with Miss Redgrave: one that did not—could not—show her dancing yet that showed why she was fearless; that showed her as an artistic force; that showed her private life as inevitable for a woman with her hierarchy of values, her extravagances as the frenzy of genius; that showed her as one of the cultural proofs that the twentieth century exists. This long but tiny film—no matter who did what to it—is a mockery of her.

Stefan Kanfer

DAUGHTER OF BACCHUS

Isadora drank too much, she couldn't keep her hands off good-looking young men, couldn't bother to keep her figure in shape, never could keep track of her money

But a great sense of health
filled the hall
when the pearshaped figure with

the beautiful great arms
tramped forward slowly
from the back of the stage.
She was afraid of nothing;
she was a great dancer.

JOHN DOS PASSOS, in *U.S.A.*

Her youth was *fin de siècle;* her philosophy was *fin du monde*. She was an earthly personification of Emily Dickinson's inebriate of air and debauchee of dew, stoned on life and art. In answer to the question, "What gods has mankind worshiped?" Dancer Isadora Duncan once replied: "Dionysus—yesterday. Christ—today. After tomorrow, Bacchus at last!" In short she was the quintessential bohemian, and the ideal subject for a screen biography. *The Loves of Isadora* supplies the ideal object: Vanessa Redgrave, whose enactment of Duncan carries with it both an exquisite sensitivity and a formidable intelligence.

That intelligence can seldom shine through the film. Director Karel Reisz (*Morgan!*) has found an appropriately Proustian mode in which to tell the story, pouring time forward and then reversing it, like the sand in an hourglass. But he places Isadora, the first natural dancer, on a background of numbing artificiality and casts her opposite a series of unconvincing poseurs and popinjays. The baroque scenario—radically cut from 170 to 131 minutes—is florid without being literate, essentially true to the events, but essentially false to the tragicomic character who made them happen.

As a child in San Francisco, Isadora burned her parents' marriage certificate to free herself from moral convention. She yielded to the tyranny of official paper only once thereafter—when she married her Russian lover in order to bring him into the U.S. Between those parentheses, she ransacked the temples of Hellenic culture, switched from dresses to togas and from shoes to scandals. In America, the bourgeois dismissed her as a wanton. It was in Europe that she won her recognition—and lost her life when her trailing scarf wound around a racing-car wheel. Her last words seem written in art-nouveau script: "*Adieu, mes amis, je vais à la gloire.*"

Duncan's first love affair was with Stage Designer Gordon Craig, whose electric presence is dimmed in the film to about 40 watts by James Fox. Her most celebrated amour was Paris Singer (Jason Robards), the sewing-machine heir. Singer's idea of a bauble was a ten-diamond pendant; Robards' idea of acting is to bark his love scenes tersely, as if ordering a gross of No. 11 needles. Isadora had a child by each of her lovers; both children died in an absurd and macabre automobile accident in France. From then on, it was a long *bourrée* downhill. "I love potatoes and young men," she sighed, "that's my trouble!" Calories and sycophants attended her decline. Choreographer George Balanchine recalled her Russian dance recital in 1921: "Absolutely unbelievable—a drunken, fat woman who for hours was rolling around like a pig."

It is in those wasted, final years that Redgrave gives the film its ironic dimension. Isadora, in a flutter of unpaid bills and lisping parasites, refuses to give way to age. Her hair is dyed a defiant red, her face is a map of cracks and hollows—but the body still rages against the dying of the light. Although thin herself, Redgrave miraculously conveys grossness. As she writhes and leaps in Duncan's unique free-foot choreography, the actress further illuminates Isadora as a reconciliation of opposites—a naive sophisticate, a Continental hick, a selfless egotist who, Agnes de Mille recalls, "cleared away the rubbish. Isadora was a gigantic broom."

The film could have used that broom—most notably in the cluttered depiction of Isadora's marriage to Russian Poet Sergei Essenin. To portray the epileptic genius at high pitch, Yugoslav Actor Ivan Tchenko is called upon to leap bedward at Isadora and roar, "Ve make lawv like tigairs!" With that kind of dialogue, and no one to act against—or for—Redgrave cannot help turning the picture into a gigantic one-woman show. So, of course, was Isadora Duncan—but even she had help.

OH, ISADORA!

HOLLIS ALPERT

There ought to be a reason for doing a film biography of Isadora Duncan, and, as far as one can judge from *The Loves of Isadora* in its present considerably shortened length, the reason was her flamboyant love life. Cut down by some forty minutes, the film now concentrates principally on Isadora's affairs with Gordon Craig and Paris Singer, and her marriage to the mad Russian poet, Sergei Essenin. I rather suspect that what was left out might have helped; certainly a synopsis of the earlier version indicates that several events in her life were covered that are now left as merely large, unexplained gaps.

But the largest gap of all is in that area of motive. Why should we have a film about Isadora unless we are given some reason for her importance? If not now, at least then. Any examination of her foreshortened life story can provide several of those reasons. Perhaps the most important is the revolutionary effect she had on the art of dance. Her life style, too, was deeply tied up in the feminist revolution. The political ideas she espoused can be dismissed as naive, but her ideas about art impressed some people at the time, even though they might now strike us as gloriously phony, impossibly pretentious. It was Isadora as dancer and personality that made her interesting; far less was her love life.

So the film is off on the wrong tack (perhaps not from the beginning, for Karel Reisz is a serious and sensitive director, who must indeed have been aware of all that Isadora represented), and, for all of Vanessa Redgrave's efforts to portray her honestly, Isadora escapes. There are still hardy devotees of Isadora Duncan who would say that the lady herself willed it so, and one of them even pointed out to me that Miss Redgrave suffered a broken toe while attempting to perform the film's dances. The implication being that the accident was supernaturally arranged.

There was very little record left of Isadora's dancing. A good many drawings and some photographs exist, and Miss Redgrave claims to have seen a few minutes of a scratchy Russian film on which she has based her own interpretations. But, strangely, Isadora, for all her fame, was loathe to appear before a film camera. She wanted her methods and ideas about dance, art, and life carried on, but this was to be done through her pupils, to whom she devoted enormous amounts of her energies and earnings. Miss Redgrave's attempts to approximate Isadora's dancing are earnest, but, I am sorry to report, rather pathetic. It is here that the film falls flat on its often attractive face. If the electrifying effect that Isadora had on her audiences could have been implied somehow on the screen, we would have understood her more and been more affected by her tragedy.

As constructed by Melvyn Bragg and Clive Exton, we first meet Isadora near the end of her life, a raddled but still defiant wreck, and from there we retreat to her beginnings—not in San Francisco, but in Chicago, where she must perform a cancan (a silly, crude sequence that should have been omitted, since Miss Redgrave hardly looks like a nubile teen-ager), and from there to her emergence in England as an artist. From time to time, back we go to the Riviera, where Isadora is trying to compose the story of her life. An attempt has been made to stay true to the facts, but there were too many facts, and the selection has not always been apt. Obviously, her grand love, Gordon Craig, had to be included, and the macabre death by drowning of her two illegitimate children, one by Craig, the other by the millionaire (and already married) Paris Singer. And eventually, her startling death by way of a long scarf that wound itself around the rear wheel of an open car.

What is not in the film is what might have given it life. Isadora's lovers were far more multifarious than the film implies (one raconteur told of an entire Italian boxing team she entertained during a trip to Argentina); the coterie that surrounded her included some of the world's most august artistic names; her concerts were regarded for many years as important cultural events. She shocked, she charmed, she convinced. She was, in her way, a titan figure. And this is what the film does not give us. Admittedly, Reisz took on a large order in Isadora. So did Vanessa Redgrave. She has moments of charm, but it is quite possible she is miscast. Certainly James Fox is as Gordon Craig. As Singer, Jason Robards, Jr., plays a stock millionaire, and as Essenin, Ivan Tchenko is simply awful. Too bad. Isadora deserved better. All that was necessary for a scenario was the brief John Dos Passos biography in *U.S.A.* In a couple of thousand words it tells us far more than the movie does.

FEET

Penelope Gilliatt

The justly spectacular thing about Karel Reisz's *The Loves of Isadora* is Vanessa Redgrave's immense performance, but maybe the fundamental point about everyone's work in this intelligent film is that no one ever allows regard for Isadora Duncan's revolutionizing talent as a dancer to blunt the realization that it was part of her character. The picture is a wittily distanced account of a believable woman, and the attitude changes everything. If film biographies of the gifted are generally the dulled things they are, I think it is partly because the people making them are so concussed by awe of the gift that they separate it from temperament. The gift is exceptional, goes the unwitting response, and therefore it is secretly threatening, and therefore it had best be kept at a distance, so that the menacing possessor of it can be domesticated. Beethoven will be shown as an empty replica of Mr. Average—hating the rain, say, until the noise of the dripping slyly starts to sound like a bit of the Pastoral Symphony, when Ludwig will immediately seem to go out of his normal mind and into a spasm of art. Most film biographies look on great innovators as people subject to aberrant attacks, as though audiences needed to be calmed by reassurances that the exceptional are primarily just like everyone else and are really rather racked by their seizures of uniqueness, which put them momentarily out of control and make them not themselves until they have finished the canvas or discovered radium. But Reisz's *Isadora*—based on her autobiography and Sewell Stokes's biography, and made from a script by Melvyn Bragg and Clive Exton, with extra dialogue by Margaret Drabble—sees very clearly that when Isadora Duncan was dancing she was most herself, just as the serious intent of her High Romantic's life was to perform and behave, in an affected and constraining age, in ways that would allow other people also to be most themselves. She is admired in the film, criticized, smiled at, observantly loved, and sometimes grieved for, and everything she does seems to come out of her whole personality, so her dancing is no inscrutable gift of the gods. You feel that, given a very slight juggling of her circumstances and attributes, she might have been a potter, or an artist's model who suddenly flung it all up and went to teach birth control in China, or a valued and gradually saddened kindergarten teacher. Her feeling for simplicity is made to seem pure and urgent, but the film's notion of how character works implies that it could have taken other and minor forms if she had been, for instance, less caustic, less dazzling to audiences, less ruthless about wanting to influence whole continents, less headlong and unread about politics. There is also the suggestion that her harrowing mixture of being both a jeered-at famous lover and in fact often alone and wretched, unequipped as she was for solitude, might have worked out less taxingly without her insistence on a panache apt to go with fickleness in the men she was prepared to love.

Gordon Craig, the great visionary of theater production and design (played by James Fox, who is a good actor but somehow yeomanly in the part of this cackling maverick), seems to have understood her temperament very well. In his *Index to the Story of My Days*, an invaluable book that was published here by Viking in 1957 and is now out of print, he writes gnomishly about his expectation that the barefoot, free-love dancer from California would be a bit governessy. They had a fine time together. They agreed that it would be commonplace of them to treat one another as geniuses, although each of them was obviously secure in knowing it to be true of himself. Craig, writing in old age, sweetly calls her a genius behind her dead back, and speaks of her courage in a world that raved about her and then dumped her. And he writes:

> What is it she lacked?
> What was it she had?
> She had calm—
> No vanity—
> No cleverness—by which I mean no clever little tricks of the trade—little or no understanding of the arts—a great comprehension of nature and perhaps overmuch ambition.

It was by Craig that she had one of the two children, who died horribly, drowning, with their nurse, in a motor accident. His written descriptions of her include more fondness and insight than the man in the film seems capable of, but Vanessa Redgrave's performance embodies every word of them. The other drowned child was by Paris Singer, a rich, muddled, despotic fop, finely played by Jason Robards, who gives an astringent and rather sad interpretation of the pinch-heart locked inside the showoff who wooed her with diamonds and a bank of white roses. He nearly suffocated her with English grand living, even if he did give her twelve thousand acres to use as a dancing school when he realized that his diamonds had been a mistake. She tells him gaily, over champagne, that she doesn't like jewelry, and he takes the blow on the chin, knowing, perhaps, the reprisals that he can take later—by making her play croquet, by repelling her with his hypochondria and crimped faddishness, and by dangling before her as a potential lover a maliciously chosen pianist to accompany her lonely dance practice. Pitiless, she calls the poor hireling monkey-faced, and keeps him behind a grille while she dances. Just as characteristically, she then rides with him in a carriage and shouts to him that his eyes have the soul of a poet; he touches the skies. They have an ecstatic affair, and she forgets him. On to Russia in the middle of the revolution. There are self-mocking scenes of grand passion with Essenin, her mad poet, half her age. A Russian teacher instructing her in the usual basics of how to say "My crayon is red" is firmly told to explain instead how to tell Essenin that he has beautiful thighs.

When Isadora first went to Europe, she looked as if she longed to unlace the corsets of the art patrons whose malicious graciousness incited her to shock them. Confronted with a whaleboned gorgon dressed in black and gold, she was as outrageous as possible. Russia suited her better, but by then much had been lost and too much of her spirit wasted in hidden loneliness—Craig parted from, Singer ditched, the children drowned, another baby dead soon after birth. She had transformed dancing, and perhaps even changed something sedate in the spirit of Europe; but the film is full of a sense of the cost, and America greeted her viciously when she came back with her wild Russian husband. Her stringent gaiety in the face of the stuffy is as moving as the scenes of her dancing. Her fluency and her love for all liberators make the events of her life seem necessities. Jocelyn Herbert's designs for the film (she gave the same grave beauty to the look of *Tom Jones* and *If . . .*) speak for what Isadora wanted to do as completely as Vanessa Redgrave's dancing does. Again and again there is some image designed with unforgettable simplicity: Isadora with Craig in Berlin, wearing a deep-blue blanket and carrying a brown book; Isadora pregnant in a long white dress in Singer's baronial school grounds, teaching a swarm of children in white tunics to dance; Isadora in Russia, with her hair now furiously dyed red, a woman who would have been washed up if she had been anyone else, dancing in a cold ransacked palace with a group of Soviet children dressed in tunics the color of the burnt-orange paint on Venice *palazzi* and Kiev cathedrals. Reisz's structure for the picture has probably been traduced by the demand over here that it be drastically shortened from three hours to a little over two. I gather that many of the cuts were made in the sequences about her theory of dance, shot in Greece, and in the flash-back/flash-forward connections between the young girl and the aging, gaudy harridan, which should surely have been allowed to stay in full so as to give them the weight and meaning they are meant to have. Even now they manage to exist not as the common bridge device of movie biographies but as a reflection of Isadora's particular mind. They stand for the consciousness of lost looks and gone faculties that weighs on all physical performers, and especially on this imperious, doomed prophet of a far-ahead period that was to make a morality of the freer life she dramatized in gestures struck so boldly.

GOODBYE, MR. CHIPS

THE ONCE AND FUTURE KING?

PAULINE KAEL

An actor often comes to movies from the theater with a big reputation, plays a big movie role, and is acclaimed as a great actor. After a string of bad movies, he no longer seems so great, his technique coarsens, and his face shows the dissipation of success. There were indications that this was happening to Peter O'Toole. In weak, characterless roles, such as the one he had in *How to Steal a Million,* he had become merely a pleasant, "stylish" leading man, a walking luxury item. It was all that the role required, but he certainly didn't burst its very obvious seams. Then, last year, in *The Lion in Winter,* he gave good evidence that he could be an actor of vitality and passion—an actor in the heroic mold. Some of the best English actors—Alec Guinness, Ralph Richardson, John Gielgud, Rex Harrison, Paul Scofield—lack the kind of animal presence, the threat of violence, that makes certain roles exciting. O'Toole did what Olivier almost alone of English actors could do (and what Nicol Williamson so feverishly overdoes). An actor who can make us feel that he has "heart"—that the feelings he projects are at the center of our lives—can hold a play or a film together and make it seem major. Richard Burton seemed to have it, but in such abundance that he began to toy with it and to devalue it. Perhaps it needs to be harder won (as Olivier won it over the obstacle of his young *inconsequential* charm, his lack of *weight*). It isn't so much a matter of talent or training, or even physique, as of temperament. O'Toole's king suggested physical strength and heroic power. He could bellow. (Can one imagine

Gielgud bellowing?) He could be brutal. (Can one imagine Richardson as a brute?) The threat of violence in his king suggested that he was an actor of considerably greater range than his screen career had indicated—and of a different range. He has now taken on another role that calls for a heroic actor, though it's a quiet, unassuming role, which needs to be played at the other end of the keyboard from his roistering Plantagenet. Neither role is a great one, but O'Toole may be turning into something of a new phenomenon among movie actors—an actor who can transform lame vehicles the way great stage actors used to.

At a mere eighteen thousand words, James Hilton's *Goodbye, Mr. Chips*—an "affectionate" tribute to a small man's useful, uneventful life—was at least lightweight, and, despite its soggy gentility, it had the virtues of gentleness and modesty. It had come out as a story in 1933, but when it was put between covers the next year it looked like a novel, and it has gone through more than seventy-five printings in the United States alone. It was a durable tear-jerker and has the odd distinction of being probably the shortest best-selling novel known. The first time on the screen, in 1939, it was saved by Robert Donat's performance as Mr. Chips (which won him the Academy Award) and by a charming young actress named Greer Garson, who, however, quickly patented her charm and became one of the most richly syllabled queenly horrors of Hollywood. The weather is much rougher now, but *Goodbye, Mr. Chips* has been saved again—this time by O'Toole, by Petula Clark as his wife, and by an added character, played by Sian Phillips. The new movie is far from being a good one, but, despite its heaviness and length, and the *longueurs* caused by an atrocious, numbing score, the director, Herbert Ross (who was formerly a choreographer), has managed to keep it a gentle romance, and keep it fairly buoyant. What this all adds up to is that one can look at Peter O'Toole's performance without too much pain.

Goodbye, Mr. Chips had a core idea of immense popular appeal —the power of love to transform a person. The Chips of the story was a mild schoolmaster, a conservative bachelor of forty-eight, who, on vacation, suddenly met and married a twenty-five-year-old governess with radical-socialist sympathies. After his marriage, he won the love of his students, because he was "kind without being soft"—because he was a happy man. When his wife died in childbirth, two years later, he became an old man at fifty. But she had broadened his ideas and humanized him, and he was a mellow old man for the remaining thirty-ad-infinitum years of his life. Hilton had a commercial genius for domesticating "the impossible dream." This story must have spoken to millions of hearts: "You poor stick-in-the-mud, you may yet be saved by a Cinderella touch and have a long, wonderful, happy life and be loved by everyone."

Terence Rattigan, who did the adaptation for this new, demi-musical version, has made the young Chips a dry-as-dust martinet of a schoolmaster (much like the one in his own *The Browning Version*) who falls in love with a musical-comedy actress, marries, and is transformed (through fifteen years of marriage—a more comforting period of time) into a loving, lovable old man. The movie is a vernal romance, with a true-blue, good-to-the-last-drop heroine and an inert structure that spans Chips's unconscionably prolonged life. (His longevity must have been part of the story's appeal; Hilton immediately took perpetual life itself as the core idea for *Lost Horizon*, and made another fortune.) Rattigan promises much more than he delivers. At the beginning, when Chips says that he doesn't care if he's liked by his students as long as he can *teach* them, he suggests a genuine sense of vocation (rigid and misguided though it may be). Since the two great loves of his life are teaching and the girl he marries, we expect the crucial part of the movie to be his discovery, through his marriage, of how to be a good teacher instead of a deadly pedant. But the movie simply settles for showing how well liked he becomes, obviously on the assumption that we really don't care if he's a good teacher as long as he's popular. Nor do we discover how the young actress perceives the hidden qualities in Chips, because they are not revealed to us until much later. Flowers on the table—a token of domestic bliss—are made to stand for a happy marriage. The flowers are nice, but we want to know what the couple's life together is like. The movie gives us the courtship and the end of life, but the middle—the transformation that we've looked forward to—seems to happen offscreen. Yet even the *suggestion* that the movie is about what makes a good life is appealing. The idea of a peaceful, useful life and of a happy marriage is now almost more romantic and more desirable than Hilton's Shangri-La once seemed. It's dream enough for now.

If only we could be left alone with our feelings, we could practically entertain ourselves at this movie just mulling it all over, marveling at the appeal of its pleasantly dowdy simplicities. But periodically, almost ceremonially, Leslie Bricusse's Muzak fills the air, as if to create a mystique of sentiment, and it inflates whatever one may have begun to feel, and makes it cheap and false. This Muzak is in some neutral neo-sentimental mode that makes you feel that it's programming you to be banal, putting a pacifier in your head. And while these pitiful songs (eleven of them, as distinct one from another as sections of beige wall-to-wall carpet) are being sung, mostly offscreen, you're treated to visual Muzak—"mood" visuals —providing enough redundancy to pad the movie out to two hours and thirty-one minutes plus intermission.

One's heart may sink every time a music cue starts up, and the picture lingers on long after it should end—and I haven't told *all* the worst—but O'Toole and Petula Clark play together so well that one smiles, wanting to accept the romance, wanting to believe in this middle-class fairy tale. Miss Clark is not very good at the beginning, when she's supposed to be a young girl (she's done up in short curls and looks too much like Mary Martin), but she improves when the romance begins to take hold, although her role is a cut-rate version of one of those sickeningly intuitive James M. Barrie heroines. She has a lovely glow in the Second World War period of the film, when she's supposed to be the age she actually is. She relaxes then, and one begins to believe in her as a truly happy woman. One wonders why the adapter, in changing the character to provide an excuse for Miss Clark to sing, didn't eliminate the age difference. Before their marriage, when Chips was explaining to her that he was too old for her, I kept waiting for her to correct him. As Miss Clark is actually about the same age as O'Toole, the supposed difference puts a strain on our credulity and on her performance. If she were older, it would improve the movie, by explaining her willingness to give up her career. The *implications* of the change haven't been worked out, either. Surely it would not be difficult, in substituting an actress for a governess with progressive ideas who liberated her husband, to show how a more worldly wife might broaden a schoolmaster's outlook, but nothing is done with this, so one gets the impression that the actress is drawn to the safety and protective comforts of a narrow academic life. That leaves Chips's transformation to be a pure miracle of love, and it makes the movie more complacent toward Chips's stuffiness than the story was.

Though Chips's role isn't particularly well thought out in the writing, O'Toole gives an extraordinarily detailed performance. He stays in character, and he resists the temptation (which can easily be imagined) to patronize Chips. The reserves of strength within gentleness are not easy to demonstrate, but he does it; his Chips is diffident to the point of disappearance, yet you still know there's a man there. O'Toole treats that man with such extraordinary respect that Chips grows in stature as the character *must* grow if the movie is to succeed as romance. And when Chips stops growing, O'Toole manages, through what in an actor is heroic intelligence, not to make him an endearing, stomach-turning old codger. There is, of course, all too much precedent for praising an actor when he plays a role such as a crusty, crotchety, noble old schoolmaster, especially if he gets a chance to age onscreen and quaver a bit. But O'Toole plays the part without seizing all the depressing opportunities or puttying himself up with wrinkles and wattles. He plays the role from within, and the externals are kept to a minimum. It's a romantic performance, not a bathetic one—a "little" man played by a very large actor—and the finest performance I've seen on the screen this year.

There is a third star—one who isn't billed that way but is felt that way. Sian Phillips (she is Mrs. O'Toole), who has had unattractive roles, such as the wife in *Laughter in the Dark,* is cast as Ursula Mossbank, an actress friend of Mr. Chips's wife. Sian Phillips's Ursula is a Beardsley vamp—theatrical in that witty, stilted way that has already become one of the small but true treasures of the past—and she gives the movie a few desperately needed shots in the arm. *Goodbye, Mr. Chips* keeps going on what used to be called charm, but it's heaven to have Miss Phillips around to needle it. Here is the actress who might have played Gertrude Lawrence as the great Camp-vamp star she was.

OLD MASTER

STEFAN KANFER

"The schoolmaster who imagines he is loved and trusted by his boys is, in fact, mimicked and laughed at behind his back," recalled George Orwell in *Such, Such Were the Joys*. James Hilton took the opposite view. The schoolmaster who thought himself mocked was actually loved. Orwell's essay may have been what the public needed to know. But Hilton's 1934 novel was what it wished to read. *Goodbye, Mr. Chips* rapidly passed from sentimental classic bestseller to sentimental classic movie. In the title role, Robert Donat won an Academy Award, and Mr. Chips achieved legendary status as the old master of the schoolboy soul.

Students, teachers, England and the world have altered considerably in 35 years. But Brookfield School remains a tranquil antechamber to gentlemanhood, where the master now reigns in the person of Peter O'Toole. Discarding the shy, dry Donat approach, O'Toole becomes his own man, a conflicted figure changing imperceptibly from instructor to institution, like an elm turning, cell by cell, into petrified rock. The result is one of the slyest and subtlest performances in his career.

Unhappily, he is contained in a clumsily updated block off the old Chips. It is no longer the Great War but World War II that punctuates the scholastic calendar, Chips's missus (Petula Clark) becomes the victim not of childbirth but of a V-1 rocket. Still, the boys are the same deferential crew; the school is ivied and kind, an eon removed from the kind of place Orwell considered "a tightrope over a cesspool." The only instance of sadism, in fact, is the disastrous decision to make *Goodbye, Mr. Chips* a musical. As a result, Leslie Bricusse was given license to inflict ten songs. Like the pupils' Latin lessons, the lyrics will not pass scrutiny ("He smiled. I smiled. We smiled. And the sky smiled too."); the melodies are scarcely more tuneful than a piece of hard chalk drawn across a blackboard. Even with O'Toole's oddly moving *Sprechgesang* and Clark's perfect phrasing, the numbers never add up to a score.

In such an intimate story, all other characters are subordinate. But one actress has taken a minor part and nearly made off with the show. As Mrs. Chips's bony crony, Sian Phillips (Mrs. O'Toole offscreen) moves like Garbo, hoots like Tallulah, and seems quite the most animated skeleton since Halloween.

In his first directorial assignment, Herbert Ross lights Clark's songs as if she were doing a turn on *This Is Tom Jones,* and tends to place his camera at jarring angles. He even mounts it on the V-1, making the viewer feel like a patient of Dr. Strangelove. No matter. It is one of the graces of group art that if any one can destroy a project, so any one can save it. *Mr. Chips* is barely enough because Mr. O'Toole is more than enough.

Superstar: The Streisand Story

JOSEPH MORGENSTERN

By any standard but raw musculature, Barbra Streisand is the most powerful entertainer in America today. She could get financing if she wanted her next movie to be based on Van Nostrand's Scientific Encyclopedia. (Not such a bad idea: We open on "Photosynthesis," with Barbra in the greenhouse dressed in silver lamé gardening togs . . .) She's seen on the screen in *Hello, Dolly!* in 70-mm. Todd-AO, she's heard on records in 360 Stereo Sound and she's dissected by gossip columnists in 8-point malice. The movie version of *Funny Girl*, her first star vehicle, which won her an Academy Award, is still playing on Times Square. *On a Clear Day You Can See Forever* will be released next spring, and she's now shooting *The Owl and the Pussycat* in New York.

Several of her TV specials have been stunning. Her records have sold nearly 9 million copies. She seems to be seen everywhere, and the volume of copy is vast about what she does, where she goes and with whom. How she wields her personal power is one thing. How she uses her artistic power is another, though, and it is the essential thing about her, as it has been ever since she appeared on Broadway more than seven years ago as Miss Marmelstein in *I Can Get It for You Wholesale*. What matters most about her is her gifts, or her art, or whatever you want to call it. It's how she's able to make such a lot go such a long way.

She made her Miss Marmelstein entrance in a swivel chair: Yetta Tessye Marmelstein, a bizarre, beehived, unbeloved child of 19, swooping and swiveling toward us to ask why other girls get called by their first names right away. "Oh, *why* is it always Miss Marmelstein . . . ?" She chose that preposterous chairbound entrance because she was too scared to face her audience standing up and because most secretaries, she figured, spend most of their time in chairs anyway. A great performance is a collection of such precisely right choices: theatrical, extravagant, but above all true. She rolled on stage, and then the most peculiar thing happened. This beehive office girl who really seemed to have come out of an office put on a whole little musical by herself. It was heroic, in its way, and desperately funny.

The heroine that she so quickly became had a particular desperation all her own. She was a wallflower. She had this Jewish problem, and this homely problem. "Nobody Makes a Pass at Me," she sang in the 25th anniversary recording of *Pins and Needles*, a garment workers' union show with a charming score by Harold Rome, who also did the *Wholesale* score. It was much the same character that Rome had written in the Miss Marmelstein number, except that Barbra threw new anger into it, comic self-hate and harsh self-appraisal. "Just like Ivory soap, I'm 99 and 44/100ths per cent pure," she wailed, and the "pure" came out as a filthy word. *PURE!*

She was purely her own invention, nothing prefabricated, no resemblance to starlets living or dead. She was a regular person with a genuine past from a real place that happened to be Brooklyn, which made people laugh. She really was pure, but pure what, exactly? Her first starring role, Fanny Brice in the Broadway production of *Funny Girl*, supplied one answer—pure oddball. It was such a persuasive answer that it seemed for a time to be the only one.

"When you're younger," she said slowly and cautiously in a long discussion of her work one recent evening, "you have only your imagination to draw on, so what happens is it transcends reality, it almost makes its own art." She was talking, at this point, about her work as an acting-school student of sixteen or seventeen. (According to a friend who knew her then, she was the only one in the class who asked questions, who wasn't passive, wasn't awed by the teacher or the material.) "As you get older," Barbra said, "reality sets in."

Whatever its shortcomings as a cohesive piece of theater, *Funny Girl* made remarkably shrewd use of its star. The choreography gave her a chance to do some sublime clowning in the "Beautiful Bride" number, in which Fanny, surrounded by long-stemmed beauties, sang sweetly that she was the beautiful reflection of her love's affection, which was all well and good except that the girl was visibly, hugely pregnant. Isobel Lennart's book gave her an antic façade and a romantic, passionate spirit. The score, by Jule Styne and Bob Merrill, gave her two distinctive ballads—"People" and "The Music That Makes Me Dance." Most shrewdly of all, the score provided an opening number, sung not by Fanny but by her friends and neighbors, that briskly explored the problem of success, sex and the homely girl: "If a Girl Isn't Pretty" ("If a girl's incidentals aren't bigger than two lentils. . .").

In her own opening number she sang wistfully, comically, that she was the greatest star but no one knew it. By the time the movie version of *Funny Girl* came out in 1968 almost everyone knew it. Rather, they knew with more than a little skepticism that she was supposed to be the greatest. But Barbra had never made a movie, and cameras are notorious unmaskers of fraud. The cameras in *Funny Girl* unmasked an artist even more gifted than she was supposed to be. I remember worrying about superlatives in my review. Would I make a fool of myself by calling it the most accomplished, original and enjoyable musical comedy performance ever put on film? I searched my memory and finally decided that, what the hell, it simply was the greatest; why not say so?

But what do such superlatives mean? What did she *do* that was so good? A fair question to ask and a hard one to answer, since the one thing she didn't do was hold still long enough for the categorizers to draw a clear bead on her. She did a livepan deadpan, a deadpan livepan. She had her ethnic material at least both ways, comedy and parody plus a bit of self-parody thrown in whenever she wanted to play dummy to her own ventriloquist. She worked a warm, romantic singing voice against a taut, comic speaking voice. Her transitions from one mood to the next were instantaneous and dazzling. In the scene leading to "Don't Rain on My

Parade," she put her hands over her ears, shook her head and said "Don't tell me" as her fellow Follies girls tried to convince her that her man, Nicky Arnstein, was a stinker. Suddenly, without warning, she was into her song, repeating "Don't tell me" with an explosive "*Don't*" that carried her all the way to a tugboat deck and intermission.

Her energy was limitless, her sense of fun almost infallible. And at the end of a movie that didn't have its own dramatic end—poor pasteboard Nicky comes back to Fanny from the hoosegow but their marriage has nowhere to go—Barbra sang "My Man." She had the sound recorded live, an artistic gamble which most movie stars wouldn't dream of taking. She wore black against a black background: nothing to be seen or heard of her but two hands, a face and a voice. She started small, injured, all trembly-tearful as if there were nothing else to do with an old chestnut about a lovelorn lady. Before the end of the first chorus, however, her funny girl made a decision to sing herself back to life. Her voice soared defiantly, a spirit lost and found in the space of a few bars, and since you'd paid your money you could now take your choice of being wiped out by the sheer, shameless sentiment of the situation, or by the virtuosity of an actress looking lovely, feminine and vulnerable at the same time she was belting out a ballad with the force of a mighty Wurlitzer.

We talked about typecasting. Italian audiences had no interest in seeing Marcello Mastroianni's superb performance in *The Organizer*. They wanted their romantic leading man, not a union organizer out of the smoky past. American audiences were indifferent to Cary Grant's fine work in Clifford Odets's film about an ill-starred Cockney, *None but the Lonely Heart*. "I suppose the audience just didn't buy it because they want what they understand," Barbra said uncertainly, with no pleasure at the thought. "But . . . I can't buy that either. I always think if something's really good and right they've got to buy *that*. I mean I want to play all different kinds of parts: you know, from bitches to sweet girls to stupid girls to bright girls to every kind of girl. 'Cause I have all these possibilities. I'm slightly dumb, I'm very smart. I'm many things. You know? I want to use them, want to express them. It's kind of funny, because I'm in these sort of big pictures and yet I'm an odd . . . I'm an odd ball. I mean, I'm not a Doris Day or a Julie Andrews. That's what's weird about it. I don't know how I got into these things. Honestly."

She mistrusts the press but trusts the audience. "The audience is the best judge of anything. They cannot be lied to. I mean, this is something I discovered . . . not discovered . . . but after almost two years on the stage one learns that. The slightest tinge of falseness, they go back from you, they retreat. The truth brings them closer. A moment that lags, I mean, they're gonna cough. A moment that is held, they're not gonna cough. They don't know why, they can't intellectualize it, but they know it's right or wrong. Individually they may be a bunch of asses but together as a whole they are the . . . wisest thing."

Of all the gossip that's gossiped about her, the most intriguing part is her reputation for being difficult to work with. She has this habit, people say, of directing her directors. People often say that about stars. Power is a fascinating subject, and people love to think of moviemaking in terms of power and nothing but power, as an epic struggle between egomaniacs: on one side the director, wearing jodhpurs, boots, riding crop, monocle and leer; on the other side the star, fussing with her face and refusing to play her scene in the county workhouse unless they let her wear the Golden Fleece. One never knows the truth of these things. The actor-director relationship is uniquely intimate. One can only make guesses based on the movie's end result.

Her director in *Funny Girl* was William Wyler, a man of vast experience and proven artistry. He'd made some 40 movies before this; Barbra had made none. She, on the other hand, had created her own role, had played it 798 times on Broadway and in London and knew more about it, instinctively and intellectually, than anyone else on earth. There was every reason for these two artists with complementary equipment to collaborate on the film and—based on the strong end result—every reason to believe they did collaborate. Not without anger or pain, surely, since stars and directors are both playing for high stakes in such elaborate productions, but not without purpose either.

As a matter of fact, if Barbra directed Gene Kelly, her director in *Hello, Dolly!*, she should have done a better job. There's no evidence that he or anyone else directed this great, plodding dinosaur of a film. It's there because it's there, an impressive industrial enterprise in which everyone came dutifully to work in the mornings and picked up where they'd left off the day before. Kelly stages his turn-of-the-century comedy in late 1940s style, as if movie musicals stopped growing when he stopped dancing in them. Like Michael Kidd's choreography, Kelly's technique is antique at best, incompetent at worst. Several shakily written comedy scenes are just as shakily performed because no one knew how to direct or cut them. The "Hello, Dolly!" number comes in fits and starts because no one knew how to make it build, visually or dramatically. The 40 million extras in the big parade scene look like a routine rabble because no one knew where to put the cameras.

Like her co-stars—Walter Matthau as Horace, Michael Crawford as Cornelius—Barbra has an uphill fight with the foolish material and the flatfooted style. She needs help and doesn't get it, and it hurts. In search of a center for the character of Dolly Levi, she finds two, three or four centers and therefore none: Mae West, Vivien Leigh, Fanny Brice, even Barbra Streisand. She's too young for the part of this doughty Mrs. Fixit, so she does some of her best work out of character. Yet the movie dies utterly when she's offscreen and comes obediently back to life when she's on. She may be in trouble from time to time but she bails herself out, and the movie as well, with great resourcefulness.

She spoofs the dumb material, or goes with it, or plays with and against it almost simultaneously. "Such a long life line!" she cries in mock amazement as she reads Matthau's palm, then continues to read it like a hip Gypsy. Leaving Matthau in the second act, she does another lightning transition from speech to song—"So Long Dearie"—with seven preposterously impassioned good-byes that she sings, trills, yodels and groans in the styles of Piaf, Marlene Dietrich and, for all I know, Lucrezia Borgia. Trapped by a scene in which Dolly teaches the waltz to an actor we know perfectly well is a professional dancer, she shows him the first rudimentary *one*-two-three, stands back while he does some exuberant look-Ma-I'm-dancing adagios, and then cuts through the whole choice idiocy with a muttered ad lib: "I think he's been holdin' out on us."

As in *Funny Girl*, she does a parade number, "Before the Parade Passes By," for her first-act curtain. She's alone on the screen at first, a warm, throbbing body in coarse cartoonland. Her Dolly is trying to gather her forces in this first chorus (force gathering is what first-act curtains are all about) so she can make her way back into the parade of life. Then there's a drum, and then an elephantine production number that takes the metaphor of the song literally: a parade with 76,000 trombones and the entire membership of the Screen Extras' Guild. And the most amazing thing of all is that the parade itself, for all its blare and vulgar trappings, never comes up to the power of Barbra's performance in the first chorus, just as the whole "Hello, Dolly!" production number adds very little to the outlandish delight of her entrance, a middle-aged marriage broker being played by a sexy young woman in a sparkling gold gown. The girl is human, the production ain't. Who needs it?

That's an odd thing for an oddball to be taxed with, looking sexy and young. Was it done with mirrors, or with Irene Scharaff's costumes, or with Harry Stradling's photography? No, the suspicion doesn't withstand scrutiny because the girl does withstand it. She looks lovely on screen and off, so much so that you wonder what happened to her and when. Had she been taking ugly pills for the *Funny Girl* role and then quit cold turkey? The answer, of course, is that her publicity and her material in the first few years of her career told us she was an oddball, so an oddball is what we saw. She looked lovely in all but the most antic comedy routines of *Funny Girl*, yet the material kept saying Homely, Clumsy, Gawky, Screwy, so we took our cues. On records she was singing "Lover, Come Back to Me" with superbly dirty sexuality five years before *Funny Girl* hit the screen, and singing her slow, sensual versions of "Happy Days Are Here Again" and "Who's Afraid of the Big Bad Wolf?" six months before that. The main and basic source of the confusion was that she'd started her Broadway career as a little old maid. Only later did she youthen.

What kind of actress is she? Where do her strengths lie? "Elliott [husband Elliott Gould] once took his great-grandmother to see me and she was about 85, and she said she liked me because I was so natural—so *natchel*. And I liked that. I guess my best attribute is my instinct. It just . . . it hurts me if I hear a wrong line reading or something. And there is no such thing as a wrong line reading, only there is. I mean, everything is so damned . . . needs to be qualified so." A line reading that didn't work, then? "Yeah. Right. It's like music. I mean, acting is even like music. Because I believe in rhythm, you know? Everything is so dominated by our heartbeats, by our pulses, when one goes against certain rhythms it's jarring, it's unnatural, unless we use the dissonance."

She was squirming now and embarrassed by herself. "I'm not articulate and I'm not eloquent. This makes it sound like a lot of crap. It just sounds awful. I mean I hear it! But the point is I read a script and I just hear and I see what the people are doing, and I'll have an idea right off the bat, and it's always my first instinct that I trust. I'm also very lazy so I don't delve much further."

When her first flop comes, what kind does she want it to be? "A big one," she grinned. "So I can have a good comeback."

What about other styles of acting? She didn't feel close to actors with "thought-out line readings—you know, they know exactly where the intonation goes, what the key word in the sentence is, what they're reaching for in their speech or whatever. I'm more moved when I see Brando, when I can't quite define his moments, when I see just *a* life, *a* mind, *a* personality. Brando is stronger than any of the characters he plays. There is a difference between preconceiving everything and having it in control, and when it's slightly out of control."

We talked about specific performances, agreeing on Jeanne Moreau's mercurial work in *Jules and Jim*, different from one second to the next and yet a perfect whole. She expanded on it enthusiastically. "Anything carries when you have conviction. You can be totally different or have the moods change or switch from serious to comedy if you believe it, and everybody will go along. One little shred of doubt, though, and you've lost them all, you know? You have to just *do* it. It's wild, you know? I mean, the strength of the will, the strength of conviction. I don't know, what *is* conviction? Is it red or blue? It's so intangible. What . . . what chemical transmits itself in doubt? One flicker of doubt and everybody—gets doubtful. And most people are followers. They need you to be sure. They might resent you for being sure but they need you to be sure. They would fall apart if you weren't sure."

She isn't altogether as free as she'd like to be yet in her performances; the rehearsals are still sometimes better than the takes. She still worries about the way she looks, and worries about worrying about it. Every actor, man or woman, is a narcissist by trade. The trick is to accept this concern with one's body and put it in the proper place—concern and body both. She thinks of herself primarily as an instinctive actress, and her instincts are indeed phenomenal. Yet she can also get hung up temporarily on irrelevant details—a question of gum chewing or something, or the arcane symbolism of some costume. And this confusion is compounded by the fact that irrelevant details may also be crucial in their way. Barbra has an extraordinary grasp of how costumes can define character, and an actress who's worried about gum-chewing techniques in a particular moment may actually be freeing herself to do the important work in the scene without thinking about it.

Her completed movie work to date consists of three elaborate musicals: *Funny Girl, Hello, Dolly!* and *On a Clear Day You Can See Forever,* which was directed by Vincente Minnelli. Barbra and musicals have done well by each other. But she's ambivalent about her singing now. She seems to be suggesting that she doesn't want to do any more musicals—no more pat, flat spectacles, the kind with the backgrounds in focus. She knows there are less rigid, less predictable ways of making movies these days, and she'd like to join in the fun. But First Artists, the new movie company she formed six months ago with Paul Newman and Sidney Poitier, has not yet announced a single production, and her own methods for searching out new material are haphazard.

In the meantime, however, she's gainfully and happily employed on *The Owl and the Pussycat.* She plays a hooker, Doris ("I'm an actress and a model . . ."), to George Segal's Felix, a pseudo-intellectual, in this movie version of Bill Manhoff's Broadway play. Neither Barbra, director Herbert Ross nor anyone else connected with it would represent *The Owl and the Pussycat* as a piece of avant-garde filmmaking. It's a romantic comedy, and it's intended to make people laugh. But it does represent a significant step in her career. It's an intentionally small-scale movie being shot under extremely low pressure at several New York City locations and mainly in a dinky studio on Manhattan's West Side. Its characters and dialogue have some basis in reality, if not necessarily in natchelism. It's not a musical, though she hums a bit. She has some near-nude scenes in it, and the movie, to her great pride and pleasure, is X-rated.

She even enjoys the unnude scenes. She's at ease with herself on this film. She says she's getting increasingly lazy in her work, but what that means is that she's getting decreasingly compulsive about details that don't matter. Notoriously late in the past, she's a model of promptness on the job. She respects her director and leading man and takes pleasure in a well-founded belief that the feelings are mutual. She likes working in New York, where the men on the crew talk like she does and she can go home after work to her apartment and her 3-year-old son Jason. Up in Central Park for location shooting one recent afternoon, she looked too pretty to not touch in a brown and white Dynel imitation lynx coat and white boots. She and Segal were shooting a scene in which he throws her to the ground and humiliates her until she cries. The scene was difficult for several reasons. It was freezing cold. A pot of charcoal embers hung under the Panavision camera to keep it warm, but there wasn't any charcoal for the actors. They had to make their wrestling look spontaneous and free while at the same time hitting their marks to be in focus. Finally, Barbra had to cry at the moment that the camera moved in for her close-up.

Even the lowest-pressure production can put the squeeze on an actor. The afternoon sunlight was failing and here they were with nary a wet eye in the house. Cry and the world smiles with you. But she couldn't cry, and she couldn't forget that she was supposed to appear a few hours later at the première of *Hello, Dolly!* at the Rivoli Theater on Broadway. She racked her brain for a way to make herself cry. The device she claims to have found was the thought of how guilty she'd feel if she went to the première of another movie and hadn't done her work properly on this one. It may not be so, but it makes a good story. The fact is that the camera turned, the tears flowed, the shot was made and the girl went home. Smiling.

"I can't tell you how marvelous she's been," said Ross, a tall, soft-spoken man who has known her since he did the musical staging in *I Can Get It for You Wholesale.* "It all comes out sounding like platitudes, but she's so generous—willing to do it my way or George's way. She has a feeling not that everyone loves her but that she's one of us." He spoke of one scene with Segal and Barbra in bed "where she takes off her bra, and it wasn't easy for her at first. She had so many inhibitions to throw off. You know, 'What would my mother think of this?' Once she did it the first time it was easy for her, but it really cost her."

Ross had directed Peter O'Toole in *Goodbye, Mr. Chips,* and he said O'Toole and Barbra were the two best actors he's ever worked with. "She isn't technical the way Peter is, a highly disciplined, highly trained actor. She has this ability to make right choices intuitively. But they're both alike in a way. They're never unprepared. They always know who they are and what they're doing. There may be areas within a scene that she's a little fuzzy about, and sometimes she'll get hung up on a little thing, a trifle, but the essentials are always clear." Before doing this movie, he said, he wouldn't have known what to think about her future. "But now I think her range is incredible. She's really what acting is all about—*being*. The more she tests her range the more expanded that range is going to be."

The most frightening part of stardom, superstardom or whatever the position is that Barbra occupies at this point in her professional life is that it inhibits growth. The historical pattern is plain. A star succeeds, repeats the success, varies the repetition slightly but insignificantly and ends up in a prison of self-parody. The most promising part of Barbra's case is that the pattern may not apply. She seems genuinely eager to test and expand her range, to grow in many directions. If she's only now beginning to be free as an actress, then the best is yet to come.

There would seem to be an undeniable logic to what she's doing now, getting out of those lavish musicals while the getting is good. The studios are collapsing and the studio chiefs, in self-preservational frenzy, are blaming it all on big-budget productions. The true culprits, however, have been *bad* big-budget productions. *Funny Girl* has made a fortune for its producers, despite its initial cost. Thanks to her presence, even *Hello, Dolly!* has a chance of making back its $25 million cost, though the logic of that budget is, of course, indefensible. To judge from the production photos, *On a Clear Day You Can See Forever* has invested a queen's ransom in costumes, as well as salaries, but there's no reason to think the ransom won't be recouped.

Hopefully, Barbra will do plenty of small movies that leave her free to explore character, reality, the finer texture of life. Hopefully, too, though, she'll be able to think big and sing big and work big again if she wants to. It was great fun seeing her on that tugboat with the Statue of Liberty in the background—in focus. It should be greater fun to watch her pump new life into the musical-comedy form and find new ways to use music in movies; any movies. When a girl can sing "Any Place I Hang My Hat Is Home" the way she does, her voice ought to be free to pop out of its cage at will.

John Wayne as the Last Hero

STEFAN KANFER

At the edge of a birch grove, four mounted outlaws try to stare down the aging lawman.

"I mean to kill you or see you hanged at Fort Smith . . ." barks Marshal Rooster Cogburn.

"Bold talk for a one-eyed fat man," the bandit leader sneers.

"Fill your hand, you sonuvabitch!" Cogburn answers, clamping his reins in his teeth and letting loose with a two-handled fusillade from his Winchester and long-barreled revolver.

At the end of the battle, four villains—and one horse—lie punctured and defunct upon the ground. "Dammit, Bo," says Cogburn to his mount as he lies pinned beneath it. "First time ya ever gave me reason to curse ya."

Self-parody is the price of style. Hemingway verged on it in his later novels; Presidents Roosevelt and Eisenhower accomplished it in their later speeches. John Wayne charges into it in his latest movie, *True Grit*. Like all consummate stylists, he remains unharmed. Only the enemy is hurt.

The broader the parody, the bigger the self. Wayne has been honing and buffing that self in some 250 pictures—mostly westerns—for 40 years. He has become the essential American soul that D. H. Lawrence once characterized as "harsh, isolate, stoic and a killer." Superficially his films have been as alike as buffalo nickels.

Only the date changes; even the Indian looks the same. Yet through the decades there has been a perceptible alteration. The public, riding along in movie houses or taking the TV shortcut, has watched the celluloid Wayne pass through three stages of life. In the '30s, he was the outspoken, hair-trigger-tempered son who would straighten out if he didn't get shot first. By the late '40s, he had graduated to fatherhood: top-kick Marine to a platoon of shavetails or trail boss to a bunch of saddle tramps. In *True Grit* his belt disappears into his abdomen, his opinions are sclerotic and his face is beginning to crack like granite. Audiences now recognize him as a grandfather image, using booze for arterial Antifreeze, putting off winter for one more day. They also recognize Wayne as an actor of force and persuasion. And the frontier town of Hollywood—which has never granted Wayne a single Academy Award—has begun to realize that it might just be a little behind in its payments.*

On one side of the screen, Wayne has often appeared to be loping through his roles. But on the other side, it seems, there has always been an exacting competitive performer. In *McLintock*, recalls Actress Maureen O'Hara, "he didn't like the way I was doing a scene, and he said angrily, 'C'mon, Maureen, get going. This is your scene.' I said I was trying to go fifty-fifty. 'Fifty-fifty, hell,' he said. 'It's your scene. Take it.' Then he added under his breath, 'If you can.'" The master of the western, Director John Ford, calls Wayne "a splendid actor who has had very little chance to act." Agrees Director Andrew McLaglen: "All of a sudden they're saying that he's an actor. Well, he always was." Even such an anti-Establishmentarian as Steve McQueen is a Wayne buff. "Sometimes kids ask me what a pro is," he says. "I just point to the Duke."

No leading man retains prominence without a strong and basic sex appeal. Wayne's has been uniquely conservative. "In a love scene, Clark Gable always forced the issue with a girl," observed Director Howard Hawks (*Red River*). "Wayne is better when the girl is forcing the issue." The romantic backlash has been operating for two generations on audiences—and on his female co-stars. Says Actress Vera Miles: "They used to say of the old West, 'Men were men and the women were grateful.' Well, that's how he makes you feel as a woman."

* Paid in full on Academy Award Night, 1970.

If Wayne stands to the right in sex, he is an unabashed reactionary in politics. A rapping Republican and flapping hawk, he has made the Vietnam war his personal crusade. Yet his rigid, Old Guard style still wins salutes from the New Left.

Terry Robbins, a Chicago coordinator for the radical S.D.S., considers Wayne "terrific and total. He's tough, down to earth, and he says and acts what he believes. He's completely straight and really groovy. I mean, if they really want to make a movie about Che Guevara, they ought to have Wayne play him."

Says Abbie Hoffman, leader of the yippies: "I like Wayne's wholeness, his style. As for his politics, well—I suppose even cavemen felt a little admiration for the dinosaurs that were trying to gobble them up."

Even Paul Krassner, editor of the black-comic book the *Realist*, makes his broadside sound like a grudging salute: "Wayne is one of the floats from the Macy's Thanksgiving Day parade."

Krassner has a point. John Wayne has become one of the pop-artifacts of contemporary life. He carries with him the unmistakable aura of camp and comic strip, as if his conversation came in balloons. As if when he slugged the opposition there would issue forth a thunderous THWACK! and SOCKO! In person, the seamed, leathery face seems an extension of his saddle. A handshake lets the visitor know how a baseball feels when it is swallowed by Frank Howard's glove. True, the unwigged forehead goes clear back to his crown, but the size-18 neck defies collars, and at 6 ft. 4 in. and 244 lbs., Wayne remains gristly underneath the adipose. Even so, Wayne is a bit like Clark Kent waiting to change into Superman. The real man seems to be the one onscreen. Up there, equipped with a rug and a role, 60 feet tall and stereophonic, he assumes his rightful proportions.

At his bay-side house in Newport Beach, Calif., Wayne, in Clark Kent disguise, recently recalled his spiral career in a series of flashbacks. Iowa-born kid turned U.S.C. football star, the former Marion Morrison began in films as a part-time prop man. He fell into bottom-of-the-bill cowboy pictures and made a few better-forgotten films in civilian clothes. "They had a college picture about girls playing basketball," he recalls. "The man in charge was a little dance director. Everything he did was by the count—one, two, three, four—and then your line. I was completely embarrassed, and that's when I walked down the street talking to myself. Will

Rogers went by and he says, 'Hey, Duke, what's the matter?' And I started to tell him and he says, 'You're working aren't ya? Keep it up.' "

An admirable philosophy, one the actor still clings to, along with an advisory from his druggist father. Though it was made in this century, it has the terse ring of orders from Davy Crockett: 1) always keep your word; 2) a gentleman never insults anybody intentionally; 3) don't go around looking for trouble. But if you ever get in a fight, make sure you win it.

Part 3 became the cornerstone of the Wayne tradition. "When I came in," he claims, "the western man never lost his white hat and always rode the white horse and waited for the man to get up again in the fight. Following my Dad's advice, if a guy hit me with a vase, I'd hit him with a chair. That's the way we played it. I changed the saintly Boy Scout of the original cowboy hero into a more normal kind of fella."

In the distinctive Wayne drawl there is the implication that somehow it would be effeminate to pronounce the *ow* in fellow or the *f* in of. In a field where male stars are constantly rumored to be epicene, Wayne's masculinity is incontestable. As a boy he owned a dog named Duke. The child became Big Duke, and the sobriquet stuck. By 30, Big Duke was a looming figure of contained violence waiting for a place to let loose. "I was in a saloon once where a guy shot all the way down a bar," he once complained to a director during a western fight scene. "And I wanna tell you, those extras aren't moving fast enough." The trick was to release the violence in neighborhood theaters. But somehow the oversized part continued to elude the outsized Wayne. The first picture he made for Monogram literally took place in a one-horse town; the budget did not allow for any more livestock.

In the 80 or so features that followed, Wayne earned his head-'em-off-at-the-passport, but his salary and his reputation remained minuscule. In one he suffered the ultimate indignity as Singin' Sandy, the screen's first melodious cowpoke. The hoarse opera was swiftly dubbed, and Wayne returned to the role of Speakin' Star. The movies soon found an acceptable substitute: fella named Gene Autry.

Wayne never did jump from the treadmill. He was lifted off by John Ford, who had become a poker-playing buddy. "I had been friendly with Ford for ten years," recalls Wayne, "and I wanted to get outa these quickie westerns, but I was damned if I was gonna climb on a friend to do it. He came to me with the script of *Stagecoach* and said, 'Who the hell can play the Ringo Kid?' " It was a part that called for a strong, inarticulate frontiersman vengefully seeking his father's killers. "I said there's only one guy: Lloyd Nolan, and Ford said, 'Oh, Jesus, can't you play it?' "

Yes, he could and yes, he did. The film became a classic of the genre, and Wayne changed to archetype casting. Following the wheel marks of *Stagecoach*, he became the essential western man, fearin' God but no one else. Tough to men and kind to wimmin, slow to anger but duck behind the bar when he got mad, for he had a gun and a word that never failed.

The films of the westerner have seldom been sullied with fact. As Historian Joseph Rosa showed in *The Gunfighter: Man or Myth?* (*Time*, May 16), "the so-called 'Western Code' never really existed. Men bent on killing did so in the most efficient and expeditious way they knew how. Jesse James was shot in the back. Billy the Kid died as he entered a darkened room. Wild Bill Hickok was shot from behind while he was playing poker. In each case the victim had no chance to defend himself."

No matter. In the province of the Old West, truth is a dude. The good and bad men who belong are necessary fantasies of the national mind. The public pays to see the Wayne western as a native morality play. The greatest good vanquishes the deepest evil and walks into the gaudiest sunset. The difference between Wayne and his audience is that they leave the illusion behind when they exit from the theater. The Duke has always taken it home with him.

During World War II, the western dwindled in popularity, but the hero could pull more than one trigger. Wayne switched from Colt to M-1 and became a screen soldier. He was a bit unsteady out of the saddle, but there was conviction behind his "Let's get the Nips!" rallying cry. Part of it came from his disappointment at missing the action. He was too young for World War I. As father of four, he was draft-exempt during the second. Still, he treasured a notion of himself in officer's garb. "But I would have had to go in as a private," Wayne says. "I took a dim view of that." Nobody took a dim view of Wayne for staying out. In the '50s, General Douglas MacArthur told him, "Young man, you represent the cavalry officer better than any man who wears a uniform."

But by 1948, the rawboned soldier-cowpoke was no longer raw or bony. The eyes had begun to puff, the flesh was settling. The walk away from the camera was a little too distinctive. From the back, the Wayne Levi's sometimes resembled two small boys fighting in a tent. His eleven-year marriage to Texas-born Josephine Saenz had quietly clopped off into the sunset; she got custody of their four children. After a stretch of popularity, Wayne looked less a Duke than a commoner. He was No. 33 on the list of box-office stars.

This time Wayne was rescued by Screenwriter Borden Chase, who created a role that Wayne could play, he predicted, "for the next 20 years." The movie was *Red River,* a western version of *Mutiny on the Bounty* with the range as the ocean and John Wayne as a pistoled and Stetsoned Captain Bligh. Wayne was at last allowed to play his age (41). Like a man loosening his belt and taking off his tie after a day in the office, the Duke was relaxed, secure and solid. The kid had gone respectable and become a father. *Red River* was a critical and popular smash. In 1950 the Duke was on top as No. 1.

Offscreen he had almost as much clout. It is axiomatic that in order to be a conservative, the individual has to have something to conserve. Wayne had made more money on horseback than Eddie Arcaro. He had property, a big rep and a new wife, Mexican-born Actress Esperanza Baur. He was Hollywood's super-American, whose unswerving motto was "Go West and turn right."

"There's a lot of yella bastards in the country who would like to call patriotism old-fashioned," grouses Wayne today. As he sees it, yesterday was even worse. "With all that leftist activity, I was quite obviously on the other side," he recalls. "I was invited at first to a coupla cell meetings, and I played the lamb to listen to 'em for a while. The only guy that ever fooled me was the director Edward Dmytryk. I made a picture with him called *Back to Bataan.* He started talking about the masses, and as soon as he started using that word—which is from their book, not ours—I knew he was a Commie."

Senator Joseph McCarthy and the House Un-American Activities Committee were uncovering more leftists back East, the Hollywood Ten were cited for contempt, and Wayne decided that it was time to help out. "An actor is part of a bigger world than Hollywood," he announced. Together with Scenarist Chase and such rigid stalwarts as Actors Adolphe Menjou and Ward Bond,

Wayne helped to form the Motion Picture Alliance for the Preservation of American Ideals. Wayne may have seen himself as a patriot. But next to some of his red-white-and-blue-blooded colleagues he looked a little pink. "We had a split in the group," Chase later reported, "the once-a-Communist-always-a-Communist group and the group that thought it was ridiculous to destroy some of those who, say, joined the party in the '30s in Nazi Germany. Duke and I were in the latter group." A risky place to be; when Wayne praised Larry Parks for admitting his Old Left indiscretions, Hedda Hopper bawled out the Duke publicly. He got the message. "I think those blacklisted people should have been sent over to Russia," he now declares. "They'd have been taken care of over there, and if the Commies ever won over here, why hell, those guys would be the first ones they'd take care of—after me." Still, even when he became president of the alliance, Wayne viewed politics as a necessary evil. "My main object in making a motion picture is entertainment," he confesses. "If at the same time I can strike a blow for liberty, then I'll stick one in."

Grinding out his two or three epics a year, Wayne feinted a jab with *Big Jim McLain*, the story of a ham-fisted HUAC investigator. It failed because Wayne was as uneasy in mufti as he was playing Genghis Khan in *The Conqueror*. In that film, Mongolia became westernized when Wayne announced to Tartar Woman Susan Hayward, "Yer beoodiful in yer wrath."

In the troubled '60s, Wayne the political theorist and Wayne the filmmaker formed a merger. After mulling over the drama for 14 years, Wayne produced, directed and starred in *The Alamo*—as Davy Crockett. The picture was about the Texans v. the troops of Santa Anna, but it was also, he said, "to remind people not only in America but everywhere that there were once men and women who had the guts to stand up for the things they believed." As Wayne saw it, the Alamo was a metaphor for America. There was Mexicans and there was Us, there was black and there was white. "They tell me everything isn't black and white," complains Wayne. "Well, I say why the hell not?"

In *Anti-Intellectualism in American Life*, Richard Hofstadter once defined the fundamentalist mind as "essentially Manichean; it looks upon the world as an arena for conflict between absolute good and absolute evil, and accordingly it scorns compromises (who would compromise with Satan?) and can tolerate no ambiguities."

Wayne's fundamentalist character was not against the American grain; it was in it.

Aging and raging, he began to take on all enemies in the same spirit: Commies, Injuns, wrongos, Mexicans—and his wife Esperanza. "Our marriage was like shaking two volatile chemicals in a jar," he said. She recalled the night he dragged her around by her hair. He countered with a claim that when he was on location she had a house guest named Nicky Hilton. During the divorce proceedings, Wayne uttered an aside that could have come from one of his early oaters: "I deeply regret that I'll hafta sling mud."

Though in the divorce his name had been linked with such luminaries as Marlene Dietrich and Gail Russell, Wayne had a different altar ego. His new wife—like the others—was of Latin extraction: a Peruvian ex-actress named Pilar Palette. "Just happenstance," he claims. "Whenever I've had free time I've been in Latin America."

In 1964, for the first time in his life, Chain-Smoker Wayne began to feel kinda poorly. Pilar persuaded him to consult a doctor. He dropped out of sight for a few months, then surfaced after a successful operation at Good Samaritan Hospital to utter his most quoted line: "I licked the big C." He was minus one lung, but his energy had not diminished one erg.

Obviously, a man who can vanquish cancer is indestructible. Still, even if he was immortal, he wasn't getting any younger. There was catching up to do. At a time when other men start to think about bifocals and social security, Wayne began to learn his lines for *The Sons of Katie Elder,* a typically nuance-free Wayne western about four lusty, brawling brothers. But that was just for loot. Now that he was back on his feet, some things were griping him. The moral backslide, for one. He stumped for his friends Barry Goldwater and Ronald Reagan. "I said there was a tall, lanky kid that led 150 airplanes across Berlin. He was an actor, but that day, I said, he was a colonel. Colonel Jimmy Stewart. So I said, what is all this crap about Reagan being an actor?"

Another thing that bothered Wayne was the war. He was for it. When ordinary men feel that way, they sound off at home or in saloons. Wayne did it in a picture. *The Green Berets* was probably the only prowar movie made in the Sixties. It was so pro that New York Congressman Benjamin S. Rosenthal accused Wayne and the Army of conspiracy. The movie, claimed Rosenthal, "became a useful and skilled device employed by the Pentagon to present a view of the war which was disputed in 1967 and is largely repudiated today."

"Nonsense," says Wayne, or words to that effect. "*The Green Berets* made $7,000,000 in the first three months of its release. This so-called intellectual group aren't in touch with the American people, regardless of Fulbright's blatting, and Eugene McCarthy and McGovern and Kennedy. In spite of them the American people do not feel that way. Instead of taking a census, they ought to count the tickets that were sold to that picture."

Nonetheless, *Berets* was an expensive production. Warner Brothers, which distributed it, will end up with some profits. Batjac, the Wayne-owned company that produced it, will just about break even. The old Hollywood axiom still holds: "If you've got a message, send a telegram." In the territory of *True Grit* he can safely espouse the hard line without having a Congressman on his back. "In spite of the fact that Rooster Cogburn would shoot a fella between the eyes," theorizes the law-and-order man, "he'd judge that fella before he did it. He was merely tryin' to make the area in which he was marshal livable for the most number of people."

Down at Newport Beach, Wayne also makes it livable for the most number of people. Out in Newport Bay bobs his boat, *Wild Goose II*. Lesser men would have a yacht; Wayne's craft is a converted minesweeper. His house overflows with memorabilia and sentimental tributes from institutions as far apart as *Good Housekeeping* and the U. S. Marines. His collection of Hopi Indian kachina dolls is probably second only to Barry Goldwater's. Though the family car appears to be a standard Pontiac station wagon, it was custom built. "I wrote to the head man at G.M.," he beams, "and said, 'I'm gonna have to desert you if you don't stop makin' cars for women.'" They fixed him up with a model deep enough to accommodate him, Stetson and all. Three of his seven children live with him: Aissa, 13, John Ethan, 7, and Marisa, 3. Two older sons, Pat and Michael, run Wayne's Batjac film-production outfit. And sixteen grandchildren frequently wander around the spacious house. No one has counted all the people on the payroll: there are the folks at Batjac, the moviemaking cronies who travel with Wayne from picture to picture, the employees on his cotton and cattle ranches, one of which covers 60 square miles. Plus assorted domestic servants.

At home, playing grandpaterfamilias to the world, he watches his country in motion, hoping it will move into the sunlight where the contrasts are clear. He will never fill up another ashtray, but he still manages to empty a few bottles. "Getting out with my comrades," he says, "and talking revolution, jeez, I'll hit it pretty good." Forever the superpatriot, he once refused to let a bandleader play his favorite tune because "everybody would've had to stand up." Yet beyond the self-parody, beyond the fifth-face-at-Mount-Rushmore pose, there is a heroic essence that Wayne manages to convey. Today, like "war," the word "hero" is usually preceded by a disinfectant: "anti." Not to the Duke. Conflict is made to be won; heroes are created to be the uncommon man sans imperfection. "I stay away from nuances," he says. "From psychoanalyst-couch scenes. Couches are good for one thing only." As Wayne sees film heroism, "Paul Newman would have been a much more important star if he hadn't always tried to be an anti-hero, to show the human feeta clay." No one will ever see Wayne's feeta clay—and no one wants to. His politics seem to date from the Jurassic period, and from other men they might appear dangerous. But as expressed by the Duke they are the privately held opinions of a public man and they have the quality of valid antiques.

Robert Frost summed up old age:

No memory of having starred
Atones for later disregard.
Nor keeps the end from being hard.

Better to go down dignified
With boughten friendship at your side
Than none at all. Provide, provide!

The boughten friendship goes on at the box office; Wayne will continue to provide, provide at the rate of two pictures a year. And at the final fadeout? "I would like to be remembered—well, the Mexicans have a phrase, '*Feo, fuerte y formal.*' Which means: he was ugly, was strong and had dignity."

It is a well-deserved epitaph for a great gunfighter. Sorta gives a man something to shoot for.

VII:

SKIN

Whatever it did or didn't do for the audience, *I Am Curious* (*Yellow*) evoked epic lust from distributors and operators whose theaters weren't playing it. The American public was obviously willing to pay premium prices for what it had been led to think was premium pornography. Sex films in all their ingenious permutations were bigger business than ever. X-ratings, issued by the Motion Picture Association of America's self-censors for skin but rarely for violence, were a badge of honor. Advertisements for naughty 16-mm peep shows often dominated a newspaper's entertainment page and gave the impression that the Clothed Cinema was a thing of the past. Yet the nation and its courts were in an increasingly conservative mood and deeply troubled by the ancient conflict between public morality and private delectation. Critics, spectators and legislators were struggling with the questions of redeeming social and artistic value and contemporary community standards, and the only workable definition of pornography to emerge in 1969 was that which a great many Americans condemn for others after seeing for themselves.

J.M.

I AM CURIOUS (YELLOW)

NOT GREAT, BUT DECENT

JOHN SIMON

After one has testified for it in court and seen the testimony excerpted and misprinted in a book; after one has spent an evening in Stockholm discussing it with its maker, Vilgot Sjöman; after one has written a polemical piece defending it in the *Times* and stood up for it in a radio debate—one is somewhat tired of *I Am Curious* (*Yellow*) and would just as soon not have to review it.

Sjöman's controversial film concerns the quest of a girl called Lena Nyman for her selfhood: political, social, and sexual. Politically, she demonstrates for various Left-wing causes, especially nonviolent resistance; socially, she has organized a group of young people to go around with tape recorders and interview people about whether Sweden is a classless society, the findings to be studied by the Lena Nyman Institute; sexually, she is experimenting in depth with a lover, her 24th. Lena also has family problems with her father, in whose house she lives: He had gone to fight Franco in '37 but quit after a couple of weeks; now he works in a frame shop, is mistrusted by his daughter and despises himself.

The film functions on several levels. There is Lena as a character in the story, but there is also a real-life Lena, who has an affair with the director-scenarist Sjöman (as she did in real life), then goes on to having one with Börje Ahlstedt, the actor who plays her lover in the film. What complicates matters is that we often see Sjöman and his crew making the film and getting into the Pirandellian act; that there are as many real moments of *cinéma-vérité* as bits of staged *cinéma-vérité* and "story" sequences; that there are authentic interviews with men like the brilliant young Swedish Cabinet member Olof Palme, and imaginary ones with Evtushenko, Dr. Martin Luther King and the King of Sweden; and there is even a fantasy where the government adopts nonviolent resistance as the official policy. It becomes hard, indeed impossible, to tell which level is up; whether, for instance, a lovers' quarrel is part of the fiction or of the framework, and whether the framework itself isn't really fiction.

Sjöman achieves a hyper-Pirandellian conundrum, some of it amusing and some merely a bother. Nevertheless, the point that fantasy, fiction, wishful thinking, and reality are all equally meaningful and, in some senses, interchangeable, is made well enough. And Lena's struggles to achieve nonviolence in her various selves—as a political and a private person, as mistress and daughter—are animatedly chronicled in their partial victories and considerable setbacks. Particularly fine are the scenes with the father (played touchingly by Peter Lindgren), full of unresolved conflict and, on his part, scrupulous evasiveness. Scarcely less good is Lena's imaginary encounter with the King, and some of the responses of anonymous interviewees are of all too human interest.

But these things tend to escape notice, for attention avidly focuses on the sex scenes. Lena and Börje make love in various places, moods, and positions. There are tender lovemakings and querulous ones; some in fun, some in fury. There is oral sex and, in a dream sequence, castration. Defiantly, the lovers copulate on the balustrade of the Royal Palace; experimentally, in what is said to be Europe's oldest tree. Though varied, the sexuality is never erotic. (Whether that makes the film better or worse is a question I leave open.) Unerotic, first, because neither of the young people is particularly attractive—Lena, in fact, is downright bovine, but her liveliness is almost as good as loveliness. Unerotic, secondly, because the sex scenes are full of humorous or unglamorous details, which prove distinctly anaphrodisiac.

Artistically, the film has its weaknesses. Sjöman shot too much footage, so that he ended up making two versions of *I Am Curious*, *Yellow* and *Blue*, named after the colors of the Swedish flag. I have seen *Blue*, a much weaker film though not without its moments, and must regretfully report that some pieces that belong in one film have ended up in the other, contributing to the depletion and confusion of both. For example, an infestation with body lice that Lena passes on to Börje in *Yellow* is explained by a dalliance *à trois* with a married couple in whose car Lena hitches a ride in *Blue*. And there are motifs that seem insufficiently developed, while others are dawdled over.

Peter Wester's cinematography, which tries for a spontaneous newsreel look, is at times a bit too slapdash. Finally, the film never probes deeply enough, precisely because it probes away in so many directions. But *I Am Curious (Yellow)* is interesting in its shimmering, multifarious approach to life in Sweden today, in its frankness about sex, and in the considerable step ahead it marks in Vilgot Sjöman's artistic development.

LETTER FROM THE FLICKS: MANHATTAN, SPRING, 1969

PENELOPE GILLIATT

So, well, the stock in Grove Press has gone up X points since the opening of its notorious import, the puny-hearted *I Am Curious (Yellow)*, almost as if the people of the city were prepared to swallow any old hootch under the rule of some wild thirst during a time when sex is placed as alcohol was during Prohibition—which is quite a fantasy of privation. And I have been to, and quit, three glum movies about homosexuality, one of them set in a laundry of lesbians and full of frightful tiffs amidst the washing. And the spring rains have been heavy, though they were held to be good for agriculture. In the meantime, town living is far from bucked up by the witless libertarianism of the wave of rotten pictures hopefully called sexy by the public. They mostly have effects that are anti-erotic in the extreme, and they are about as accessible to criticism as an egg-and-spoon race or a trot round the reservoir. After any time spent in their company, you have a strong impression that sex is on its last legs and will soon die out, like crochetwork. Language sometimes seems to be finished, too. Last week, a play in

Manhattan was closed by the police for offenses that included "consentual sodomy." One of the many, many reasons why pornography is in such a bad way now may be that its mere pompous name gets everyone down. Funniness might well not have survived if it had been a topic for pundits and been called "risibility."

This is a time of transition, though, and the winds of change are whistling through the corridors of power and the concrete jungle and other places of cliché, and the age of neurosis is having its agonizing reappraisal. That is to say, cant is flourishing, and many things to do with going to the pictures are all to pot—for instance, ticket-buying. You are quite likely to be kept out of the theatre if you make the mistake of saying "please" to one of the stone women in box offices, because she may then take you to be a murderous nut who is having her on. Yet at the same time, in this half-world of the business of pleasure, some sweet and inapt vestiges of old manners remain. A couple of weeks ago, for instance, reading one of the questionnaires about obscenity and nudity that pour in from academic institutions and learned journals at the moment, I got to a sheet that said solicitously: "As a woman in the cinema, *when confronted by blatant sex* [my itals], do you feel obliged to respond asexually?" I didn't know what it meant, but the middle part sounded protective, as if women were being sent into the trenches. Another set of demands asked, "What is your opinion of pornography? When is it good? When is it bad?"

(Q.: Discuss [my question].

A.: Humor is good when it is funny and bad when it is not funny; by extension, pornography is good when it is erotic and bad when it is not erotic. I put this forward as a possibility.

No. Erase.

A.: I have thought about this and I have no thoughts.)

For inanely diligent reasons, I put myself through the trial of seeing *I Am Curious (Yellow)* twice. I went to it first in the customs building, invited by Grove Press as a possible expert witness for the defense when the film came to trial for obscenity. As far as I could judge, the movie only went to show that the Swedes can be as chic and mannered as anyone else. It is decked out with a lot of idiot sociology and seriously marred by its mock humor, which has the discomfort and occasional ugliness of a jape by a meagre-spirited schoolmaster. I told the Grove Press lawyers that I was prepared to argue strongly against censorship in general but that I knew this was no good to the film, since the law asks such a case to be fought on the plea of redeeming social and artistic value. On these grounds, it won—earnestly, doggedly, and with immense profit in publicity. Well, O.K. But the second time I saw it I arrived for the last five minutes of the previous showing, and noticed that there were no subtitles. So I talked to the projectionist, and he adjusted the lens so that the subtitles suddenly burst on the audience, who had been sitting through the length of this Swedish-language film and losing all the redeeming social worth of its hours of puerile street interviews without missing redemption one bit. The people there seemed happy enough with the pittance they were being handed out, but who can tell what joy there might have been in a film more grown up, more free, less peekaboo, more risky about clinging to its nature instead of courting sociologists' compliments? It seeks favors, and it swims with fins of lead.

GIVING THE PUBLIC WHAT IT WANTS

HOLLIS ALPERT

Our television newscasters (along with dozens of newspaper columnists) have already taken note of the long lines at two New York cinemas showing *I Am Curious (Yellow)*. Recently I had a telephone talk with the owner-manager of a Washington "art house" who has been showing the same film for the past month. "We turn them away by the hundreds at night," he reported. "The afternoon matinee is usually sold out, and we have half a houseful for our 10 A.M. showing. On a seat-by-seat comparison, we're outgrossing *The Sound of Music.*"

On opening day a half-dozen anonymous hate letters arrived and a few equally anonymous phone calls were received; after that, there were no complaints, except for one strange happening. One man ran screaming from the theater. It was learned afterward that his family immediately had him committed. The counterreaction has been sparse in New York, too: some thirty hate letters received to date, and the lady manager of one of the theaters showing the film was slapped in the face by an irate woman who was curious and then regretted it. A court case looms in Philadelphia (the third city to play the film): Two policemen saw the film and reported that it had no artistic merit.

Artistic merit or no, *I Am Curious* must be considered significant, and in other than cinematic areas. Grove Press, the film's distributor, went public prior to the film's opening and since then has tripled in value (at this writing). And there has been a kind of spin-off effect in magazine circles. Several large-circulation magazines have taken advantage of the *I Am Curious* phenomenon for feature spreads on the so-called sex wave in movies, theater, and art.

It would appear, then, that those who would treat sex with seriousness, intelligence, humor, and/or artistry are giving the public what it wants—certainly, the buying public. One wonders, therefore, what community a Philadelphia district attorney is supposedly representing when he brings suit against the film. After all, no one is being dragged off the street, forced to shell out cash for admission, then strapped in his seat until the film ends. But let's not assume that the basic ingredient of what a large segment of the public is buying is anything but sex.

Actually, it has always been so with the cinema, even at its silliest. It was only fear that prevented moviemakers from catering more frankly and bluntly to the voyeuristic bent of its audiences. Greta Garbo was one kind of sex heroine. Dumpy little Lena Nyman is another. In a way, she's more preferable to today's audiences because she's a lot more honest about her sexuality, and doesn't think there's much to hide. Not all of what's happening in the current sex cinema is regrettable. On the other hand, we're bound to be in for some curious examples of what might be termed, politely, "art-eroticism" films featuring flesh and fantasy in supposedly meaningful terms.

One now at hand is *Succubus*, a German-made weirdie, featuring Janine Reynaud as a sadistic, murderous sexual demon in her subconscious life, and a nightclub performer on the more "real" plane. Berlin and Lisbon are the backgrounds, and both are found to be rife with decadence, ranging through orgies, Lesbianism, sadism, but of the kind less apt to be imagined by the heroine than by the screenwriter and director. Plainly hokum, it parades its erotic wares under a guise of being artistic. The credits appear against classic works of erotic art, the musical score is by, of all people, Friedrich Gulda.

From Denmark, where just about all is legally permissible, comes *People Meet and Sweet Music Fills the Heart*. Here the direction and scenario are by Henning Carlsen, who made the estimable *Hunger*. It might be mentioned that his new film was held up by U.S. Customs until the U.S. Circuit Court made its determination in the case of *I Am Curious*, although *People Meet* has little total nudity. The sex acts in it are numerous, though, several of them participated in by Harriet Andersson, who does much to give the film humor and even a certain amount of charm. Carlsen's aim was to blend erotic comedy and fantasy into a stylish whole, but his sense of humor is often heavy, and his imagination hardly flowers into brilliance. He does, however, have some excellent actors, among them Eva Dahlbeck and Prebin Neergaard. Such story as there is—about a young student who runs afoul of the amoral dancer played by Miss Andersson and yearns for her ever after—soon runs out of purpose, and the movie gives off only fitful gleams, some of them fleshy, after that.

COMING APART

SACRED BULL

JOSEPH MORGENSTERN

Mirror, mirror on the wall, who is squarest of them all? Me, I guess. For the first few minutes of *Coming Apart*, a movie shot almost entirely at crotch and couch level through the wall-size mirror of a Manhattan apartment, I thought I was seeing a rich satire of neo-nudie films. I thought *Coming Apart* was taking apart those obsessively sexual little stinkers with the sociophilosophic overlays, the panting underlays and the steadfastly unfulfilled promises of unlimited perversion. I forgot, if only for a few minutes, that sex is our civilization's sacred cow, or bull, and that sex and insanity together are the least laughable, most solemn themes that a modern movie can ponder, or mount.

As the movie begins, Rip Torn is heard over a black screen quoting Pascal: "I am frightened, and wonder to find myself here rather than there." Very serious, that, even though the first scene finds Torn couched with an ardent, undressed young lady. The second scene finds him couched with an even more ardent lady (Lois Markle) with cigarette burns all over her chest and an apparently insatiable appetite for pain. She's splendidly funny as she implores Torn to abuse her. He's funnier still as he plays the scene straight, discussing depravity calmly, apparently putting her on, describing some trick he's heard of that involves human genitals, a live duck and a dresser drawer. "Would you like that?" the girl asks eagerly. He's flabbergasted by her eagerness and, in one of the great and only intentional gag lines, says: "I mean, where would we get a duck?"

Now, that really is a great gag, but it soon becomes clear that *Coming Apart* is no laughing matter. It's as serious as Pascal led us to believe. It's the diary of a madman—a mad psychiatrist, if you please—as recorded by a hidden camera. The psychiatrist has hidden the camera himself so he can act out his sexual fantasies in front of it. You may think that's a healthier approach to stardom than hanging around a Hollywood drugstore until a talent scout finds you, but Torn's schizy shrink isn't interested in playing love scenes for their own sake. He only wants a witness to his inexorable dissolution, a silent and unblinking eye that will play analyst to his own analysand.

You may also think this is a promising approach to cryptopornography, a Candid Camera setup in which a nut case lures a succession of unsuspecting ladies to his lair. And the ladies do come, do disrobe, do use candid language to describe our hero's multiple hangups, and do strike poses that look promising when displayed as still photographs in a "special movie edition" paperback that's being put out along with the movie (or is the movie being brought out to accompany the paperback? How can you ever unmix mixed motives?). The cruel fact of the matter, though, is that very little happens in the movie to animate the stills.

These people all seem to have more time than we do. The logic of the fixed camera position is ingenious, but there's no action to speak of. You wish the psychiatrist would make love, not film. There's not much language to speak of, either. Most of the supposedly serious dialogue, as written and directed by Milton Moses Ginsberg, makes you yearn to hear more about that duck. What's left, if the movie is to be taken seriously at all, is the acting, and I'm not at all sure how to judge it. Sometimes it seems wonderful, yet almost all the excitement is generated by scenes in which the characters played by Torn, Sally Kirkland and others are drunk or stoned. In days of yore you would regard such scenes as simulations and judge the actors on their simulative techniques. Today it's as likely as not that the actors are genuinely zonked, caught by the camera in the process of being rather than simulating. Is that really any of our business? I didn't think so in *Easy Rider,* where the material was so strong that we were more interested in what the actors were doing than in how they actually managed to do it. In *Coming Apart,* however, the material is weak to the point of self-parody, and the performers are left to their own devices, and we're left to wonder just what those devices are.

CRACKING UP ON CANDID CAMERA

RICHARD SCHICKEL

I suppose most of the discussion of *Coming Apart* will revolve around whether it violates "contemporary community standards" in its treatment of sex. That is, let me say, a fair question, because the movie is extraordinarily blunt about, and singularly preoccupied with, naked bodies and with certain widely practiced, but rarely photographed, uses to which those bodies can be put by libidinous human beings. Indeed, in its unwillingness to avert its eyes from them the film can only be compared, alas, to *I Am Curious (Yellow)*. Still, contemporary community standards are in such a shambles that no honest man can say with certainty whether an object of art (or commerce) really violates them. Moreover, *Coming Apart* does, at least, deal with *our* community, not Sweden's, and it does so, I believe, in a way that is altogether more interesting, psychologically and cinematically, than *Curious.*

Coming Apart is, in fact, one of the few illuminating—not to say harrowing—portrayals of a schizophrenic crack-up that I have ever seen on the screen. The fellow coming apart is a married psychiatrist (Rip Torn) who has taken a bachelor pad where, for reasons of illusion and delusion, he pretends to be a photographer. It is equipped with a hidden movie camera with which he records the results of his unscientific but dedicated study of a cross section of New York feminine life that he lures into its range. The film we watch is supposed to be the film that camera has exposed, and that is where the technical interest of the film lies. For Director Milton Moses Ginsberg must hold our attention over a long span using only the one fixed angle available to this camera and without any of the editing devices usually available to directors. I won't dither on about the inventiveness with which he varies his work—staging action at different distances from the camera, utilizing the edges of the frame and off-camera voices. I will point out, however, that technique is of consequence only if it reinforces our comprehension of a director's larger meaning. This one does.

That hidden camera is the logical extension—no, the *reductio ad absurdum*—of our age's insistence that experience must be passed through some recording-communicating medium before it can become completely real to us. Of course, the end result of our media madness may very well be the opposite of what is intended: It is likely that it is a dissociative force, preventing us from getting in touch with emotional reality.

Certainly Mr. Ginsberg wants us to note the correlation between our coolly voyeuristic state as we watch the hidden camera's film unroll and that of the psychiatrist who has, with similar coolness (even coldness), decided to act out his fantasy life in front of it, regardless of its effect on his partners or his loved ones offstage.

It's all right for him in the beginning, when the emotional stakes are low. A casual encounter with an aimless chick who used to be one of his patients, a comic engagement with a masochist ("Hurt me," she cries; "How?" he asks, eager to please), a sad encounter with a teeny-brained teeny-bopper who develops inhibitions when she remembers her baby is asleep nearby. The trouble develops when the chick (played by Sally Kirkland with a perfect air of dumb desperation) would have him take responsibility for her. That, of course, is precisely what he is trying to avoid, and things start to come unstuck quickly. An ex-mistress and then his wife appear in his lair and observe that he is rather farther gone than he knew. The point is that man cannot live by fantasy alone; reality, dismal as it is, sustains us. And when Miss Kirkland returns finally to wreck his little world, and him with it, we see just how fragile fantasy is.

It is not, I think, a tragedy, which may be its chief defect. It is merely an ending. And the same point could have been made without so much explicit sexual activity. Easily. Surely the motives of the film's makers must be questioned. Surely the motives of anyone who decided to avoid it could not be questioned. But the film's effect is powerful, not least because of Rip Torn's brilliant performance as he transforms himself from a man making a half-serious experiment in living to a creature ensnared in a trap of his own devising.

I recognize the paradox that works of art that offend traditional morality are often more deeply moral than those that do not dare such transgressions, but I despise the current trend to abuse it for sensation's sake. And yet in honesty it must be recorded that *Coming Apart* does have a morally instructive dimension. It may or may not have been made in the spirit of art, but for me it has the effect of art, and very troubling art at that.

ABOUT THE CONTRIBUTORS

Hollis Alpert is a film critic for *Saturday Review*. The author of four novels; a collection of essays, *The Dreams and the Dreamer*; and a biography, *The Barrymores*, he has taught at New York University and Pratt Institute.

Harold Clurman is theater and film critic for *The Nation*, and Visiting Professor at Hunter College. An active stage director, he was one of the co-founders of The Group Theatre and has been a film producer and director. He received the George Jean Nathan Prize for Dramatic Criticism in 1958, and the Sang Prize for Dramatic Criticism from Knox College in 1968. His published works include *The Fervent Years, Lies Like Truth, The Naked Image*. He has written articles for *The New York Times*, the London *Observer*, *Harper's Bazaar*, *Partisan Review*, and others.

Penelope Gilliatt, film critic of *The New Yorker*, was formerly film critic of the London *Observer*. She has written two novels, *One by One* and *A State of Change*. A book of her short stories is entitled *Come Back if It Doesn't Get Better*.

Philip T. Hartung, film critic of *Commonweal*, has contributed articles on film for the *Encyclopedia Americana* Annuals and *The Book of Knowledge* Annuals. He has also reviewed movies for *Woman's Home Companion, Charm, Scholastic Magazines*, and *Esquire*.

Robert Hatch writes film criticism for *The Nation*, and is executive editor of that magazine.

Pauline Kael reviews movies regularly for *The New Yorker* and has been a movie critic on the *New Republic* and *McCall's*. She has written film criticism for *Partisan Review, Sight and Sound, Atlantic Monthly*, and *Harper's Bazaar*, and is the author of three critical collections, *I Lost It at the Movies, Kiss Kiss Bang Bang*, and *Going Steady*.

Stefan Kanfer is film critic of *Time* magazine. He has contributed articles to *Life, Harper's Bazaar, Esquire, Atlantic Monthly* and *Playbill*.

Stanley Kauffmann is the film critic of the *New Republic*

and one of its literary critics. He is the author of *A World on Film* and has been a Visiting Professor in the Yale School of Drama.

ARTHUR KNIGHT is a film critic for *Saturday Review*, a professor in the Cinema Department of the University of Southern California, and a member of the board of trustees of the American Film Institute. He is the author of *The Liveliest Art* and co-author with Hollis Alpert of *The History of Sex in the Cinema* and has contributed to the *Encyclopaedia Britannica* and *Collier's Encyclopedia*.

ROBERT KOTLOWITZ is the managing editor of *Harper's Magazine* as well as a frequent contributor on "Film and Performing Arts."

JOSEPH MORGENSTERN is the film critic of *Newsweek*. He has been a reporter for *The New York Times* and a film and drama critic for the New York *Herald Tribune*. His novel, *World Champion*, was published this year.

ANDREW SARRIS is film critic of *The Village Voice*, Associate Professor of Cinema at Columbia University, a member of the Program Committee of the New York Film Festival at Lincoln Center, and a Guggenheim Fellow. His books are *The Films of Josef von Sternberg* (1966), *Interviews with Film Directors* (1967), *The Film* (1968), *The American Cinema: Directors and Directions 1929–1968* (1968), *Film 68/69*, co-edited with Hollis Alpert (1969), and *Confessions of a Cultist: On the Cinema 1955–1969* (1970).

RICHARD SCHICKEL is film critic for *Life* magazine. His books on movies include *The Disney Version*, *The Stars*, and *Movies: The History of an Art and Institution*. He was co-editor of the first volume in this series, *Film 67/68*, and his most recent work was *The World of Goya*, a biography of the painter.

ARTHUR SCHLESINGER, JR., who formerly reviewed films for *Show* magazine, is now a reviewer for *Vogue*. He is also a historian and writer.

JOHN SIMON is film critic of the *New Leader* and drama critic of *New York* magazine and the *Hudson Review*. He has taught at Harvard, the University of Washington, M.I.T., and Bard, and is the author of two books of criticism, *Acid Test* and *Private Screenings*. He was the winner of a Polk Award in criticism for his articles in the *New Leader* in 1968.

INDEX